China in the World

SINOTHEORY A series edited by Carlos Rojas and Eileen Cheng-yin Chow

China in the World

Culture, Politics, and World Vision

Ban Wang

Duke University Press Durham and London 2022

Printed in the United States of America on acid-free paper ∞
Designed by Aimee C. Harrison / Project editor: Annie Lubinsky
Typeset in Portrait Text Regular and Helvetica Neue by Westchester
Publishing Services

Library of Congress Cataloging-in-Publication Data
Names: Wang, Ban, [date] author.
Title: China in the world : culture, politics, and world vision / Ban Wang.
Other titles: Sinotheory.
Description: Durham : Duke University Press, 2022. | Series: Sinotheory |
Includes bibliographical references and index.
Identifiers: LCCN 2021021969 (print) | LCCN 2021021970 (ebook)
ISBN 9781478009801 (hardcover)
ISBN 9781478010845 (paperback)
ISBN 9781478012368 (ebook)
ISBN 9781478092452 (ebook other)
Subjects: LCSH: China—Foreign relations. | China—Civilization—
20th century. | China—History—20th century. | China—Politics and
government—20th century. | China—Civilization—21st century. |
China—History—21st century. | China—Politics and government—
21st century. | BISAC: HISTORY / Asia / China
Classification: LCC DS775.8 .w364 2022 (print) | LCC DS775.8 (ebook) |
DDC 327.51—dc23
LC record available at https://lccn.loc.gov/2021021969
LC ebook record available at https://lccn.loc.gov/2021021970

Cover art: Arnold Chang and Michael Cherney, *After Huang Gongwang #6*,
2014. Courtesy the artists.

This title is freely available in an open access edition made possible by
a generous contribution from Stanford University.

Contents

Series Editor's Foreword | CARLOS ROJAS

Matteo Ricci's introduction to his 1603 Chinese-language catechism *The True Meaning of the Lord of Heaven* opens with the binome *pingzhi* 平治—in which the first character, *ping* 平, is short for the phrase *ping tianxia* 平天下, meaning "to make peaceful all under heaven," while the second character, *zhi* 治, is short for *zhiguo* 治國, meaning "to govern the nation."[1] The phrases *ping tianxia* and *zhiguo* are paired in many classical Confucian texts—including, mostly famously, in the opening section of *The Great Learning*, one of the canonical "Four Books" within the Confucian tradition—and in alluding to these phrases here, Ricci was attempting to draw on the intellectual authority of Confucianism in order to promote Christian thought in China.

Ricci was one of the most important early Jesuit missionaries to visit China. He first arrived in the Portuguese settlement of Macau in 1582, and the following year he traveled to China, where he remained until his death in 1610. Ricci completed the first draft of *The True Meaning of the Lord of Heaven* in 1596, based on conversations he had had with several Chinese thinkers, and in the text, he draws heavily on Confucian vocabulary and concepts to introduce Christian ideas, specifically to make the case for the existence of

God. In 1603 Ricci added the introduction and published the catechism as an independent volume.

The term *tianxia* (all under heaven), embedded within the very first character of Ricci's introduction, also resonates with the first term in the text's Chinese title, *Tianzhu shiyi*—which uses *tian* to refer to the "Lord of Heaven" (*tianzhu*), the term that the Jesuits had adopted to refer to God in Chinese. In both *tianxia* and *tianzhu*, the initial character, *tian*, has a hybrid significance, alluding to the culturally specific concept of "heaven" within both the Confucian and Christian traditions, while simultaneously gesturing to the possibility of establishing an umbrella concept that might bridge these two worldviews. Indeed, the explicit objective of Ricci's text was to present a series of dialogues between himself and Chinese interlocutors, in order to find common ground between the Confucian and Christian traditions.

Often translated as "heaven," the term *tian*, in early Chinese thought, referred both to the sky and to a divine power associated with the sky, while the binome *tianxia* began to be used as early as the Warring States period (roughly, the fourth century BCE) to refer either to the territory controlled by the Zhou kings or, more generally, to the (proto-)Chinese society that operated under Zhou values.[2] To the extent that *tianxia* came to refer to a culturally specific realm associated with what is now known as China, however, it is intriguing to consider that the term *tian* itself may be etymologically derived from "non-Chinese" origins like Mongolian (*tengi*) or Tibetan-Burman languages like Adi (*taleŋ*) or Lepcha (*tă-lyaŋ*), and that as early as 1613 (just three years after Ricci's death), the first of several versions of the Chinese term (spelled "tayn") had entered the English language as a loanword.[3]

This hybrid significance of *tian* as a figure of both universality and cultural specificity, of continuity and transformation, is also the focal point of Ban Wang's 2017 edited volume *Chinese Visions of World Order: Tianxia, Culture, and World Politics*, which traces the evolution of the Chinese cosmopolitical concept of tianxia from the early Zhou up to the present. While this edited volume is sensitive to the ways in which the term's meaning has changed over time, the book as a whole also highlights the important continuities in the ways that the concept has been understood and deployed from early China to the present. With respect to the modern and contemporary periods, meanwhile, the volume also underscores the apparent paradox that *tianxia* designates universality ("*everything* under heaven") as well as sociocultural specificity ("everything under [a specifically Chinese-conceived] heaven").

In the current volume, *China in the World*, Wang focuses more narrowly on the period from the late Qing dynasty (i.e., the late nineteenth and early twentieth centuries) to the present day. He argues that during this tumultuous period of political transformation, China not only emerged as a modern nation-state but also continued to draw on a notion of polity derived from its premodern dynastic and imperial roots. As Lucian Pye puts it in a line that Wang cites in his opening paragraph, "China is not just another nation-state in the family of nations. China is a civilization pretending to be a state," and Wang argues that this is true at the level not only of political sovereignty but also of ideology and political philosophy.

At its heart, accordingly, *China in the World* is concerned with the relationship between the two interlinked Confucian concepts to which Ricci elliptically alludes in the first two characters of his seminal 1603 text: "to make peaceful all under heaven" (ping tianxia) and "to govern the nation" (zhiguo)—including attendant questions of the relationship between universalism and particularity, continuity and transformation, inner and outer, self and other, and nation and world.

Acknowledgments

This book was underway when I began teaching the seminar "China in the World" at Stanford University in 2008. The students who participated in this seminar, repeated a few times with variations, are too numerous to list here. I express my gratitude to all the participants for their input, discussion, and writings. I hope the students will recognize something of their own when they have a chance to read this book.

I would like to express my deep gratitude to Kenneth Wissoker of Duke University Press for his patience, advice, and wise steering of this manuscript through two rounds of review and revision. My thanks also go to three anonymous readers for their suggestions and comments, which made me improve the arguments and analyses.

Empire, Nation, and World Vision

Introduction

THE RISE OF CHINA has generated intense debate on the country's power and worldview. Some fret that China's economic power is turning into military might and territorial ambition, threatening to repeat old-fashioned interstate conflict. Whether perceived as a threat or benefit, an empire or nation-state, modern China has been an unsolved mystery. Regarding China as a civilizational state in national disguise, Lucian Pye writes, "China is not just another nation-state in the family of nations. China is a civilization pretending to be a state."[1] China's "One Belt, One Road" initiative traces back to the ancient Silk Roads across Eurasia and sea routes in maritime trade in Asia and Africa. The proposal by the Chinese leadership for a "Community of Common Destiny with Mankind" rests on a belief that a global order of interdependence and cooperation will temper interstate rivalry. In taking the lead on climate change, China calls for a new power relation alternative to the interstate system. These engagements with the world invoke the ancient visions of *datong* 大同 (great unity) and *tianxia* 天下 (all under heaven), bringing old worldviews into the twenty-first century.

While the debate on China's place in the Western nation-state system dates back at least to the Qing dynasty, it came to a head during the Cold War. In 1968, when the Cultural Revolution and the Third World movement were making waves, John Fairbank warned that the Chinese vision, indebted to tianxia and empire, posed a challenge to the system of nation-states and national discourse rooted in "concepts such as nation, sovereignty, and equality of states." The nation-state paradigm is "ill-equipped to deal with the body of thought and practice" associated with the Chinese outlook.[2] Recently, Martin Jacques retraced this worldview to its imperial roots and ancient political culture, which served to "cohere an enormous population otherwise fragmented by dialect, custom, ethnic difference, geography, climate, level of economic development and disparate living standards."[3] Nowhere is the world vision more vividly orchestrated than in the 2008 Olympics opening ceremonies under the rubric "One World, One Dream." Directed by Zhang Yimou, the spectacle goes backward to China's past and deploys ancient resources to forge spectacular patterns.[4] But perplexing questions remain: Does the spectacle project China as a hegemon or promote a cosmopolitan unity of all nations? Does it flaunt leadership or imperialist power?

The question "What is modern China?" has been a vexed issue for more than a century. As the Qing empire was thrust into the world of nation-states in the late nineteenth century, Chinese thinkers recognized the necessity of engaging and adopting the nation-state as an effective model for competition and survival in the forest of nations. Yet confronted with the colonialist nations as aggressors and a source of global conflict, they often looked to cosmopolitan prospects beyond the national border. Observing the League of Nations in 1919, Liang Qichao wrote that the league, for all its unfair, backroom manipulation detrimental to China, heralded a dream of reconciling cosmopolitanism and nationalism. Referencing Immanuel Kant's idea of eternal peace, Liang applauded the league's initiatives as a vista of "a grand human community" (*quan renlei da tuanti* 全人類大團體)—an echo of China's classical vision of tianxia and datong. The Chinese tradition, wrote Liang a few years later, had never conceived the self-contained state, be it an ancient kingdom or modern nation, to be the ultimate unit of human society, and had always held tianxia to be a higher order over separate polities.[5]

In *Ou you xinying lu* 歐遊心影錄 (Travel impressions of Europe), Liang gave a favorable appraisal of the league's promotion of diplomatic reciprocity among nation-states and curtailing of their claims of absolute sovereignty. In a section titled "The Cosmopolitan State" (*shijiezhuyi de guojia* 世界主義的 國家), Liang asserts that a nation is not the paramount polity but a threshold to datong cosmopolitanism. The nation-state's raison d'état is not self-interested and chauvinistic but projects a planetary ethic. Progressing in a spiral from the individual and family through nation-state, a nation should cooperate with other nations so that all people would unite and culminate in a unitary world. Drawing on the Confucian doctrine "Cultivate the self, order the family, govern the country, and bring peace to all under heaven" (*xiuqizhiping* 修齊治平), Liang pictures a self that is not self-serving but sociable, and a nation-state that is not aggressive but a team player. This moral trajectory ascends in a spiral from the individual to family to nation-state, culminating in a peaceful and unified world.[6]

> The ultimate aim of an individual's life is to make contribution to humanity as a whole. Why? The reason is that humanity as a whole is the upper limit of the self. If you want to develop yourself, you need to move in that direction. Why must the state exist? The reason is that with a state, it is easier to rally the cultural power of a national group; to perpetuate and grow it so that a country will be able to contribute to humanity as a whole and help the world grow as well. Building a state is thus a means of advancing humanity, just as the coordination of a municipal government with self-governing local regions is a means of building a state. In this light, individuals should not rest content with making their own state wealthy and powerful but should instead make their nation an addition to humanity. Otherwise, the state is built to no purpose.[7]

Liang is projecting an image of the cosmopolitan state with the full force of the tianxia tradition behind him. Rather than a "civilizational state," which traces a direct line from tribalism, ethnicity, and culture to nation-state, the cosmopolitan state transcends the clash of civilization thesis and is open-minded toward other civilizations.[8] While attracted by transnational elements of "cosmopolitanism," the thinkers tapped into classical traditions to inject new meanings into the concept of nation-state. The ancient notion of tianxia has elicited a spectrum of interpretations lately. Literally "all under heaven," the term is essentially a conjunction of political system and moral authority, its meanings ranging from an imperial apparatus to a unified state equipped with an elaborate bureaucracy, a regime of value, an overarching quasi-religious authority, and a world vision distinct from the Western interstate system.[9] Though often invoked together with "empire" and datong, tianxia leans toward datong but is distinct from empire in its stress on morality, culture, and authority. Empire marks an administrative and military mode of governance capable of holding vast regions and diverse populations together, and is often mentioned in the same breath with tianxia. Yuri Pines has written that the Chinese empire remained intact throughout periodic disorders for two thousand years, until 1912, and some of its elements remain active in modern times. Defined "not only as an administrative and military entity," tianxia is "also an ideological construct" and was accepted as the means for the "political unification of the entirely known civilized world." The idea of tianxia, indeed, is eminently moral, cultural, and ideological: it has served as "building blocks of Chinese political culture"—a cluster of "ideals, values, and perceptions that laid the intellectual foundation for imperial unification."[10]

Conventional wisdom has it that the Chinese nation-state came about by breaking away from the empire and its political culture. Yet the leading thinkers, such as Kang Youwei, Liang Qichao, Sun Zhongshan, and Mao Zedong, often invoked the terms *tianxia* or *datong* in their thinking about national projects, seeking a broader passage to global outlooks. This hybrid of tianxia and nation-state becomes crystalized in the term *tianxia state*.

Echoing Liang's cosmopolitan state, Luo Mengce 羅夢冊, a high-ranking official and political theorist in the Guomindang, coined the term *tianxia state* (*tianxia guo* 天下國). In his 1944 book *Zhonggou lun* 中國論 (On China), Luo conceived a multiethnic, cosmopolitan Chinese republic. At that moment, China's impending victory in the War of Resistance against Japanese Aggression and abolition of foreign extraterritoriality began to worry the observers. Was China rising as a national power or was it restoring the oriental empire? Refuting this national lens, Luo argued that China was not a mere nation-state. Neither would it be an imperialist power, much less an ancient empire. China's new identity owed much to the tradition of tianxia and should be defined as a "tianxia state." But a tianxia state would grow and rise not by clinging to the past but by moving forward. While memories of tianxia come alive in modern times, the Chinese should transform their country into a modern state through "national consciousness and state thinking." By achieving sovereignty, industrialization, and modernization, China must strive to find its place in the world and make its contribution.[11]

The refrain of tianxia state recognizes the nation-state not only as a vehicle for survival and struggle but more important as a road to a higher end. To many Chinese thinkers, the nation was but a way station toward a unified world of datong. Over and above the nation hovered a vision of human flourishing and planetary harmony. As Benjamin Schwartz noted, Kang Youwei, Liang Qichao, Yan Fu, and others envisaged "a vast cosmic-social process leading mankind eventually to the realization of unimagined possibilities of human achievement or even to a utopian resolution of all human problems."[12] In his *Datong shu* 大同書 (Book of great community), Kang painted a trajectory of the world forging ahead—with China as one major mover and shaker. Instead of clashing nation-states, world history presented a "moral drama leading to a spiritual moral solution."[13] Promising to deliver men and women from the bondages of family, gender, class, and above all the nation-state, Kang's vision projected a cosmopolitan harmony among individuals, people, and nations by "sinking into the ocean of humanity."[14]

China's position in the world has been a fiercely debated issue in recent decades. Theodor Huters has shown the dilemmas over absorbing Western culture at the expense of the ancient heritage.[15] Lydia Liu addresses the agency of Chinese writers in the translation of Western learning and interstate antagonism as imperial claims on sovereignty.[16] Rebecca Karl analyzes popular nationalism in Asian colonies by showing that the "Chinese, in concert with Asian nations, could act against global unevenness."[17] Kun Qian's *Imperial-Time-Order* brings to the fore a persistent imperial pattern under tianxia in Chinese Marxism, nationalism, and literature, and Nicolai Volland has explored literary circulation and cultural diplomacy in socialist cosmopolitanism during the Cold War era.[18] Viewing China's rise as a second coming, a regaining of "its former preeminence after one and a half century's decline," James Hsiung suggests that "we cannot grasp China's present without taking due account of its long past" and outside its civilizational context. Distinct from the Westphalian interstate system, China has long cherished aspirations for "citizenship in the international society," which derives from the millennial and modern visions for social unity, distributive fairness, and political culture.[19]

Gaps remain, however, in the study of China's engagement with the world. To deepen this inquiry, it is imperative to explore the dialectic interplay between nationalism and cosmopolitanism and the persistence of the classical traditions. Indebted to the idea of tianxia, Chinese writers saw in cosmopolitanism or internationalism reincarnations of the classical notion. They yearned for a supranational community, shared interests, and solidarity beyond national borders. But cosmopolitanism would be wishful thinking and empty talk without the backing of national strength, independence, and influence. The architects of the nation grappled with the stark reality of a weak and colonized China and realized that the way to the cosmopolitan dream must go through the buildup of a strong nation-state. "If we are to promote cosmopolitanism," declared Sun Zhongshan, "we must first strengthen nationalism."[20] This national-international nexus was taken up by Mao, who asserted that "only China's independence and liberation will make it possible to participate in the world communist movement."[21] Thus, this study probes the dual track of nation building and cosmopolitan aspirations.

This book examines the way Chinese thinkers and writers draw on the classical vision of tianxia in imagining and projecting China's place in the world. Examining a series of empirical cases, this study addresses the paradox of nationalism and cosmopolitanism by delving into their entwinement and interplay. I deal with these questions: How did nationalism and cosmopolitanism interact and clash during the transition from empire to nation-state? How did China's national project align with its world visions? How did each term interact with the other in reciprocity and tension? How did the Chinese Revolution resonate and connect with world revolution? How did national literature find a place within world literature? How did socialist ethnicity policy hark back to the millennia of multiethnic coexistence? How did the Third World relate to China's economic development and Maoism? How did China's assistance to the Tanzania-Zambia Railroad trace back to the arrival of the Ming admiral Zheng He's fleet in Africa? As China becomes integrated into the capitalist world, how does globalization shape the perception of China and Chinese studies in the United States?

Scholars in the Confucian tradition tended, writes Wang Gungwu, "to admire a remote Golden Age in the distant past and to use that image to guide and correct actions in the present."[22] A utopian image of peace and harmony, tianxia holds out an inclusive vision of cultural and political unity over fragmentation and conflict. Touted as China's soft power, the idea is being salvaged from oblivion as a metaphysical and nostalgic image. Such approaches, however, shed little light on the rugged terrains of China's journey into the modern world. Instead of a gaze back at the hoary traditions, this book traces modern reinventions of the past and explores how the old ideas experienced new leases of life as a source of inspiration for modern intellectual trends and cultural practices. Rather than a "Chinese essence," I treat expressions of classical visions as a historically fluid and volatile activity, not reincarnations of some timeless wisdom. Driven by political contingencies and social practice, Chinese writers articulated world visions through frequent returns to the past. But each return to the ancestor home was a leave-taking—a round trip of refurbishment in order to travel further into the outside world. Invocations of the classical heritage are not meant to boost national pride but to place Chinese history in the broad narrative of world history.

Wang Hui's work has brought to light the ancient motifs in weaving a broad narrative of China in the world. Challenging the European dichotomy of nation-state and empire, Wang looks at residual elements of empire that inform China's national project and have delineated an evolving China as a nation-state with a broad spectrum of international outlooks.[23] Building on Wang's leads, in the next section I take a closer look at the relationships between nation and empire.

Empire and the Nation-State

Since the Peace of Westphalia in 1648, the West has enshrined the nation-state as the basic political unit and accepted the interstate world as the universal norm. To Immanuel Wallerstein, this universalism has spread as a civilization on the scale of humanity at the expense of non-Western world-views. Rooted in rationalism, individual autonomy, science, and sovereignty, the international norm has prevailed over prior civilizations.[24] Key to this universalism, the nation-state has preoccupied thinkers and statesmen as a fundamental category for understanding issues of law, politics, economy, ethnicity, language, history, and international relations. On the cusp of transition from empire to a nation-state, Qing China was struggling to fit into this norm. But its millennial imperial tradition remained so intransigent as to make the country unfit for the modern system. In the eye of Han nationalist thinkers like Zou Rong, overnight the empire became an alien regime ruled by the Manchus. But as William Rowe explains, the Qing had already attained the umbrella of tianxia as a "multinational, universal empire" and successfully "expanded the geographical scope of 'China' and incorporated non-Han peoples such as Mongols, Jurchens, Tibetans, Inner Asian Muslims, and others into a new kind of transcendent political entity."[25] Consciously and unconsciously, ideas and institutions of empire had a staying power and drove reformers to push beyond the envelope of the nation. The challenge, writes Wang Gungwu, was to "deal with issues like building a nation after having been an empire for 2,000 years." Beset by the difficulty of "reconciling their republic with the political culture they inherited," reformers thought that China was "neither empire nor nation-state" and attempted to "renew the Chinese state through a civilization of industry and science fused with the best of their heritage."[26] To understand the dilemma, we have to look at the empire-nation nexus.

Based on "ethnicity, territory, religion, and language," the European nation-state model has proved inadequate for understanding modern China. Setting empire against the nation-state, Wang Hui addresses the productive tension and linkages at a deeper level. The imperial legacy persisted and allowed reformers and revolutionaries to articulate and weave tianxia, empire, and nation-state into a new synthesis. The concept of empire (*diguo* 帝國)

represents both a political structure and an ethical orientation. The political aspect describes an "overarching, absolute imperial sovereignty and a form of power based on the unified state." A unified state needs shoring up against centrifugal forces of usurpers, hegemons, and kings in their endless struggle for power. The ethical side refers to the virtuous rule of a regime by means of culture, beliefs, and custom—an ability to "employ virtue to do battle" as opposed to the deployment of armed forces.[27] In other words, "empire" denotes a unified "political form" of an overarching centralized administrative system constantly in tension with local feudal estates. The system's other pillar features an "ethical orientation," a structure of virtue and morality essential to tianxia—"a formation of moral authority with religious significance, and a cultural strategy for political legitimacy."[28]

An order at once political and moral, the tianxia regime governs not merely by coercion but more through assimilation, culture, ritual, gift exchange, tributes, and mutual recognition. Theoretically, diverse cultures, traditions, and ethnicities could coexist in the realm of all under heaven. Through "kingly transformation" and spreading moral values, the regime draws people from afar to the shared values, yet different ethnic groups keep their historically distinct ways of life.

The Qing empire's collapse made Chinese thinkers realize that the only way to preserve the country was to transform the empire into a nation-state. By building national institutions and acquiring modern knowledge, China would join the ranks of major nations. But stepping into the world does not mean abandoning the indigenous tradition. Unlike European nations that had splintered from the old empires, Chinese nation builders, writes Wang Hui, "took certain contents and characteristics of a syncretic universal imperial system and brought them into the inner structure of the nation-state."[29] What emerged was an entity that was neither an empire nor a Western-style nation-state—an anomaly that has confounded the national perspective rooted in the empire-nation binary. Through a tortuous process of reform and revolution in the first half of the twentieth century, China has entered the world as the only society in the world that "has retained, within the structure of a sovereign nation-state, the territorial area, population, and political culture inherited from an empire that existed before the nineteenth century."[30]

Sun Zhongshan's notion of a transnational Asia is instructive. In a 1924 speech in Kobe, Japan, Sun posited the idea of "Greater Asia" to distinguish from Japan's program of Greater East Asianism. Recognizing the urgency for China to become a modern nation, Sun lauded Japan's victory in the Russo-Japanese War of 1904–5 as a triumph of national sovereignty and power. But Sun strove to go beyond the Japanese model. The architect of the new nation urged that China should be able to rally Asian nations to forge an intra-Asian network of self-rule and resistance. Following the Confucian Kingly Way (*wangdao* 王道) and ideas of virtue and morality, Asian nations would assist each other, join hands, and make common cause against imperialist domination and colonial subjugation. Motivated by the principle of self-determination, Asians would rise up against the hegemonic way (*badao* 霸道) of colonizer nations. The emotional structure of virtue and morality encouraged one person to empathize with pains of another, be compassionate with others, and come to one another's assistance. The Asian network is "a culture that rebels against the hegemonic way" and strives for "the equality and liberation of all peoples."[31]

Based on transethnic and cosmopolitan premises, Sun's Asianism sought to bring the multiregional, multiethnic groups and relations into a unified intra-Asian linkage. The plan envisaged a new Asia where multiple national and ethnic identities could coexist, merge, and coordinate in a common project. The far-reaching pluralism included "Japan in the East, Turkey in the West, and nation-states with traditions of Hinduism, Buddhism, Islam, Confucianism and other cultural heritages."[32] Rather than a source of division, cultural specificity and national difference were the foundation for shoring up unity. Taking over multiethnic landscapes and demography from the prior imperial dynasties, the Manchus of the Qing had managed to cement their legitimacy as a "Chinese" dynasty by incorporating diverse ethnic communities, populations, localities, and religions "into a flexible and pluralistic political structure."[33] Although Sun wielded Han nationalism strategically in the anti-Manchu campaign, the newborn Chinese republic quickly implemented the policy of "five races under one union," comprising the Han, Manchus, Mongols, the Hui, and the Tibetans to preserve the empire's multiethnic, multicultural framework in a modern nation-state.

Updating tianxia to Asian cosmopolitanism, Sun was proposing an alliance and solidarity among colonized nations in their struggle for national independence against the colonizers. This vision evolved and transformed in the twentieth century. Kang Youwei and Liang Qichao evinced a similar logic in their articulation of the empire-nation nexus. Kang's datong vision stemmed from a rethinking Confucian universalism in the context of moral authority and empathy that transcend national, religious, and ethnic divides.[34] Liang's nationalism called for the cultivation of a public morality (*gongde* 公德), updating the broadmindedness of tianxia advocated in *Li ji* 禮記 (*Records of Rites*).[35] Public morality signals a commitment beyond parochial and kinship ties, heralding a cosmopolitanism premised on mutual assistance of nations in pursuit of independence. Later in the twentieth century, the tianxia vision continued to be updated and revised to inform socialist internationalism and Third World movements.

Liberal Cosmopolitanism and Socialist Internationalism

Sun's trinity of *sanmin zhuyi* 三民主義—nationalism, democracy, and the people's livelihood—goes beyond ethnonationalism and includes colonized Asian nations, gesturing toward socialist internationalism. Socialist internationalism, the major subject of this study, is often confused with liberal cosmopolitanism. A distinction needs to be made.

In the early twentieth century, liberal cosmopolitanism flourished on the presumption of nation-states' equal access to and participation in global trade and culture. Liang Qichao's novel *Xin Zhongguo weilai ji* 新中國未來記 (The future of New China, 1902) offers a glimpse of it. In its opening passages, world leaders come to attend a peace conference in Nanjing and an exposition of trade and commerce is in full swing in Shanghai.[36] Scholars from all over the world participate in seminars and talks, and diverse schools of thought engage in dialogue. Marveling at this massive interchange, Liang exclaims "datong" to capture a freewheeling sense of cosmopolitan cultural flows and exchange. World trade and commerce, as Adam Smith and Immanuel Kant hoped, would be an effective conduit for international hospitality and connectivity.[37]

Chinese liberal cosmopolitanism had its halcyon days from the 1930s to the 1940s. Based in Shanghai's foreign settlement, the intellectual trend was dubbed by Joseph Levenson a "cosmopolitan fringe."[38] Drawing on ancient motifs of tianxia, the cosmopolitan writers believed in the cross-fertilization and fusion of diverse traditions from East and West and upheld a humanism that transcended national cultural particularities. Zhou Zuoren, the best-known figure, was steeped in classical traditions yet commanded a wide range of modern knowledge such as anthropology, psychoanalysis, and aesthetics. A leading May Fourth thinker and activist along with Hu Shi and Chen Duxiu, Zhou took a transcendent liberal-humanist stance and called for a humane literature (*rende wenxue* 人的文學).[39] Humane literature valorizes the individual as the fundamental unit of humanity. Like a tree in a forest, the human person sinks biological roots to the animal kingdom, yet culture uplifts the person and allows him or her to evolve morally from lowly strata to ascend to the ideal life. Literature is meant to depict the ideal pattern of human life as well as expose inhuman behavior and corruption.[40]

As speedy communication and flows of knowledge offered the possibilities of understanding among nations, Zhou noted, literature would foster a catholic taste for all varieties of experience and transcend local preferences, allowing individuals to "move gradually together." Although there are "the Peters and Johns in the West, and the Zhangs and Lis" in China, they are all "units of mankind, all endowed with emotions and natural dispositions."[41] Their pain will be my pain. Humane literature entails a form of cosmopolitan intersubjectivity, premised on moral sensibility and far-reaching empathy. A leader of the Peking School (*jingpai* 京派), Zhou espoused a cosmopolitan humanism free from nationalistic affiliation even in its appeal to "Chinese" motifs. As Shumei Shih has noted, instead of retreating to the past, jingpai insisted that the universal qualities of naturally endowed emotions are the foundation for a cosmopolitan world.[42]

Lin Yutang, another leading cosmopolitan, struck a "middling path."[43] Born of a Christian family in Fujian province, Lin attended St. John's University in Shanghai and Harvard University, receiving his PhD at Leipzig University in Germany. Inspired by Harvard professor Irving Babbitt, he co-founded the *xueheng* 學恆 (review of classical learning) society with the mission to reassess and revive classical culture for the modern world. Self-styled as a scholar with "two feet crossed on both Eastern and Western cultures" and writing mostly in English, Lin eschewed the notion of "Chinese essence" by Babbitt and developed a "cross-cultural aesthetics." Like Zhou, he managed to steer a path between nationalism and communism, championing individual autonomy in quest of commonalities between West and China and blending the two into a higher cosmopolitan synthesis. "To Lin," writes Qian Suoqiao, "both Chinese and Western knowledge has to be selectively absorbed and contested in the process of its incorporation into modern China" through piecemeal reconciliation and contestation.[44] The highest caliber of a writer is the ability to "take modern culture as shared culture of the whole world, a cosmopolitan culture belonging to all," while preserving his own national culture.[45]

Liberal cosmopolitanism was exemplified by Lin Yutang's career as editor, critic, and board member of two English-language magazines, *The China Critic* (1928–45) and *T'ien Hsia* (1935–41). In Shuang Shen's insightful study, these magazines were the flash point of Shanghai's cosmopolitan public spheres. Nestled in the foreign settlement, they offered a public forum for the cosmopolitan synthesis of East and West. Western educated and well versed in Chinese classics, the writers fused Western knowledge and Chinese tradition, promoted cultural exchange, and advocated world peace. Instead of imitating Western cosmopolitanism, they valued national heritages and saw the nation as a step toward cosmopolitanism. As a columnist for *T'ien Hsia*, Lin adhered to the belief that liberal humanist education, cultural exchange, translation, and the study of foreign languages were key to achieving cosmopolitanism. Mutual learning and understanding would "alleviate cultural misunderstanding and abolish extraterritorial privilege."[46]

Although *T'ien Hsia* and *The China Critic* used English as the principal medium, the writers viewed the English language as an opportunity rather than a repressive tool of colonialism. The colonialists might wield English in their domination, but the English language might be employed as a weapon of critique and resistance in the hands of the colonized. More important, English enabled Chinese writers to have their voice heard in a global vernacular and lay claim to cosmopolitanism.[47]

The liberal cosmopolitanism of Shanghai, however, has large blind spots and is implicated in the myth of culture as a form of capital and commodity. The expansion of global capitalism, wrote Karl Marx, not only has "given a cosmopolitan character" to local economies but also facilitates the circulation of culture: "In place of the old local and national seclusion and self-sufficiency, we have intercourse in every direction, universal interdependence of nationals. The intellectual creations of individual nations become common property . . . and from the numerous national and local literatures, there arises a world literature."[48] Wary of the inevitable loss of deep-seated national culture and tradition in commodity circulation, Levenson called this cosmopolitanism the "silk fan" approach. Equipped with transcendent aesthetic patterns, this style attempts to "construct a culture out of selected values from particular histories, so that a cultural Esperanto will accord with the new technological universe."[49] The term *technological* here points to the formal and abstract patterns expurgated of particularities and complexities of a lifeworld, pointing to Levenson's insight of museumization of culture as relics for a detached taste.

The process of museumization, aided by commodification and canonization, consecrates formal properties of literature and arts and elevates them to an exalted space of "the world republic of letters."[50] Literary values accrue to a reserve of cultural capital and become reified into a currency. Composed of discrete tropes, styles, schools, and aesthetics, such cosmopolitanism is illusory and becomes vulnerable, as Pheng Cheah puts it, to "the manipulative constitution of taste, desire, and opinion by the global commodity circuits of image production."[51] Disengaged from the struggle and lived experience of a semicolonized nation, aesthetic works are celebrated as something pure, free, and universal. Writers turn away from the reality and became aficionados trading on commodities and currencies in a literary marketplace. At the risk of simplification, one may say that liberal cosmopolitanism in Shanghai was contemplative and obsessed with a syncretic spectacle of colorful diversity. Humanist and individualistic, it valorized a transcendent subject capable of cherry picking timeless cultural essences from national traditions and adding them to a world repertoire.

The ivory tower of cosmopolitanism ignores this question: Who is the ruler, and what kind of power structure dominates the garden variety of world culture? It averts the eye from the stark reality of the unequal relations governed by colonial control over peripheral territories, markets, and culture. As a semicolonized country, China was far from being an equal party and had no access to this freewheeling conversation. For all their rich heritage and long tradition, Chinese writers were unable to gain a hearing. The truism that diplomacy is not an option for a weak country applies just as well to writers of a colony intent on promoting the visions of cosmopolitanism.

A movement to overcome the unequal conditions of colonialism and imperialism, the Chinese Revolution pursued a different cosmopolitanism: socialist internationalism. To be sure, liberal cosmopolitanism shared with socialist internationalism certain aspirations and a common origin in the European Enlightenment. In Henri de Saint-Simon's utopian vision, socialist internationalism called for a European Parliament in which people's activities could "extend beyond their own country" and achieve the universal outlook.[52] China's May Fourth or New Culture movement cherished cosmopolitan dreams. Li Dazhao, a leading socialist, for instance, lumped liberal cosmopolitanism together with communism and socialism in extolling the October Revolution. His cosmopolitanism gathered into one package humanism, universal principles (*gongli* 公理), pacifism, democracy, freedom, the red flag, working classes, enlightened citizens, and world leaders such as Woodrow Wilson.[53]

But the growing aggression of colonialism and imperialism forced revolutionaries to approach China's future along the lines of internationalism. Tackling the dual task of national independence and social emancipation, revolutionaries became both nationalist and internationalist. They mobilized a wide swath of the population for national liberation from colonial rule and against Japanese invasion while forging alliances and solidarity among workers of the world.

Given the close links between national liberation and internationalism, the idea of nation takes on prominence in theories of socialist internationalism. Long a lacuna in orthodox Marxist internationalism, nationality is disengaged from social and class emancipation. Marx famously remarked, "The nationality of the worker is neither French, nor English, nor German, it is labor, free slavery, self-huckstering. His government is neither French, nor English, nor German, it is capital."[54] When the capitalist system exploited workers everywhere and divided the world into a bourgeois upper class and a proletarian underclass, workers' national identity seemed a matter of no importance. Workers of one nation shared a common fate with those of other nations, becoming a universal, world-historical class regardless of national identities.

This is why internationalism and nationalism have been viewed as antithetical. The former refers to a supranational world order, whereas the latter is rooted in a particular national community. Throughout this book, however, I examine how this binary is crossed and how two terms interact and transform each other over time. In the context of revolutionary China, what seals the bonds of nation with socialist internationalism was the rise of a national liberation movement: the Chinese Revolution. On the one hand, colonized China must combat colonialism and build a sovereign nation-state. On the other hand, the nation's laboring classes were to be mobilized as participants in nation building and social emancipation, laying the foundation of a people's republic that is a socialist state. Thus, the Chinese Revolution embarked on the dual track of national liberation and class emancipation, taking on the double features of nationalism and internationalism.

What made this dual task visible and urgent was the watershed event of the October Revolution of Soviet Russia. Identifying domestic class oppression with colonial subjugation by foreign powers, Chinese socialists redefined the nation: the nation was to be constituted by a coalition of working classes seeking both social emancipation and national liberation. As John Fitzgerald puts it, the Chinese Revolution "seems to have delivered the awakening message to class and nation at the same time."[55]

Premised on a cosmopolitan future made possible by national liberation and class emancipation, socialist internationalism, in Wang Hui's words, "stems from linking the liberation of one's nationality with that of others rather than from an amnesia about national identity."[56] The term *class nation* expressed this duality and gained prominence, opening the door to a sense of the common fate of working classes across national, racial, and ethnic lines. Revolutionary thinkers extended the concept of class nation to align with oppressed classes of other nations and ethnic groups. Affinity and solidarity linked them in a common fight against global capitalism, imperialism, and colonialism, warranting a passage through national to international struggles.

In "On New Democracy," a speech delivered in Yan'an in 1940, Mao Zedong stated, "The Chinese Revolution is part of the World Revolution."[57] China's nation building, from the Opium Wars to the late Qing reform and the Republican Revolution of 1911, had centered on the bourgeois nation-state, with the express goal of fitting China into the capitalist world system and turning her into "an independent, democratic society."[58] World War I pushed China in a different direction. The deepening crisis of capitalism, the plundering of the colonies, and the birth of the first socialist state in Russia redrew the battle line between global capitalism and the international proletariat. The bourgeois project was "to clear the path for the development of capitalism," but Chinese revolutionaries looked forward to a working-class nation aligned with its counterparts in both the Western metropolises and far-flung colonies.[59]

The 1931 Constitution of the First All China Soviet Congress declared this world-class subjectivity and projected the united front of working classes beyond China. American journalist Edgar Snow captured this internationalist sentiment at the grassroots level. In Yan'an, the birthplace of the socialist nation, national and cultural prejudices are "sublimated in class antagonism that knew no national boundaries." The Chinese peasants hated the invaders from imperialist Japan but knew that "the Japanese masses were their potential allies."[60] They treated oppressive foreign capitalists with as much hostility as they did Chinese landlords and compradors. Seeing themselves as part of a broad-based movement, they realized that their revolution was not isolated and that "hundreds of millions of workers, not only in Russia, but also throughout the world, are anxiously watching them, and when the time comes will emulate them."[61]

The vision of the world splits in this shift from liberal cosmopolitanism to revolutionary internationalism. To be sure, capitalist modernity is nothing if not a world-making process. Capitalism by nature must extend capital and production around the world in search of markets, raw materials, colonies, and domination, remaking the world after its image. Yet such a world deepens rivalry, exploitation, inequality, and poverty. Spreading Western culture in the name of cosmopolitanism, the capitalist world order justifies the legitimacy and structure of colonial domination. In contrast, socialist internationalism cherished a dream of a subaltern coalition of national people composed of working classes—an alliance that heralded the Third World and the Global South. The twin theme of class emancipation and national liberation undergirded Mao's claim that the Chinese Revolution is part of world revolution.

Levenson was probably right in suggesting that Mao's melding of nationalism and internationalism was to redeem the ancient dream of China's world leadership. Although "communist cosmopolitanism" derived from a Marxist worldview, it "compensates for Confucianism lost," serving "national enhancement and defense."[62] As I show in this book, the ancient motifs have persisted and inspired Chinese thinkers to engage the nation-state while articulating world visions.

Chapter Overviews

Focused on Kang Youwei's *Datong shu*, chapter 1 discusses an updated Confucian universalism—a hybrid of ancient and modern ideas. Faced with interstate conflict and realpolitik logic, Kang drew on the classical ideas of *gong* 公 (public), benevolence, empathy, and aesthetic pleasure to construct a datong order. Resonating with the Kantian notion of *sensus communis*, Kang proposed that moral empathy and aesthetic communication could bring people and nations together. The Confucian classic *Chunqiu* prioritizes moral assessment as the guiding spirit of the tianxia order. Rooted in benevolence, equality, and popular sovereignty, this order treats democratic values as universal rather than of Western provenance. Kang's Confucianism called for the curbing of monarchal power and religious authority by promoting social mobility, land redistribution, popular sovereignty, and meritocracy.

Chapter 2 examines how Liang Qichao grappled with tensions between nation-state and tianxia while attempting to reconcile them. Analyzing the novel *Xin Zhongguo weilai ji* and the treatise *Xinmin shuo* 新民說 (Discourse on a new people), the chapter reveals the contradiction between nationalism and cosmopolitanism. Liang advocated the idea of public morality as opposed to private morality. Through moral reform and commitment to the common good, a national people would emerge imbued with a public ethos. The new people not only constitute a nation but are ready to embrace the tianxia outlook. Public morality fosters far-reaching compassion and empathy, manifest in the internationalism of mutual assistance among independence-seeking and decolonizing nations. This blended into Liang's discovery of socialist precursors of harmony, equality, and redistribution in the Confucian classics.

Looking at the world literature seminar taught by novelist Zhou Libo, chapter 3 articulates a new configuration of humanism, nationalism, and internationalism. Teaching European fiction in the Lu Xun Academy of Arts in Yan'an, Zhou evinced a shift from romantic humanism to class-based, socialist humanism. In his lectures, Leo Tolstoy's penetration into socioeconomic inequality in Russian land ownership transcended the sentimentalism of European novels. The wartime urgency of national survival intensified the debate on the national form and worldwide socialist movements. The national form came to be conceived as the creation of a modern people, not passively received heritages. The idea of class nation viewed the toiling peasant class, not the national elite, as the mainstay of a nation. As the national independence movement paralleled working-class emancipation, nationalism paired with socialist internationalism.

Chapter 4 addresses the interplay of national defense and internationalism in the Korean War. The film *Heroic Sons and Daughters* weaponizes the spirit of self-sacrifice based on patriotism and internationalism. A continuation of the Chinese Revolution, China's involvement in the war extends class liberation beyond its borders. The politics of spirit bolsters the fighting spirit and inspires moral power over weaponry. Embodied by what Schwartz called the "reign of virtue," the empowered spirit illustrates Mao's strategy of the people's war and extols mass power as a spiritual atom bomb against imperialist superpower.[63]

Chapter 5 addresses the multiethnic conditions of the imperial legacy that informed China's minority policy. Refuting the ethnonationalist lens, the film *Five Golden Flowers* (1959) portrays ethnic diversity and warm interaction between the "Han" cultural professionals and Bai minority workers. Propagating laughter, enthusiasm, and hard work through eulogistic comedy and across ethnic lines, the film highlights the inclusion of ethnic minorities into economic production and socialist communities. "Han" artists associate with minority people as humble pupils eagerly absorbing local ethnic culture, and national unity is anchored in multiethnic diversity.

Chapter 6 addresses the linkages among Third World internationalism, socialist development, and global Maoism. In opposition to the uneven, neocolonial regime, the hegemonic powers, and the modernization paradigm, China pursued a different path of social economic development. Driven by the Maoist mass line, self-reliance, and the faith in the masses, the socialist development sought to combine social and economic progress to bridge the divides between city and countryside, industry and agriculture, and mental and manual labor. The valorization of the peasantry's revolutionary potentials and mass-line mobilization appealed strongly to the Third World and, during the heady days of May 1968, inspired Alain Badiou's critique of dogmatic Marxism and the rereading of Maoism.

The rise of the neoliberal empire in the wake of the Cold War erased the memory of Third World collective politics and reshaped Chinese studies in the United States. Addressing the interplay of capital and geopolitics, chapter 7 shows the rise of capitalist cosmopolitanism and its depoliticizing tendencies. The trashing of memories of socialism and the Third World to the dustbin of history hollows out the subjective agency and transformative energy of collective movements. A new cosmopolitanism premised on possessive individualism and neoliberalism has reshaped the study of Chinese culture in the American classroom.

Chapter 8 concludes with a reexamination of key ideas and frameworks underpinning the historical case studies throughout the book. Many terms—empire and nation-state, ethnicity, universalism and cosmopolitanism, value and history, culture and politics, nationalism and internationalism, depoliticization and globalization—are fundamental to understanding China's past and ongoing engagement with the world. They have undergone controversy and distortion but maintain certain lines of consistency. Sharing Wang Hui's definition of Chinese modernity as a "modernity against modernity," the chapter delves into the discursive frameworks, historical practices, and polemics of these conceptual frameworks and clarifies their meanings, uses, and variations in history. The book ends by asserting China's deep yearning to be recognized as an equal part of the world. Involved in a national-international nexus, Chinese thinkers and modernizers have striven, in Perry Anderson's words, to "transcend the nation-state toward a wider community."[64]

Morality and
Global Vision in
Kang Youwei's World Community

IN THE WORLD TODAY, the rhetoric of interstate cooperation and inter-dependence barely masks increasing tensions between nations and people. Digital media and connectivity, standardized lifestyles and tastes, rapid flows of information, massive immigration, and expanding global trade are fully matched by divisive nationalism, protectionism, identity politics, religious fundamentalism, and geopolitical rivalry. Torn between cooperation and self-interest, between universal norms and particularistic attachment, how can an individual relate to strangers of a different nation? How can a group interact, communicate, and coexist productively with other groups? Since the advent of the Westphalian system, attempts to address these questions have generated a variety of world visions. Cosmopolitanism, a faith in humans' capacity to coexist and work together, is the most prominent and enduring. In the aftermath of the Cold War, political life for a moment indulged in a euphoria of global harmony and cooperation, as developed and emerging economies intersected, markets expanded, goods circulated, and people immigrated across borders. But the euphoria quickly retreated to the particularistic attachment of ethnonationalism and tribalism. The essence of nationalism rests on the claim that "a person's most fundamental political obligations are interconnected with the form of social life of which he is part, and which his political structures are obliged to protect."[1] By contrast, cosmopolitanism proposes that a person can be both a national citizen and a human person, contrary to the nationalist priority of particularistic fealty.

Conventional political theory in the West has been skeptical of cosmopolitanism as a principle for international order. Although global thinkers since Kant have upheld the possibility that different societies might interact, communicate, and coexist, mainstream political philosophy has favored the sovereign nation-state as the fundamental unit in the international order. This focus prompted Martin Wight to declare that international theory leaves no room for a prospect of world community and that "a tradition of speculation about the society of states, or the family of nations, or the international community . . . does not, at first sight, exist."[2] Instead of being construed in a language of law and morality and based on humans' rational capacity to coexist globally, the interstate space has been viewed as a field of struggle for survival, rivalry, and domination. The sovereign state as the principal power player in the Hobbesian jungle has preoccupied political thinkers and suppressed alternative world visions.

Anticipating the impending collapse of globalization in the wake of September 11, 2001, John Mearsheimer asserts the great powers' tendency to act aggressively toward each other in the struggle for hegemony. Global trade networks and social interaction are illusory and belied by perpetual conflict between nations. The accelerated pace of economic globalization has misled many to believe that peace among the great powers would be around the corner, and that the horizon of a family of nations was tantalizingly in sight. But expanded military bases and arms buildup, the translation of economic power into military might, and the fiercely competitive penchant of the powerful states only amplify the perennial doctrine of political realism: "international politics has always been a ruthless and dangerous business." Great powers always fear each other and aggressively compete for hegemony. The top priority of each state is to maximize its share of world power at the expense of other states.[3]

Realpolitik is also at work in culture. In his influential *Clash of Civilizations and the Remaking of World Order*, Samuel Huntington highlights the conflict of civilizational and cultural identities. Relations among nations and people always hinge on a rigid definition of who "we" are as opposed to "them": "People define themselves by reference to ancestry, religion, language, history, values, customs, and institutions. They identify with cultural groups: tribes, ethnic groups, religious communities, nations and at the broadest level, civilizations."[4] The primacy accorded to particularistic loyalty to the state, nation, and cultural patrimony has reinforced the experience of political separateness, moral tension, racial divides, and geographical isolation. All these run counter to the cosmopolitan vision of an interconnected world.

Alternatives to political realism, however, have been proposed and practiced in the East and the West. Rather than aggressive power competition and paranoiac divisions, thinkers have envisioned international relations based on rationality and moral improvement. Faced with the eighteenth-century world marked by accelerated interaction of people in travel and commerce, Kant realized that human beings could not remain in their separate spheres of identification and value but had to learn to live and work together. Kantian cosmopolitanism rests on a belief in humans as "self-developing and self-directing beings with the possibility of transforming existing relations of intersocial estrangement into relations of familiarity."[5] Now this vision of relations between nations and individuals provides a comparative perspective for appreciating similar world visions of Chinese thinkers. Although the Qing empire's encounter with the international system dealt a traumatic blow to the traditional tianxia worldview, modern Chinese thinkers have searched for a politically viable world by revitalizing the ancient tradition.

Confucian thinkers cherished the ideal of the whole world under heaven and an outlook beyond local community and ethnic lineage, projecting a unified worldview inclusive of different cultural and ethnic groups. Unlike the menacing spectacle of national-cultural chauvinism attached to China today, Confucian universalism stems from a scheme of a ritualistic empire, which is at odds with the modern empire rooted in power alliances, strategic balance, and pursuits of hegemony. As Joseph Levenson noted, Confucian literati accepted cultural differences as the way of the world. Although they distinguished between the civilized and barbarians, they were aware that "the barbarians are always with us." Rather than a structure of domination, the tianxia order appeared to be "a criterion, a standpoint, not a point of departure." Chinese left home to travel and settle in other countries, but "not one had any Confucian pretensions to be bearing out a Word," as did Christian missionaries.[6] At the time when thinkers like Kang Youwei began imagining a viable prospect of the world, however, Confucian universalism was challenged and threatened by Western powers.

This chapter considers how Kang Youwei revised the Confucian moral tradition of datong and formulated cultural exchange as bridges to a common world. Kang's ideas resonate strongly with the Kantian notion of aesthetic humanity. In Kang's utopian imagination, moral vision and aesthetic sensibility emerge as an antidote to the realpolitik international relations.

The Public Principle, Selfishness, and Equality

In *Datong shu* (Book of great community), Kang Youwei projects a world society by abolishing nation-state boundaries, gender barriers, political and social hierarchies, class stratification, and racial divides. Premised on a broadly public principle of *gong* 公, this ideal dates back to the Confucian classic *Records of Rites* (*Li ji*), compiled during the Han dynasty (206 BCE to 220 CE). Invoking a golden age, the ideal society raises the prospect of a public community governed by equalitarian principles, a commitment to common goods, and a sharing of natural bounty and fruits of labor. It is a community where each person has his or her interest cared for and is able to care for others in an extended family. Fruits of nature and products of labor are distributed, and there is no waste and no private hoarding of wealth.

> When the Great Way was practiced, the world was shared by all alike. The worthy and the able were promoted to office and men practiced good faith and lived in harmony. Therefore they did not regard as parents only their own parents, or as sons only their own sons. The aged were cared for till the end of their lives, the able-bodied pursued proper employment, while the young were nurtured in growing up. Provisions were made to care for widows, the orphaned and the sick. Men had their tasks while women had their hearths. They hated to see goods lying about in waste, yet they did not hoard them for themselves; they dislike the thought that their energies were not fully used, yet they used them not for private ends. Therefore all evil plotting was prevented and thieves and rebels did not arise, so that people could leave their outer gates unbolted. This was the age of the Great Community.[7]

Gong means "sharing by all," "universal," "fair to all," "common goods," or "public and communal space." In an essay on gongli (public principle), Kang defines the term by treating humanity as a biological, evolutionary process. Scientific, natural laws lay the ground for human laws, and human institution must fit into the lawful texture and rhythm of nature. Yet natural laws impose necessary limits, and human laws entail freedom and innovation.

Recognizing the split between humans and nature, Kang concludes that the public principle signals ethical freedom that is bonded by natural law on the one hand and public policy beneficial to all humanity on the other.[8]

Kang pits gong against si 私 (private). Politically, si refers to self-interested oligarchy, the family or a dynasty house and its monopoly of power; socially, it denotes a class bent on its own advantage; economically, it implies the hoarding and plundering of public resources and concentration of wealth. Si thus describes how self-seeking states, families, and individuals maintain a private sphere and are bent on seeking power and profit at the expense of the common good. The private pursuit undermines the public principle, plunging humans into a divided, unequal, and competitive struggle. Nation-states are also regarded in terms of si, since they are self-interested and hungry for power and territory. Nation-states should be abolished, so that there would be no more interstate war; families should go too, for there would be no disparity of love and affection among family members. Self-gains should be banished, so that resources, goods, and services would not be used for private ends.

Of the boundaries to be erased, Kang names the nation-state as the major stumbling block to the rise of the great community. Whether it is the belligerent kingdoms in China's Warring States era or the modern nation-states vying to gain territories and markets, the nation-state seems to be most selfish, destructive, and oppressive. "Once a state is established, patriotism is born. Everyone must be loyal to and work for the advantage of their own state and aggresses against other states."[9] Constant interstate rivalry breaks the moral fabric of human society and has proved ecologically damaging. Citing examples from Chinese and Western histories, Kang condemns extended interstate warfare and bloody battles that killed millions of soldiers and innocent people, disrupted the normal production of life, and savaged natural environments. Both human bodies and natural environments fell prey to war and massacre. In the wake of battles, the mutilated corpses are strewn in the wilderness, rivers run with blood, disease and plague sweep across the land, and the forests are burned and charred.

The root cause of destructive war is the selfish pursuit of power and wealth by the nation-state. Each member of the nation feels attached to their country, because the nation protects their private interest. Morally upright persons cannot but swear allegiance to the state and accept killing other people and gaining territory as the reason of the state (68; 79). Narrow-minded nationalism and patriotism become the incentive for citizens to gain the honor of heroism. The Warring States' scramble for power and wealth interrupts everyday economic life in grassroots communities, pillages natural resources in order to supply ever growing armies and military buildup, incurs excessive expenditures, and lays waste the land and farms (68; 79).

Kang pits the public principle against the nation-state's self-aggrandizement. This alludes to a perennial debate in Confucianism about the conflict between utilitarian interest and political morality. Confucianism defines the morally virtuous ruler as rooted in righteousness, which entails the public principle of caring for the whole community and providing for economic reproduction of livelihood. Mencius elaborates on this principle with reference to wars in the *Book of Mencius*. To stop a war between the Qin and Chu states, an advisor argues that the war would not be in the states' interest. Continued fighting would impoverish people, diminish their wealth, and ultimately weaken the states, proving detrimental to all warring parties—a lose-lose outcome. To this utilitarian argument, Mencius answers that if utilitarian self-interests of security, wealth, and prestige are arguments against war, these considerations will not work, because power-seeking states would make haste to realize their short-term goals here and now. "The notion that in basing morality on the pursuit of interests men can be led to support the universal interest over particular interests is a chimera," wrote Schwartz.[10]

By attacking the self-interest of Warring States, Kang affirms that the morality of the state is not to aggrandize private interests in pursuit of wealth, power, and territory but to take care of the well-being of all lives under heaven. This constitutes the essential feature of the public principle: the sharing of all bounty and resources equally, regardless of social status and individual ability. Natural bounties and fruits of labor belong to the commons, and goods are to be equally distributed. The pursuit of self-interest and private pillaging and possession of public assets violate the public principle and social harmony, breaking the communal fabric and fragmenting social ties. Kang recalls the foresight of *Records of Rites* about the evil of self-seeking. The golden age of the public community begins to fray and break down as individuals and vested groups gravitate toward self-interest and a selfish agenda.

Now the Great Way has fallen into obscurity, and everything under Heaven is the possession of private families. Each regards as parents only his own parents, as sons only his own sons; goods and labor are employed for selfish ends. Hereditary offices and titles are granted by ritual law, while walls and moats must provide security. Ritual and rites are used . . . to set up social institutions, organize farms and villages, honor the brave and wise, and bring merit to the individual. Therefore intrigue and plotting come about and men take up arms.[11]

Kantian cosmopolitanism insists that moral sympathy and aesthetic communication could build bridges among people and nations. Sensitive to the power of cultural exchange, Kang Youwei also focuses on aesthetic sensibility as bridges to a world community. Kant's aesthetic notion of *sensus communis* resonates meaningfully with Kang's world community to be achieved through closer ties in morality, culture, and aesthetic experience.

In its power to forge moral empathy and sensibility between different subjects, aesthetic consideration seems to be a universal discourse, eminently capable of breaking out of the particularistic closet on the way to a common world. The rise of aesthetic discourse in Europe was concomitant with the disintegration of the religious, unitary order. While European societies emerged from the ruins of the theocratic regime, modern market society was constantly torn asunder by rival interests and agendas. Divided feelings and conflicted pursuits plagued individuals and states. Kant diagnosed this fragmentation and disharmony with a blanket term, *unsocial sociability*.[12] The term refers to the individual's paradoxical tendency to associate with others socially while simultaneously competing with them in self-pursuit and aggrandizement. Social members are "bound together with mutual oppositions that threaten to break up the society," and each individual pursues private agendas at the expense of others.[13] In "Idea for a Universal History with a Cosmopolitan Purpose," Kant extends this domestic antagonism to that of mutually opposed, self-serving states in the international arena. Although the eighteenth century saw increasing global commerce and interaction among people and nations, the world was rife with conflict and war. The aesthetic, which aspires to a shared plane of sense and sensibility over and above economic self-interest and geopolitical conflict, seems to offer an attractive solution to bridge the constant schism. Aesthetic experience in culture and the arts gestures toward a vision of rationally conceived society, where intersubjective feelings resonate and a genuinely human community seems tangible. Kant writes, "Beautiful arts and sciences, which by means of a universally communicable pleasure and an elegance and refinement make human beings, if not morally better, at least better mannered for society, very much reduce the tyranny of sensible tendencies, and prepare humans for a sovereignty in which reason alone shall have Power."[14]

A gateway of sense and sensibility, the aesthetic leads to rationality and understanding in the social sphere. Sunk in their private sphere under "the tyranny of sensible tendencies" and engrossed in material survival, humans are bound to antagonize each other like barbarians. The aesthetic elevates humans to a higher level of culture and morality. Judgments of cultivated behavior and beautiful taste point to a common ground of sociality over divisions and conflict, a platform informed by the idea of sensus communis. Rather than crudely sensuous life governed by primal aggression, sensus communis claims a moral, rational capacity that transcends one's private, particular sphere by putting oneself "into the position of everyone else, merely by abstracting from the limitations that contingently attach to our judging." To extend empathy requires a cosmopolitan mind to set the individual "apart from the subjective private conditions of the judgment, within which so many others are as if bracketed." It is to reflect on one's own judgment "from a universal standpoint" by putting an individual into others. The enlarged mind will suspend the individual's narrow-mindedness and rise above the subjective conditions.[15]

Aesthetic experience contains pleasure common and sharable among all humans, forging affective and imaginary bonds conducive to reciprocity and sociality. By means of aesthetic communication, civil society is now reimagined as a public space for experiencing shared pleasure in arts and ritual activities rather than one fraught with rivalry and conflict. A human being with aesthetic taste is sociable rather than self-indulgent, outgoing rather than inner directed.

Thus, the public sphere is pitted against the private sphere, the social against asocial behavior, broad-mindedness against the egotism of "unsocial sociability." Aesthetic experience delivers humans from this entrapment and enables us to "realize the ideal world of moral freedom in the given world of egoistic strife and unsociability through culture"; it minimizes "our natural bondage" by promoting humans' potential for moral improvement and purposeful action.[16]

Kant's idea of sensus communis, as Terry Eagleton writes, proffers a comforting fiction of the universal embedded in humanity's aesthetic existence. Taste must be universal against private pursuits and self-interest: it "cannot spring from the object which is purely contingent, or from any particular desire or interest of the subject, which is similarly parochial." Since the rational is universal and cognition is supposed to be common to all individuals, the sharable pleasure we take in the aesthetic is "the knowledge that our very structural constitution as human subjects predisposes us to mutual harmony." To be human is to engage in the aesthetic activity of shared pleasure and to be prepared to share with others the beautiful illusion of a consensus of feeling and understanding. Each of us partakes of this pleasurable communication, mesmerized by the prospect of "a universal solidarity beyond all vulgar utility." This aesthetic cosmopolitanism offers a symbolic solution to the fragmentary, divisive jumble of prejudices, custom, and parochial habits of mind.[17]

Cosmopolitan implications of the aesthetic are clear. Despite the troubling tendency toward unsocial sociability, cultural exchange could be accepted by individuals raised above the level of survival and labor. As Sankar Muthu has noted, widespread communication in the eighteenth century in salons, public places, and the arts inspired Kant with a vision of aesthetic humanity. By engaging in arts and literature, by rising over and above the interests of self-preservation and survival, individuals are deemed able to share pleasures and communicate judgment and taste, leading to a community of empathy and emotional resonance. From a broad humanistic perspective, Kant states, "Humanity [*Humanität*] means both the universal feelings of sympathy, and the ability to engage universally in very intimate communication. When these two qualities are combined, they constitute the sociality that befits [our] humanity [*Menschheit*] and distinguishes it from the limitations [characteristic] of animals."[18]

The aesthetic of humanity hinges on a broader idea of human beings as cultural agents who wield aesthetic power and remake the existing world for political freedom. Endowed with the ability to inscribe the world with human values and to transform our natural drives, the cultural agent humanizes the world with aesthetic forms.[19] The world of humanity, rising above creaturely needs and material wants, also appeals to humans' aesthetic sensibility. Rather than being a prisoner in a particular culture, the cultural agent connects the universal and the particular. The idea that all people are equally endowed with the ability to reflect on and beautify their own inherited situation recognizes the commonality of humans. Although particular agents cannot choose where they are born, and their trajectories bear particular imprints of circumstances, customs, and tradition, they can choose to reflect on and transform the world they are born into—therein lies agential aesthetic humanity. By this logic, the cultural agent should grant equal respect to all historical, cultural heritages as ongoing products derived from rationality and creativity intelligible and sharable to all. The particular is only a locus for advancing the universal, leading to a mutual appreciation of an aesthetic taste embedded in a specific historical tradition.

Kang Youwei retrieved a Confucian language of heaven to assert a similar universal logic for aesthetic communication. In response to the eclipse of the tianxia world order under the assaults of the nation-state system, Kang reconsiders a moral and political order sustained not solely by legality and coercion but primarily by ritual, music, moral patterns. Tianxia denotes a sphere of culture and value—a set of ideals and conduct to be internalized by all individuals and groups. In opposition to the Warring States in ancient China and the Westphalian system of nation-states, tianxia has recently resurfaced as the center of debate. Rooted in Confucianism and the collective unconscious, this concept, as Levenson said, describes a world "whose values were Value, whose civilization was Civilization, a transnational antithesis to barbarism."[20] As colonialism and imperialism dragged China into the forest of nations in the late nineteenth century, Kang saw the ancient order being cut down to size and noted that as "the globe is completely known, what was called the central empire [Zhongguo] and adjacent territories are but one corner of Asia and one-eightieth of the world" (69; 80). Western encroachments broke up the moral fabric that maintained traditional communities, and the Central Kingdom was in tatters. Relations between China and other countries and regions were no longer based on ritual, tributary networks, commerce, and family ties under the aegis of Confucianism but were increasingly driven by ruthless competition, conflict, and domination. Aggressive geopolitics and zero-sum competition became the name of the game and penetrated Chinese consciousness.

Datong shu assaults the reader with an excruciating list of miseries of the world: class oppression, national strife, civil conflict, natural disaster, diseases, mutilated bodies, gender and race inequality, dependence, and ignorance. Shortly after China's conflict with France in 1885, Kang fled Canton and returned to his native village to live a life of study and reflection in his ancestral house of Abiding Fragrance. Every day, when he stepped out of his quiet study, he was overwhelmed by not only the suffering and bickering of his neighbors but also the news of bloody interstate wars around the world and particularly in East Asia: "All the people of the whole world are but grieving and miserable people, and all the living beings of the whole world are but murdered beings. The azure heaven and the round Earth are nothing but a great slaughter yard, a great prison" (2–3; 63).

Against bloody conflict, Kang attempted to restore certain strands of the Confucian worldview. Along with his associate Liang Qichao, he engaged with the Qing government and devised strategies to implement modern reforms in politics, education, economy, and social and gender relations. But Kang gave priority to moral and aesthetic problems in China's encounter with the world. He raised the question of how the sensibility of one person can and must connect and resonate with another in a world divided by boundaries and conflict, and how a far-reaching sensibility can be articulated. In a world of suffering and conflict, how can moral empathy enable one individual to commiserate with another? What forms of aesthetic culture might foster this?

Like Kant, Kang thought of the world in terms of morality and the aesthetic. To him the aesthetic consists in learning from and immersing oneself in diverse cultures in a way that involves all senses, body and soul. Learning allows us to have intimate access to others and fosters sympathy and shared appreciation of pluralistic cultural forms. The way to a unitary world is through aesthetic enjoyment and circulation of cultural traditions across national boundaries.

> I have drunk deeply of the intellectual heritage of ancient India, Greece, Persia, and Rome, and of modern England, France, Germany, and America. I have pillowed my head upon them, and my soul in dreams has fathomed them. With the wise old men, noted scholars, famous figures, and beautiful women of all countries I have likewise often joined hands, we have sat on mats side by side, sleeves touching, sharing our meal, and I have grown to love them. Each day I have been offered and have made use of the dwellings, clothing, food, boats, vehicles, utensils, government, education, arts, and music of a myriad of countries, and these have stimulated my mind and enriched my spirit. Do they progress? Then we all progress with them. Are they happy? Then we are happy with them. Do they suffer? Then we suffer with them. It is as if we were all parts of an electrical force, which interconnects all things, or partook of the pure essence that encompasses all things.[21]

This passage presents a vignette of long-distance learning and exchange by way of far-reaching sense and sensibility. Broad-minded and sensitive, the aesthetic subject embraces a spectrum of cultural heritages across the globe. Appealing to the senses as well as the intellect, the approach to foreign cultures involves the five senses, the imagination, and the soul. The lessons and wisdom are highly revered—the best that has been written and thought and preserved by "old men, noted scholars, famous figures, and beautiful women." "Beautiful women" serves as an aesthetic metaphor for cross-cultural experience. Far from being dry and pedantic, learning is pleasurable through feminine charms and fleshed out in intimate experiences of touching, joining hands, sharing meals. Moving from body to soul, the aesthetic experience expands the spirit and enhances shared happiness. The parallel progress between "they" and "we" implies a common path of civilizational advancement, projecting a normative measure for assessing each particular culture. Cross-cultural learning is an educational as well as a maturing project, akin to the program of aesthetically inspired *Bildung* in German romanticism. While Bildung cultivates civic virtue purged of unsocial sociability, Kang's moral and aesthetic progress aims at the cultivation of noble virtue that may lead to intercultural understanding and sympathy.

Cross-cultural reciprocity could be mediated via the Confucian idea of *qi* (氣), often translated as "electric energy or vital forces." Running through all boundaries of race, states, and regions, qi captures an all-embracing process and a cosmic substance, at once physical, biological, spiritual, and moral. Permeating heaven and earth, it flows through humans, animals, and plants. Similar to the concept of ether, qi drives our perception and sympathy with everything and everybody else. Kang writes, "I have a body, then I share with coexisting bodies that which permeates the air of heaven, permeates the matter of earth, permeates the breath of man" (3–4; 64). Rather than a product of a particular tradition, the qi-filled body is considered under the rubric of *tianren* 天人 (heaven-endowed human) and is equivalent to another body, be it man or woman, high or low class. The heaven-endowed body functions as an equalizing principle and a source of critique of the arbitrary divisions of gender, class, ethnicity, and nation-state.

Rather than mere disembodied truth, qi is bodied forth by perception, sympathy, and benevolent social feelings under the sign of *ren* 仁 (benevolence, compassion, love). Ren describes an ethical sensibility and compassionate connectedness with others, regardless of their station and identity. In this sense, qi-based perception and compassion is as aesthetic as it is moral.

Invoking the mind's capacity to empathize with human suffering, Kang attributes the lack of sympathy to the absence of far-reaching sensibility. In childhood, Kang read about the well-known massacres in the Warring States period and the burning of France's city of Sedan by Otto von Bismarck. But in his uncultivated, immature sensibility, he remained tone-deaf to those horrendous events. Kang attributes this lack of perception and feeling to the inadequacy of humanity, since all human beings under heaven are brothers of "the same womb" (5; 65). Humanity consists in sensitive awareness and outreaching compassion: "hence, if men sever what constitutes their compassionate love, their human-ness will be annihilated, and return to barbarism" (5; 64).

The principle of benevolence is key to Confucian morality embodied by the Kingly Way (wangdao). As a foundation for benevolent governance, the Kingly Way denotes a capacious sensitivity to people's pain and suffering, expressed by the Mencian motto "All men have a mind that cannot bear [to see the sufferings of] others" (人皆有不忍之心). *The Works of Mencius* illustrates this principle with an intriguing scenario. When King Xuan of the state of Qi saw an ox being led to sacrifice, he could not bear to see "its frightened appearance, as if it were an innocent person going to the place of death."[22] The king immediately ordered that a sheep should replace the ox. Mencius advised that this was a sign of the king's "unbearing mind," and if he could only apply this sensitivity to the state and the people, he would have the Kingly Way and attain orderly government. The king was not sure he could do that, because, like any other selfish man, he loved wealth and female charm. Mencius replied that all men had similar desires, but if the king understood that other people's desire was as valid as his own, he would take measures to satisfy popular desires and thus attain the Kingly Way, which is nothing but benevolence put into practice.

Rather than an administrative or legal entity, the politics of the Kingly Way is primarily a moral one. If Kantian aesthetic experience facilitates social cohesion and sustains reciprocity of nations and people, Confucian benevolent government resorts to ritual, music, sensitivity, and compassion. Its object is the human body in all its creaturely, sensuous, and emotional attributes. As Eagleton observes, the aesthetic concerns "nothing less than the whole of our sensate life together—the business of affections and aversions, of how the world strikes the body on its sensory surfaces, of that which takes root in the gaze and the guts and all that arises from our most banal, biological insertion into the world."[23] This aesthetic politics presumes a close fit between the well-being of a private body, whose welfare is the central focus of a kingly order. No political order could flourish that fails to take care of the lived experience of people.

In addition to caring about the material well-being of the population, benevolent government promotes shared pleasure and forges emotional solidarity. *Mencius* offers another scenario that illustrates shared aesthetic experience as part of the Kingly Way. When the king of the state of Qi conveyed his worry about his indulgence in music, Mencius advised him reassuringly: "If the king's love of music were very great, the kingdom of Qi would be close to a state of good government." But it made a huge difference whether the king enjoyed music alone and with a select few or shared music with the majority of the people. In the former case, people would complain that the king, absorbed in pleasures enjoyed privately with a crony, ignored their distress and needs. The deprived people would frown on other aesthetic privileges, such as the beauty of the royal plumes, horses, and entourage. But if the king shared music with his people, and if the high and low all had equal access to music, the people would enjoy music as much as the king. The people would then rejoice in looking at the majestic beauty of the king's carriages and other pleasures.[24]

Shared joy in music is more than entertainment. It is both moral and political: bodies and hearts are connected in emotional empathy, reciprocity, and conviviality. Mencius's moral precept enjoins: "Treat with reverence the elders in your own family, so that the elders in the families of others shall be similarly treated; treat with kindness due to the young in your own family, so that the young in the family of others shall be similarly treated—do this, and the empire may be made to go round in your palm."[25]

Extending these moral convictions to the conception of good government in modern times, Kang bases politics on the aesthetic principle of removing pain and seeking pleasure. In a way that resonates with the idea of natural right, he brings the notion of the pleasurable body to Confucian political culture. The standard for assessing the legitimacy of governance is not only political and moral but also aesthetic, emotional, and bodily. This standard derives from the aesthetic experience of shared pleasure and collective ritual. A legitimate political order increases people's pleasure and reduces their distress.

This sensibility informs an unbroken chain of being extending from person to family to community and government, all the way to all humans under heaven. Kang depicts a rising scale of obligations from the lowest human unit to the broadest one.

> Master Kang says, being that I am a man, I would be uncompassionate to flee from men and not to share their grief and miseries. And being that I was born into a family, and [by virtue of] receiving the nurture of others was able to have this life, I then have the responsibilities of a family member. Should I flee from this [responsibility], my behavior would be false. . . . And why would it not be the same with the public debt we owe to one country and the world? Being that we are born into one country, have received the civilization of one country, and thereby have its knowledge, then we have the responsibilities of a citizen. If we flee from this [responsibility] and abandon this country, this country will perish and its people will be annihilated, and then civilization will be destroyed. (48; 65)

By this widening gyre of sympathy, imagination, and obligation, Kang Youwei suggests that a member of a local community could become a citizen of the world.

Kant argued that the republican state, based on the sanctity of right and representative government, offered the best hope for cosmopolitan world order. As citizens of a republic, the people would refuse to succumb to the arbitrary decision by a despotic ruler to go to war. They would judge a war by its potential damage to their own life and property, and hence would be less likely to be coaxed into it by some extravagant national pride.[26] Aware of ideas of the people as citizens yet reared in a different moral tradition, Kang differs from Kant in his elaboration of the ethico-political doctrine of benevolent governance. By revitalizing the Confucian notion of benevolent government, Kang extended the concept to the world in search of a vision of unified world community.

"At the very root of social relations," notes Eagleton, "lies the aesthetic, source of all human bonding."[27] This insight illuminates the intimacy of morality and aesthetics at the center of politics and makes Kant comparable to Kang. Kantian aesthetic disinterestedness does not mean self-centeredness and lack of interest in morality and politics. Aesthetic detachment means indifference to practical interests, it is true, yet not to others' interest but to one's own. The aesthetic subject is detached from one's own narrow sphere and self-absorption, from unsocial sociability. This reading of civic virtue resonates with Kang's ideas about sympathy, benevolence, and governance—and with Liang Qichao's public morality, discussed in the next chapter. Civic virtue is a "passionate affection for his fellow citizens and for shared conditions of their common life."[28] The aesthetic sensibility stems from the pity we feel for each other in the state of nature and is based on the empathetic imagination, which makes us capable of "transporting ourselves outside ourselves, and identifying ourselves with the suffering animal, leaving our being, so to speak, in order to take his. . . . Thus no one becomes sensitive except when his imagination is animated and begins to transport himself outside himself."[29] In both Kang and Kant, the aesthetic raises the possibility of fostering a civic virtue of benevolence extendable to different peoples and communities in the world.

Revitalizing Confucian Morality

In the Confucian tradition, self-cultivation internalizes normative moral principles. But rather than personal perfection, spiritual practice must extend to social and political realms. Private learning needs to be upgraded to the scale of moral and social improvement. This underlies the ethico-political core of social order. In actual dynastic changes, however, the moral core and sociopolitical practices diverged and split and took the form of a divorce between names and substance, an estrangement of morality from warped institutions. In the Spring and Autumn period, early Confucianism, exemplified by the classic of *Chunqiu* 春秋 (*The Spring and Autumn Annals*), arose as a form of moral, political critique against the collapse of ritual and music (*libeng yuehuai* 禮崩樂壞). The *Chunqiu*-style critique sought to reinstitute a proper ethico-political order on the model of the golden age of the Three Dynasties. The scholar-officials over the centuries continued to exercise this ethico-political perspective and pass judgment on rulers and social ills. This sense of a split between the ethical principle inherent in ritual and music, on the one hand, and institutional corruption, on the other, ran through several schools of thought but came to self-consciousness in the perennial project of commentaries on Confucianism.

Kang Youwei updated the Confucian critique of the separation of music from society, and morality from politics. His accounts of the historical evolution of the Three Ages (三世) in his commentaries of Confucianism begins with the golden age of antiquity, when Great Peace (datong) prevailed. But the Three Dynasties in antiquity witnessed a devolution to the age of lesser tranquility, when people loved only their own kin and family and pursued private gains. This age declined further to the Age of Disorder in the times of Confucius. The process then gradually rose to the Age of Rising Peace and culminated in the Age of Great Peace. This narrative portrays an ascending scale of moral principles, embodied by successive forms of social and political order. The Three Dynasties trajectory arose in his short book *Renlei gongli* 人類公理 (Public principles of humanity) and was given fuller expression in *Shili gongfa quanshu* 實理公法 (Book of substantive public law).[30] After the failure of his petition for reform, Kang began to move away from metaphysical arguments to a historical account of the evolution of government and society. Drawing on the New Text School of commentary of the Han dynasty, Kang built on the interpretations by Dong Zhongshu 董仲舒 and the Gongyang and Guliang commentaries. For the New Text School, *The Spring and Autumn Annals* was as an activist, reformist work of historiography, figuring Confucius as a reformer. According to He Xiu, the earliest of the three forms of governance was one of decay and disorder. In order to rectify the political disorder, Confucius devoted all his energy to restructuring the state of Lu by recovering and transmitting the ritualistic principles of the Zhou order. This proactive agenda is followed by the era of rising peace, in which Confucius extended the local principles to all other states, thus bringing peace and order in the Middle Kingdom. The apex of moral triumph is "universal peace," in which "the whole world, far and near, great and small, is like one."[31]

This reformist image of Confucius informs Kang's book *Confucius as Reformer*. In it, Kang claims that while competing with a wide array of contradictory theories, Confucius did not simply transmit prior bodies of thought but revamped the ethico-political principles of the Zhou order, using an imagined past to transform the present.[32] As the uncrowned king (*suwang* 素王), Confucius rearticulated the Kingly Way through his study of institutional changes in the state of Lu. In the book *Li yun* (禮運), the Three Ages followed one another in a descending order. The sage rulers of the Three Dynasties had presided over an era of less tranquility or *xiaokang* (小康), marking a downward turn from the golden age to "a world marked by both military power and ritual morality," a time during which "the empire became a world of families where people love only their own parents and their own children [and] goods and labor are used only for private advantage."[33] Yet these forward and backward pointers along a historical timeline are not important. Instead, an upwardly spiraling narrative rises above historical reality according to a teleology. Due to the distortions coming from outside Confucianism and internal institutional corruptions, Chinese culture for thousands of years had remained at the xiaokang stage. The modern period, however, was one of transition "away from a social system based on patriarchal clans and tribes and a corresponding political system based on the despotic authority of rulers over people or nobles over commoners." Yet from the xiaokang society, there would "emerge a world where the hierarchical distance between peoples and their rulers and between different individuals in their social relations would be markedly diminished." The political form embodying this new relationship would be the nation-state and constitutional monarchy.[34]

Some regard Kang's reading of the Confucian tradition as conservative, and others view his appropriation of Western democracy as a misguided cosmopolitanism. These two extreme views obscure Kang's universal and moral aspirations. Bogged down in a narrow view of morality, detractors miss the universal ethical orientation of Confucius as the uncrowned king and the politically comprehensive visions in Kang's reading of *The Spring and Autumn Annals*. The uncrowned king deserves credit and admiration from posterity, because he did not embody and defend the established institution of power and the entrenched core values tied to a specific time or kingdom. Without constraints of official title and position, the sage was free to articulate and project a new set of values. Though embedded in the *Analects*, these values are nowhere to be found in a given institution or practice in empirical reality. Against the vicissitudes of political order depicted in *The Spring and Autumn Annals*, Confucius attempted to advance the normative principles that, though derived from the reading of specific circumstances, were broad enough to transcend the actual conditions and applicable to other periods and states. In Kang Youwei and the New Text School commentary, Confucianism separates value from fact, and extracts the genuine content from the institutional forms, distinguishing benevolent governance from its travesty in the corruption of legitimate status (*mingfen* 名份). Although as a commoner he was powerless to realize the new values within the established framework, Confucius tried to articulate what was impossible and unpractical.

Kang admired the Duke of Zhou as the paragon of ideal morality and culture, but this is not to be read as the rearguard preservation of the ancient order. Kang's elevated image presupposes that the Duke of Zhou occupied a position that seamlessly combined virtue, power, and authority (有德有位) and was capable of implementing universal public laws based on the Dao. The unity of morality and politics was precisely what Confucius looked forward to but failed to implement in his lifetime.[35]

The aspiration for normative ethical principles sets the *Chunqiu* off from the *Zuozhuan* 左傳 (Zuo commentary). Just as Kang viewed the *Zuozhuan* as a distortion of the *Chunqiu* spirit, so Schwartz expressed a distaste about the former as embodiment of an implicit might-makes-right, winner-takes-all approach to human affairs. For all its vivid accounts of alliances and counteralliances, power struggle and intrigue, and the rise and fall of states, the *Zuozhuan* reflects a "morality of pure political expediency and deplorable concern with 'success and failure' rather than with pure moral motivation." In today's language, the *Zuozhuan* narrative would be the language of realpolitik keyed to the cycle of war and peace—the currency of the Westphalian international system. On the other hand, the *Chunqiu*, while loaded with details of military strategies and brutal, contradictory human behavior, is not mired in power politics. The book can still be treated "ahistorically." Rather than plunging into the thick of melodramatic vicissitudes, the *Chunqiu* extracts moral precepts that "involved what might be called perennial and metahistorical principles of ethical and political judgment." The classical criteria of praise and blame (*baobian*) pertains most judicially and effectively at the ethical level, holding up politics and events not as a gripping, agonistic story but as a moral mirror of benevolence and justice.[36]

The critical thrust of the *Chunqiu* lies in its diagnosis of how historical reality falls short of the ethical ideals and in the ability to discern actual violations of ethnical norms. Confucian anxiety over the breakdown of order is associated with a vigorous upholding of status obligation and names. This seemingly rearguard concern came under fire by May Fourth antitraditional critiques, which condemned Kang's intellectual and political conservatism. But if he agonized over the breakdown of order and violations by the Warring

States, Confucius can hardly be characterized a defender of moribund regimes. Rather, he was grappling with and passing judgment on the status quo. In this light, Confucius might present the image of a judicious innovator, a censorious judge, and a visionary thinker. In Schwartz's reading, it is the ethico-political and nonfactual aspect of ren, not the reified institutions, that constitutes the norms by which "the monstrous behavior and caprices of the authority and power holders are duly recorded." The moral principles of justice reveal the decay of legitimate authority and depletion of normative principles, whether it is due to subversion from below or to corruption of power holders or authority figures.[37]

Following Dong Zhongshu, Kang recovered from the historical periods a set of moral principles that transcend the mutations and corruptions associated with specific institutions. He strove to extend the moral principles derived from a particular society to interstate and cross-cultural relations. Just as the ethico-political truths of Shakespeare or Aristotle are relevant to different centuries and cultures—a shared property of the aesthetic world community, writes Schwartz—so Kang Youwei's focus on the *Chunqiu* and three stages reveals an effort to apply universal standards to the world community.

Equality and Democratic Critique

Critics with nationalist sentiments have objected to Kang's attempt to follow the liberal model in the West. Liberals have charged Kang with promoting a conservative agenda of constitutional monarchy. Just as Confucius attempted to extract moral principles from the actual events of the *Chunqiu*, so Kang sought to articulate a worldview based on his experiences in the West and tease out ethical principles from Western democracy. Although he frequently referred to the United States, Germany, or Belgium as the exemplary model, Kang was interested in the democratic ethos and ideals not bounded by the institutional form of a territorial nation-state. A notion of republicanism based on popular sovereignty and power sharing enables him to envision a future society that would be united, democratic, and free. Consider his comments with regard to US democracy: "when states are autocracies, it is natural that they are self-centered" (88; 86). American democracy broke aristocratic self-centeredness, and the constitutional movement established a legal framework. When states are democracies like the United States, they are well on their way to forging federated alliances, and social harmony may be on the horizon. Similarly, the people's empowerment in the drive for freedom and equality characterizes the French Revolution as well as the national independence movements that challenged colonial rule (90; 87). This was possible because the republican principle of the people's sovereignty prevailed: "people only seek profit and benefit for themselves, and so when the benevolent men advocate the pleasure and profit of One World, it naturally accords with men's mind" (88; 86). Since the democratic impulse is universal, it is not tied to a particular interest or identity.

If the pursuit of equality and benevolence is essential to democracy—and Kang thinks it is—then the notion is disengaged from the specific Euro-American context and held up as a universal principle. This transcendent move allows Kang to critique American institutions and practices for not living up to democratic principles. Although the United States was a democracy, it failed to measure up to its self-expressed standards, especially in matters of race, class, and capital-labor relations. In terms of equality, Kang appraised the Confucian vision of the ethical bond of social harmony and portrayed the sage as a democratic thinker *avant la lettre*. In the Spring and Autumn era dominated by the feudal, hereditary nobility, Confucius originated the idea of equality: "He made clear the unity [of the empire] so as to do away with feudalism, and derided the [institution of] hereditary nobility so as to do away with heredity of office. [He transmitted the ancient] assigned-field system [so as] to do away with slavery" (213; 135). In one breath, Kang drew a parallel between George Washington and Confucius, between Confucian reform and American constitutional revolution. Confucius "wrote the constitution of the *Chunqiu* so as to put a limit to the monarch's powers. He did not exalt himself to his followers and rejected the authority of great priests. Thereby caste was completely swept out from Chinese institutions. Everyone became a commoner; anyone could rise from common status to be ennobled, to be a minister of state, to be a teacher or scholar and be soaring in the sky, unburdened by the traits of selfishness" (213-14; 135).

Speaking of the Chinese translation of Alexis de Tocqueville's classic *Democracy in America*, Gan Yang notes that the Chinese title, *Meiguo de minzhu* (美國的民主), is misleading because the adjective *meiguo* (American) confines democracy to one national territory and community and thus obscures the author's intention to discuss universal democratic principles. In his preface to the book, Tocqueville repeatedly expresses the intention to write about democracy as a "universal and permanent" question. Although the book delineates the transition from autocracies to the self-governance of the people, the French thinker claims that much of his book discusses things "being American, but not democratic." The book's second volume makes a sharper distinction between "what is democratic" and "what is only American." By this distinction, Tocqueville contends that democratization is a worldwide, irresistible trend, not a uniquely national creation.[38]

The separation of the American nation from democracy captures the way Kang Youwei approaches global democracy in the spirit of *Chunqiu* commentary. This spirit marks a critical vigilance that decouples normative values from historical practices. Yet in redressing the corruptions of a regime, the spirit seeks to reinstate and rearticulate the ideal values. Kang elevates democracy as an ideal set of principles from its actual performance, and this influenced subsequent thinkers like Liang Qichao, Zhang Taiyan, Lu Xun, and Mao Zedong. In his response to Yan Fu, Liang asserted that Western democracy, understood as the people's equal rights, popular sovereignty, and self-determination in political processes, took off only in the nineteenth century. The democracy of Greek antiquity was a form of hereditary autocracy, not unlike the political structure in the *Chunqiu*. If one judges a democracy by how much power the people enjoy and share in politics, many existing liberal democracies fall far short. But democracy seems an inevitable global process that involves not only China but also many nations striving for that ideal. Certain Euro-American nations may be ahead of China in pushing for democracy, but the gap is not absolute. In the *Chunqiu* critical spirit, Liang claims that "actually existing" democracies are still trying to achieve inherent democratic goals, and they have not yet arrived and are still struggling. More often than not, they regress from democracy.[39]

In this light, Kang Youwei does not simply draw on Confucian classics in an attempt to broaden certain normative, universal elements. His work presents a bold attempt to lay out ethical principles that are universally applicable. These principles may carry the name of the Mandate of Heaven or democracy; they may be about benevolence, equality, compassion, or aesthetic imagination, but they are not tied down to their original institutions, historical locus, and reified conditions. Rather, they are deployed to hold governments accountable and to measure the distance between the articulate moral goal and institutional practice, between moral imperatives and political performance. Ethical principles, whether embodied by Confucianism or democracy, are not the exclusive, unique property of one particular nation-state and product of one cultural community. This transcendent ethico-political imagination constitutes the key to Kang's vision of the great community.

Nationalism, Moral Reform, and Tianxia in Liang Qichao

THE FUTURE OF NEW CHINA, an unfinished novel by Liang Qichao, opens with a celebration of the fiftieth anniversary of China's reform. Set in Nanjing, the capital city of the Chinese Republic, the celebration concurs with the signing of peace treaties and cease-fire. Honoring China's preeminence, the major Western powers have sent leaders and diplomats to deliberate on disarmament. Not far from the peace-making event, a World Expo is in full swing in Shanghai, where merchants from all over the world engage in commerce and trade, with goods and commodities changing hands. Crowning the Expo is a cultural and intellectual event, complete with a sprawling platform of panels, lectures, and seminars. Scholars from different nations converge and exchange ideas, and diverse schools of thought converse and interact. In an aside, the narrator marvels at the spectacle of cultural convergency and calls it datong.[1]

In this gathering, nation-states come together under the mandate of global unity and peace. National interests and sovereignties, constantly at odds, are set aside and reconciled in a world fair. World trade and scholarly seminars testify to a marketplace of ideas and culture redolent with the spirit of cosmopolitanism. But no sooner does the cosmopolitan spectacle strike the reader than it is upstaged by a keynote speech on nationalism. The speaker, a descendant of Confucius, is named Kong Hongdao 孔弘道 with the style name Kong Juemin 孔覺民. "Hongdao" means expanding the *Dao* in the manner of the ancient sages promulgating the Way. "Juemin" alludes to enlightening the people as citizens of a modern nation. Kong's traditional lineage goes with his modern profile. A scion of the Confucian tradition, he is honored as the architect of the nation: the drafter of the constitution, educator, and historian. His speech tells a story of building a nation-state on the strength of a new people.

Although the national story does not sit well with the overall cosmopolitan fanfare, it reveals Liang Qichao as a staunch nationalist. To Liang, cosmopolitanism sounded nice but was unrealistic amid clashing nations. As China confronted the world of nation-states at the turn of the twentieth century, the urgent task was nation building, not indulging in cosmopolitanism. The national form appeared necessary as the Qing empire, faced with encroachments of colonial powers, was scrambling to be part of the forest of nations. The national status was a matter of life and death and the global norm. The world was now a stage, but only the full-fledged nations could gain recognition and enter the international arena. "The idea of nation," in Craig Calhoun's words, is "also inherently international and works partly by contraposition of different nations to each other. Nationalist rhetoric offers a way of conceptualizing the identity of any one country that presumes the existence of other more or less comparable units."[2]

However, Liang saw the Western nation-state as belligerent and aggressive—the root cause of international conflict. He harbored the datong dream that would transcend the nationalist propensities and inspire people to work together in projecting an imaginary solution to a world rift asunder by warring nations.[3] But one has to be realistic in times of trouble and frailty due to the lack of nationhood. To coexist peacefully with other nations, China had to join the world—to be a nation-state first. In this nation-cosmopolitan link, the paradox in Liang's novel becomes less jarring as the magnificent scene of cosmopolitan unity touches down to the groundwork of the Chinese nation in the throes of birth. Kong Hongdao takes the podium to speak to a cosmopolitan gathering, only to begin with a nation-building story.

This chapter asks this question: Does Liang Qichao's novel drop the idea of datong by delving into nation building? In the last days of the Qing dynasty, when the Confucian order was forced to meet the Western nation-states, the relation between nation and empire, nationalism and cosmopolitanism became a focus of debate. Liang's novel consists of a long but inconclusive debate on nationalism and cosmopolitanism. What concept of nation emerges from the debate? What elements of tianxia seep into Liang's nationalist thinking?

Nation-State and Tianxia

Aware of the importance of the nation-state to China's survival, Huang Keqiang and Li Qubing, two major protagonists of *The Future of New China*, study Western languages and enroll in Oxford University in Great Britain. Dismayed by the European prejudice against the Boxer Uprising, they feel compelled to study the secret of statecraft and institutions of Western nations. Transferring to a German university, Huang studies political theory and constitutional monarchy. Li, inspired by the French Revolution, develops radical views. Both embrace the nation-state as an effective means for national revival but debate its merits and limitations.

The major Western nation-states strike them as the prime aggressor against China. Returning home during a trip to Manchuria, the young men witness foreign occupation, the loss of territory, and the plight and suffering of local people. Ascending the Great Wall and surveying the occupied land, they bemoan the country's dismemberment. Drinking to drown his sorrows, Li expresses his frustration in a classical *ci* poem and asks Huang: "Brother, as you see it, does China now belong to the Chinese people? In all eighteen provinces, is there anyone *not* under the dominion of foreigners? It is either Russians or British, either British or Germans; either French or Japanese or Americans" (5617).

Given the annexations and infringement of sovereignty, should the Chinese emulate the nation-state as the ideal modern polity? This question leads to a discussion about the means of making regime change—through force or moral principles? Reviewing dynastic upheavals, Li contends that those changes are little more than a circulation of brutal force based on the logic of "might makes right," ravaging lives and communities throughout the imperial chronicles. The first emperor, Qin Shihuang, and the emperors of the Han and Ming dynasties took the throne by force, replacing one repressive power with a more lethal one. Trading violence with violence (*yi bao yi bao* 以暴易暴), this bloody cycle recalls Gu Yanwu's definition of *guo* (state), the power-driven polity seeking wealth and territory at the expense of tianxia's civilizational norms.[4] Liang, following his mentor Kang Youwei, routinely compared the belligerent nation-states to the clashing kingdoms in the Warring States era.[5] Although no social order could be put in place without military campaigns, legitimate change should appeal to gongli (universal principle) in an evolutionary scheme. Genuine change must work toward "replacing violence with benevolence" (*yi ren yi bao* 以仁易暴, 6521).

To Li, the principle of *ren* resonates with French Revolution cosmopolitanism. The term recalls the protagonists' prior meeting with Tan Sitong 譚嗣同 (1865–98), a revolutionary thinker who has bequeathed to them his unpublished book titled *A Study of Benevolence (renxue* 仁學). To Liang, the book is an elaboration of Kang Youwei's notion of datong and expounds the desire "to converge all wise minds of the world and to save the multitudes." Kang "promoted ren as the goal, followed the datong principle, deployed China a means to that end, and aspired to break through the private and family shackles."[6] Benevolence dissolves self-absorption and extends sympathy to pains and sufferings of others. The idea, to Li, motivates the French Revolution and drives the liberation of oppressed people. Against Huang's view of the revolution as a case of bloodshed and violence, Li maintains that under the banner of liberty, equality, and fraternity, Napoleon Bonaparte sought to transform Europe into a world republic by championing popular sovereignty and granting justice to commoners. The French leader had nothing unworthy of *tianxia ren* 天下人 (all people under heaven). The revolution entails a cosmopolitan aspiration by promoting universal laws and disseminating the spirit of freedom, equality, and fraternity to all nations (5620).

Huang seems to be brought over to the French Revolution's commitment to a unified Europe. Napoleon pushed back against the tide of parochial nationalism of his times and sought to "bring together different ethnic groups, religions, languages, and nationalities" (5620). The revolution aimed to create conditions for individuals, groups, and nations to live in a world republic, signaling the early stirrings of the European Commonwealth. Francis Fukuyama points to this cosmopolitanism as a significant legacy of the French Revolution: the first modern law, the Code Napoléon, was more transparent and uniform in its treatment of citizens than arbitrary rules of the previous feudal estates. To Napoleon, the code and the uniform administrative state were a "greater victory" than those he won on the battlefield.[7]

Converging on the idea of popular sovereignty, the debaters agree on the people as constitutive of a republic. Legitimate change hinges on the empowered people. The Chinese people, be they Manchus or Han or of other ethnic origins, can and should have equal share in government. The new national republic would gain legitimacy when different ethnic groups share power in running the country. This transethnic notion, distinct from the ethnonational idea of identity rooted in ethnicity, language, and custom, would integrate multiethnic groups into a unified Chinese nation.

The image of a multiethnic nation anticipates Sun Zhongshan's multiethnic nationalism. Although he was the leader of a national revolution, Sun kept datong cosmopolitanism in view and regarded nationalism as a means to that end. The October Revolution of Soviet Russia had achieved national self-determination by building a modern nation-state. Vladimir Lenin's notion of self-determination fueled the movement of national liberation in combatting the domination of imperialist powers. Calling for mobilizing and assisting the twelve hundred million people fighting the two hundred million oppressors, Sun held that national self-determination of weak nations is the basis for broad internationalist alliance and movement. But hostile to national self-determination of the colonized, the colonial powers spewed the smoke screen of cosmopolitanism to maintain their domination. Suspicious of colonial rule masking as cosmopolitanism, Sun believed that it was premature for colonized Chinese to indulge in that fancy talk. The urgent task was to promote nationalism and achieve national independence. In a talk titled "Nationalism Is the Basis for World Unity" ("Minzu zhuyi shi shijie datong de jichu" 民族主義 是世界大同的基礎), Sun explains nationalism's relation to cosmopolitanism.

Today we should revive China's lost nationalism and rally people of four hundred million strong to fight for peoples of the world in the name of justice. . . . Out of fear of this thinking, the imperialist powers come up with a dubious doctrine and seek to trick us with cosmopolitanism. They say the world must progress, that humanity's vision should be far and wide, and that nationalism is too narrow. . . . It is under such misleading influence that some Chinese new youth advocate a new culture and oppose nationalism. But the doctrine of cosmopolitanism should not be accepted by a subordinated nation. We are a subordinated nation, and we must restore our nation to the status of equality and freedom with other nations before we discuss cosmopolitanism. If we are to promote cosmopolitanism, we must first strengthen nationalism.[8]

To achieve "the status of equality and freedom with other nations," China must first become a nation—a nation strong enough to promote the cosmopolitan ideals of equality and freedom. Sun's appeal to datong—a world order of peaceful coexistence and mutual respect among nations—implies a dialectic view that deepens the connections between nationalism and international outlooks. Assisting the weak and saving the fallen (*jiruo fuqing* 濟弱扶傾), Sun asserts, is "what a strong nation is supposed to do," which lays the groundwork for "ordering the nation and preserving the peace for all under heaven" (治國平天下).[9]

Private Interest, Public Morality, and Tianxia

Through Kong Hongdao's nation-building story, Liang's novel articulates a new concept of the people. Rather than a privileged, elite group, the Constitutional Party, which is the leading nation builder, engages the grassroots population and keeps in touch with all social strata. By mobilizing the people's energy and power, the party takes the lead to build a nation of the people, by the people, and for the people. The success of a nation-state, Liang notes, "depends on all people who make it their own country" by their own hands.[10] This popular nation makes a distinction between a nation ruled by the elites and one that is mass based, between a party with vested interests and one committed to fostering political subjectivity. Such distinctions herald Levenson's distinction between the nation-state as an elitist club and the people's nation.[11]

As Western imperial powers encroached on China's territory, a competitive race for power and domination among nations thrust China into geopolitical rivalry. The social Darwinist imperative for self-strengthening and survival necessitated the creation of a nation-state. While the late Qing's self-strengthening program focused on technological and institutional reform, it was the people's moral and political character that promised to be a source of power. Yet for all their faith in the people, Li and Huang lament the moral deficiency of Chinese. In modern parlance, this moral deficiency means the absence of political consciousness and civic virtue requisite for national citizenship. Nation building requires the cultivation of the people's moral mindset as the basis for a political community.

The formation of a people hinges on their moral empowerment. The Constitutional Party works with and creates the people on three cardinal terms: the people's morality (*minde* 民德), intelligence (*minzhi* 民智), and power (*minli* 民力), with the people's morality as the top priority.[12] A rallying principle of esprit de corps, the people's morality brings us to Liang Qichao's book titled *Xinmin shuo* 新民說 (*Discourse on a New People*). Written from 1902 to 1905, the book charts a course of moral reform with the goal of attaining national consciousness and civic virtue.

Discourse on a New People calls for a moral revolution. In order to revitalize the people's morality, Chinese should extract the best from ancient traditions and learn from powerful Western nations. Liang construes morality as a vehicle to reform politics by tapping into a long-entrenched tradition of the Chinese empire. In Confucian political culture, the moral is seamlessly intertwined with the political. A good political order emanates from a body of moral precepts and is to be realized in ritual and music. Morality requires daily renovation and reshaping, and only through such practices can a political order be maintained. Speaking about the moral core of tianxia, Zhao Tingyang quotes a Confucian phrase—"maintain political order by resorting to morality" (*wei zheng yi de* 為政以德)—to capture the centrality of morality to politics.[13] Kang Youwei believed in moral teachings as a means of achieving political order (*yan jiao tong zhi* 言教通治). Adhering to this ethico-political tradition, Liang proposes to renovate morality as a way of creating a robust citizenry and empowered nation.

The morality essential to the Chinese nation comes in the form of *gongde*, which could be translated as "public virtue" or "public morality." Public morality maintains that commitment, service, and devotion to the common good are essential, upholding a reciprocal relationship between the individual and the collective. Its opposite is *side* 私德 (private morality), a morality concerned with the individual's integrity and self-cultivation. Private morality is cultivated in a program of self-improvement whereby the self is thus disengaged from public affairs and unconcerned with the common good. Its most pernicious form is manifest in the single-minded pursuit of private interest and profit, a behavior that threatens and corrodes common goods and public space.

Liang impugns private morality for its obsession with the individual's moral purity and inner integrity, performed in a display of "moral graces" and gentlemanly persona. Private morality undermines common goods and leads to political decay. Rooted in interpersonal ties of patronage and favors, the private mindset, in Fukuyama's description, regulates "a reciprocal exchange of favors between two individuals of different status and power, usually involving favors given by a patron to the client in exchange for the client's loyalty and political support."[14] The emperor and his ministers, Liang insists, are supposed to relate to each other under a broad mandate of imperial-civil service and governance. But this "public" arena frequently degenerates into a private exchange of personal favors and benefits. Yet an empire is by "no means an exclusive property at the disposal of the emperor and his subjects" (*fei junchen suo neng zhuanyou* 非君臣所能專有). If the political order runs on private morality through the swapping of personal benefits, then politics is reduced to a trade-off between two private persons and has nothing to do with the totality of common goods.[15] Political institutions decay into an exchange between two self-serving individuals at the expense of public well-being. This is nothing short of stealing from public property and resources.

For millennia, Liang continues, the Chinese have wallowed in private morality embedded in patrimonial obligations to family and kin and in the bonds of local attachment. Self-centered and parochial, they are only concerned with what is best for themselves and rarely give thought to what is good for the broader community. The stock phrase *jia tianxia* 家天下 (privatizing the whole world under heaven) reflects how emperors and nobles claimed all the land and population under heaven as their own possessions. When private morality held sway, the Chinese behaved like loose sands, nonchalant about common interests beyond their local attachment and welfare. This prompted Liang to make the famous claim that Chinese, accustomed to tianxia as the norm, know nothing about *guojia* (nation-state), and attached to family and kin, have no sense of themselves as a political community.[16]

A contradiction arises here. By associating private morality with tianxia, Liang is suggesting that a tianxia order, premised on private morality, runs counter to public ethos and to universalism. This calls into question the familiar interpretation of tianxia's universality and broad-mindedness. In Zhao Tingyang's analysis, tianxia rests precisely on a broad morality as the source of legitimacy and makes appeal to the principle of *gong*. Gong means, first, that all people under heaven are the most important substance and the care of their well-being and needs is the measure of political legitimacy. Second, whoever is in charge of tianxia is not to take possession of the land and resources for his private enjoyment but to carry the Mandate of Heaven, which means winning the hearts and minds of all people and taking care of their welfare. This sweeping moral capacity constitutes the essence of *de* 德 (morality or virtue), a universal form of political morality. Citing Mencius and Xun Zi 荀子, Zhao writes: whoever loses the state loses people, but whoever gains people's support will achieve a good political order. When an emperor has de, he would have the support of people. He would have lands, wealth, and many uses. In this light, the tianxia order describes the unity of all people (*wan min* 萬民) across the realm, far and near, under *dezheng* 德政—a morally informed political order.[17]

The classical notion of gong thus comes close to the modern ideas of public space or common prosperity, and often is so translated. Frederic Wakeman Jr. translated *tianxia weigong* 天下為公 into "render public all under heaven" and "commonweal."[18] The crucial question is: Can we graft gong, an ancient motif, to the public ethos and the commonweal of a national republic? The key articulation of tianxia in *Records of Rites* (*Li ji* 禮記), a Confucian canon compiled during the Han dynasty (206 BCE to 220 CE), begins with gong. Gong proposes a tianxia world shared by all, which thrives on meritocracy, extended family ties, universal care for vulnerable members, a fair distribution of goods without waste, a commitment to the common good, and the absence of private pursuits of wealth and power.[19]

In its emotional extension, mutual care, and universal benevolence, gong resembles the civic virtue and mutual empathy of a modern citizenry in a national republic. Mandating a public sphere that breaks down the silos of familism and tribalism and exposing individuals to a common purpose, gong envisages a society in which each has his or her interest cared for and is able to empathize with other people as if all belong to a family. Resonating with Jean-Jacques Rousseau's civic virtue, the public virtue of gong, as Eagleton notes, describes a citizen's "passionate affection for his fellow citizens and for the shared conditions of their common life." It is about the pity we feel for each other and even for nonhuman animals. Civic virtue makes for "a kind of empathetic imagination" that "enables us to transport ourselves outside ourselves, identify with suffering humans and animals."[20] Loving one's parents is a form of private morality, but the capacity to extend affection to parents of others signals a broader moral compass of sociality. In this stretch of empathy, private morality, born of family and tribes, proves to be no impediment to public morality and indeed becomes reconcilable with the latter. Thus, contrary to his earlier view of tianxia as a loose aggregation of individuals, Liang concluded that "private morality is by nature not incompatible with public morality" (私德公德，本并行不悖也, 661). Filial piety, gratitude, and duty are the essence of private morality, but a citizen can cultivate these virtues and ascend from family through community to nation. A public-minded citizen would be able to push private love and duty outward in a widening circle. Just as we owe our parents our life, so we owe our well-being, identity, and protection to the community. Private morality and public morality are intertwined as two sides of one coin, extending all the way from the private sphere to the public sphere of civic virtue, community, and national ethos.

This modernized tianxia recalls Liang's trajectory of the cosmopolitan state in terms of a rite of passage. It begins the individual's moral cultivation, extends to the ability to harmonize with the family, ascends to the order of the state, and culminates in the harmony of all under heaven. In this spiral from particularistic relations to broad moral and social horizons, the patrimonial pursuit of private interests is transcended on the way to the higher ground.

Tianxia becomes modern in that the citizen is able to extend the moral scope from private to public morality, from civic virtue to the cosmopolitan ethos.

The modernized version of tianxia, however, lacks an essential modern element: a people endowed with popular sovereignty and as participants in political processes. While tianxia is concerned with all people under the care and protection of the benevolent emperors like Yao and Shun, and while the empire is supposed to be a common culture shared by all, its political structure presents a top-down governance.[21] The sage king fostered people's morality and showered benevolence on people's well-being and needs. As the "Kingly Way" (wangdao) distinct from the "overbearing way" (badao), tianxia prescribes how the wise king should educate people about moral ideas and correct conduct. But this paternalist order leaves little room for people to exercise agency and sovereignty. Liang was spot-on: the classical tianxia was "for the people and of the people, but not by the people."[22] An updated tianxia presupposes the people's capacity to build their own society and set their own agenda. Individuals, through moral reform, will educate themselves to become a people endowed with public morality. Instead of the Kingly Way showering benevolence from above, the "public" means delegating moral education to the people themselves as they cultivate themselves to be citizens. In this argument, the notion of popular sovereignty replaces tianxia's paternalistic care of multitudes.

If a national people can build a nation-state with a broad public ethos, the Chinese nation would be on the way to the tianxia state. Particularistic obligation and allegiance can be open-ended: moral sentiments can spiral from one's family to other families, from one's village to the nation, and from the nation to other nations. Tianxia's political morality not only works on behest of a nation's interest and security but also goes on to serve the interests and peace of the whole world.

National Independence and Internationalism

Written as part of the moral reform to cultivate national ethos, Liang's novel treats literature as a means to a political end. The political use of literature has drawn ire from critics in favor of the purity of literature. C. T. Hsia, for example, deplored political uses of literature as an "obsession with China" and as denigration of literary value.[23] He charged Liang with disregarding aesthetic value in favor of an instrumental agenda for fiction.[24] But the political use of literature stands in a long tradition of the unity of morality and politics. Liang construed politics not as power struggle or administration but as dynamic emanations and practical fulfillments of moral values. Morality, both an inner quality and outer action, needs to be built up by performing ritual, music, and song and by engaging in learning and aesthetic activity. Conceiving politics in terms of morality, intelligence, and power, Liang believed that a people with these qualities should be able to stand on their own feet and engage in modern politics. Literature comes in to serve these ends, moving beyond its narrow aesthetic confines and becoming a vehicle of both moral and political transformation.

In his insightful book *Global Space and the Nationalist Discourse of Modernity*, Xiaobing Tang suggests that the novel's debate attests to Liang's stance as a constitutionalist and liberal. Playing off the parliamentary view against revolution, the debate degenerates into hostile polemics and warring parties in subsequent history. Worse, in the fervor leading to the Republican Revolution of 1911, Li's radical stance anticipates a form of Jacobinism and plunges the protagonists into violence.[25]

National liberation, however, necessitates revolutionary actions. The unfinished debate, I contend, suggests that military action is inevitable and crucial in combating colonialism and building an independent nation. As the protagonists confront colonial occupation and encroachment, their thoughts gravitate toward armed struggle and rebellion. After a whole night of debate, Huang and Li travel to Dalian and Lüshun, the areas of Manchuria occupied by Russia and the battlefield of the 1904 Russo-Japanese War. They are dismayed to find the area under foreign rule. Russian troops are stationed there; Russians control the railway and business, brutalize the residents, and rape local women. The Russian language is becoming the official language. Most infuriating is the Qing government's willingness to let its sovereignty slip away to foreign powers. Further investigation reveals that Japan and Russia are in an arms race and vying for control of Manchuria. When night falls, the two arrive back in the inn. Depressed and downcast, they are suddenly lifted by someone singing. A singer in the adjacent room chants a tragic tune with accompaniment of a Western instrument.

> Such is the aspect of this shore;
> 'Tis Greece, but living Greece no more!
> . . . . . .
> The isles of Greece, the isles of Greece,
> Where burning Sappho loved and sung,
> Where grew the arts of war and peace
> Where Delos rose, and Phoebus sprung!

Eternal summer gilds them yet,
But all, except, their sun, is set.[26]

These lines, from English poet Lord Byron's *The Giaour* and *Don Juan*, articulate the poet's deep sympathy for the fate of Greece. Acquainted with Byron's work, Li immediately pinpoints the source of the lyrics. Written in 1819 on the eve of the Greek independence movement from Ottoman rule, *Don Juan's* stanzas honor ancient Greek civilization and values, lament the absence of warrior spirit, and allude to the geopolitical context of the Ottoman Empire and Russian involvement in the Greek war of independence. Byron himself traveled to Greece and joined the national liberation. A leading figure in the uprising, he was honored as a national hero by the Greeks. Geopolitically, the story is located in what the English viewed as the "Orient."

Byron's poem indicates a high ground that overlooks the lost land. A similar ritual is performed by the protagonists, as they ascend the Great Wall and survey the fallen landscape. Byron's poignant elegy bemoans the lost land and beautiful shores that are no longer "living." It strikes a chord with the intellectuals of Liang's time, who have fallen into a melancholy mood over the demise of millennial Chinese civilization. But not all is lost. They hear a clarion call to action:

Clime of the unforgotten brave!
Whose land from plain to mountain cave
Was Freedom's home or Glory's grave!
Shrine of the mighty! Can it be,
That this is all that remains of thee?
Approach, thou craven crouching slave.[27]

Challenging the listener, these lines issue a call that echoes the phrase "Give me liberty or give me death." It is not Huang the constitutionalist but Li the radical revolutionary who gets excited and begins to spell out sonorous lines from his memory to fill the gaps of singing. Although it is *wangguo zhi yin* 亡國之音 (sounds of the country's demise), the poem sounds more like a rallying call to arouse heroic passions. The melancholy song resonates with their dark mood but also provokes them into patriotic sentiment. The music and poem "sound manly and defiant, and lift our spirits," comments Li. Lines like "the musical instrument of our ancestors has fallen into our hands," "the land of slavery is not for us," and "the wine of slaves we shall not drink" all ring a bell.[28]

Finding a kindred spirit in the singer, Huang and Li meet Chen Meng in the hotel's dining room and strike up a conversation. It turns out that Chen shares their intention of investigating the colonial occupation in Manchuria. Chen stands tall as a man with a commitment to public morality and a keen sense of duty as a patriot and citizen. This recalls Gu Yanwu's moral imperative, now turned by Liang into a popular saying: "When tianxia is at stake, a regular guy should take on patriotic responsibility" (*tianxia xingwang pifu youze* 天下興亡，匹夫有責).[29]

Chen embodies both literary qualities of *wen* 文—talent in literature and arts combined with the martial spirit *wu* 武. This dual quality of warrior spirit and poetic talent exemplifies the link of aesthetics with politics. Trained as a cadet in the well-known military school in the city of Wuchang, the hub of uprisings in the Republican Revolution, Chen quits the school due to the corruption of the authorities. In his room, a Russian map hangs above the desk, signaling a deep concern about Russia's imperialist ambition in the Far East. A sharp analyst of geopolitics, Chen expounds on the encroachment of colonial powers and their growing menace, analyzing the underlying relations between global economic competition and clashes of nation-states. Denouncing the oppression of Chinese people by foreign imperialists, he rails against the Qing regime for its complicity with foreign powers and explains the need for the people to stand up to fight colonial as well as domestic oppression. Anger, fury, and passion suffuse his otherwise empirical, clear-headed analysis. Thrown into an emotional whirlwind, the two listeners feel confirmed in their own view by the patriot's assessment.

The conversation shifts quickly from geopolitics to poetry and music. Lying on the desk are two books of poetry next to a musical instrument. One is Byron's *Don Juan* and the other is a collection of poems by John Milton. Chen confesses that his love for the two English poets is more than a love of their literary imagination and genius. Responding to Huang's comments that he must be an expert in literature and music, Chen replies:

> I am nothing of the sort. When I was in military school, I got to hear foreign military music and realized that music is deeply infused with the national spirit. So I tried to study music. These two books of poetry by Milton and Byron are my favorite books. This is because Milton supported Oliver Cromwell and committed himself to the great cause of the English Revolution. Byron supported the Italian revolutionary party and gave up his own life in fighting for the independence of Greece. Such personalities and virtues fill me with admiration. And it is not simply about music and literature![30]

Byron and Milton drew a series of translation in the late Qing and Republican eras. The Byronic hero finds a rich reading in Lu Xun's long essay "Moluo shili shuo" 摩羅詩力說 (On the power of Mara poetry). In Lu's gallery of romantic poets, Byron figures as a paragon of rebellion against the religious establishments and repressive institutions of his day. Milton, celebrator of Satan in *Paradise Lost*, also figures prominently. Raising the banner of "Mara poetry," these poets critique the authorities, challenge God, cry out against injustice, and commit themselves to helping oppressed people. The rebellious characters in Byron include Satan, Cain, Japhet, Manfred, Conrad, and others. In *Manfred*, the Manfred character represents a symbol of moral autonomy. Defying the demons' attempts to tempt him, Manfred declares: "I . . . was my own destroyer—and will be—/ My own Hereafter . . . The hand of Death is on me—but not Yours!"[31] "As humans have capacity for both good and evil," writes Lu Xun, "they are supposed to determine their actions, be they praiseworthy and condemnable." As in Manfred, humans need be "intimidated by neither gods and spirits, devils or dragons, nor should we be coerced by any less powers."[32] Moral autonomy also marks the biblical figure Cain, who declares that moral good does not necessarily attach to religious authority and dominant power. With reference to Friedrich Nietzsche, Lu Xun applauds Byron's assertion of strength and autonomy: while "Nietzsche, in his desire to promote self-strengthening, praised the strong" and Byron "fought to resist the strong . . . they were in agreement that strength was both necessary and desirable."[33]

Byron emerges as a rebel leader capable of rallying the masses in resistance movements. Feeling the need to be in the vanguard, he is frustrated by the slackers—those who lack the spirit of public morality. Lu Xun's reading alludes to the sleepwalking Chinese population and the government's complacency in the face of national crisis. Just like Satan, who pushes and disciplines his followers, Byron takes the lead to "empower and rally the masses in joint resistance, so what is the point of attacking his discipline and control?" (*zhongsheng tongkang, geng he zhi yun* 眾生同抗，更何制雲).[34] Exalting power and praising the strong, the Byron image signals self-determination and revolt against colonial, domination as reflected in the American Revolution and the French Revolution.

I [Byron] love America, this realm of freedom, this green meadow of God, this land unbowed. From all these things it becomes evident how Byron could delight in Napoleon's decimation of the world, while at the same time loving Washington's struggle for liberty; how he could be fascinated by the ravages of pirates, yet go forth to single-handedly adopt the cause of Greek independence; how repression and resistance could be and were embodied in one and the same man. It is, in fact, on this paradox that his dedication to both liberty and humanity turned.[35]

Byron reproaches the Greeks for their moral weakness and prods them into action: "The sincerity of his commitment to Greece is evident in the outbursts of emotion, the strains of anger, and the notes of censure with which poems like *The Giaour* and *Don Juan* are so liberally laced."[36] In assisting the independence movement, Byron cherishes the hope that Greece might one day be restored to the splendor of Grecian antiquity.

Committed to other nations in seeking independence, the Byron image articulates a form of patriotism intertwined with internationalism. Premised on moral autonomy, national self-determination, and popular sovereignty, each nation, in combatting oppressive regimes, can also extend sympathy beyond the border to identify with the similar fate of other nations. The national citizen is able to understand and sympathize with other nationals and foster emotional and poetic affinity. Byron came to be admired by Chinese writers precisely for his romantic passion and for his generous support for a subordinated nation. The internationalism of his assistance to independence-seeking people echoes Sun Zhongshan's attempt to seek foreign support for the national cause in the hope that the Chinese revolution "should have its Lafayette no less than the American."[37]

Liang's novel brings poetry, geopolitics, cross-cultural sympathy, and internationalism into focus. Chinese nationalists—Huang, Li, and Chen—identify with Byron, merging nationalist sentiments with the poet's international spirit. Instead of a sign of liberal cosmopolitanism of high culture, the Byron image suggests an internationalism that unites independence-seeking nations. It suggests that a nation's pursuit of autonomy and independence can be inspiring and shareable for other nations in similar struggles. A concept of world culture emerges from the translation and appropriation of Byron. Rather than being an arena of conflict and domination, rather than a soft power imposing or cajoling others, world culture arises from equality, mutual respect, and sympathy among nations.

Stirrings of Socialist Datong

As an unfinished novel, *The Future of a New China* presents a brainstorm session on nation building with an eye toward a utopian future. Beginning with a cosmopolitan spectacle, the text delves into Chinese and European histories for possible solutions for besieged China. The ending urges an armed struggle against colonialism to achieve independence. The novel's cosmopolitan beginning envisages China's future as a multinational republic in the capitalist system—an image of the bourgeois "old democracy" whose goal is to fit into the nation-state system.

The calamity of World War I came as a rude awakening for Liang about that prospect. His growing doubts in the wake of the war showed signs of a critical reflection on the capitalist world system and a quest for alternatives.

As an observer of the Paris Peace Conference in 1919, Liang was inspired by the League of Nations' program to transcend the antagonist, self-serving nations. In the long essay on the league, Liang turned to the issues of labor in conjunction with socialist internationalism. Observing that "from now on the labor issue is the single most important issue for the whole world," he places labor-capital relations on a par with the issues of world peace, datong, and socialism. Reviewing a history of the European labor movement from the nineteenth century to its initiatives in the league, Liang notes that the movement arose from the workers' discontents with the antihuman (不合人道) and unfair (bu gongping 不公平) working conditions under capitalism.[38] As capital became internationalized, workers also become an international class. Quoting "The working men have no country" from Marx's *Communist Manifesto*, Liang warns that national identity is an ideology by the state to trick workers into identification with national capitalists—to the neglect of their own interests. In an insightful gloss on Marx's working-class internationalism, Liang adopts an internationalist lens: instead of using nationalist lines to "vertically" (zongduan 縱斷) map the world, the analysis must use "class" to "cut across" (hengduan 橫斷) national borders to understand workers unions and the common fight of working classes. The message from Liang's discussion is that labor issues involve a working-class movement that promises to contribute to peace and world community.[39]

Examining the documents of the International Labour Organization as a part of the League of Nations agenda, Liang draws insights about the class divide and tensions between capital and labor. The exploitive relation boils down to a matter of social justice, which is fundamental to the achievement of world peace. The labor organization in the league presents a proletarian internationalism and articulates solidarity and sympathy among workers of different nations. Liang appraises particularly two principles of the "Labor Regulation": the refusal to treat labor as commodity and the promotion of the "bodily, moral, and intellectual happiness of the workers," applauding them as a new Declaration of Human Rights of the French Revolution.

While in doubt if these ideals are feasible when the capitalists own the means of production and extract excessive amounts of "surplus value," Liang feels that the principles project a future norm for harmonious international relations and a common standard to be realized in the future.[40]

In Liang's analysis, the intractable contradiction between labor and capital extends to the unequal structure between the capitalist metropolis and the peripheral. The capitalist states, with their expansionist ambition, were going around the world in search of territories, markets, cheap labor, and natural resources, waging wars against each other if necessary. For want of a sizable capitalist class, China did not seem to be plagued at the moment by the disparity between capital and labor. But this did not mean China was free from similar class tensions and oppression. While the capital-labor conflict aggravated the gap between rich and poor and created "an oppressor class over the oppressed" elsewhere, China was trending in the direction in which "all Chinese would belong to the oppressed class" and suffer the same fate as the working class in capitalist countries.[41] While the league's deliberation of labor issues involved the question of workers' welfare and poverty, the issue was tantamount to the nation's life and death in China, as the country's very survival was under the lethal threat of capitalist colonial agenda. The writings of China's colonization were on the wall: all the important ports, infrastructure, and transportation networks had already fallen into foreign hands. Natural resources essential for homegrown industrialization were being plundered or siphoned off by colonialist traders and investments. The divide between capital and labor was making the rich richer and the poor poorer. In about a decade, Liang predicted, all capitalists in China would be foreigners and four hundred million Chinese would be reduced to wage laborers, thus spelling the death of the country. The image of a nation of working classes under colonial capital chimes in with Li Dazhao's notion of the proletarian nation as well as "class nation," a discourse of anticolonial nationalism that undergirded the Chinese Revolution, socialist internationalism, and the Third World.

In the 1920s, the Chinese Revolution embarked on the path of attacking the alliance of foreign capital and domestic landowning class. It was a movement to close the widening gulf of inequality and to dismantle the exploitive structure of capital over labor. Its socialist goal is to transform capital, power, and wealth concentrated in a few hands for the benefits of society and people. Although acutely aware that inequality was injurious to the nation's integrity and to world peace, Liang harbored half-baked socialist thoughts and remained uninterested in revolution. Nevertheless, he was sensitive to the promise of revolutionary change and yearned for a utopian society of equality and harmony. In his scholarly reflection on Chinese classics, issues of socioeconomic inequality loomed large and compelled him to tease out what he believed to be "socialist" elements in terms of datong and tianxia.

Reflecting his earlier association with Kang Youwei in Japan in the mid-1920s, Liang realized that Kang's datong idea was a cosmopolitanism with socialist implications. Liang had previously favored a narrow and even militant nationalism against Kang's cosmopolitanism. Now, glossing the classic tianxia weigong passage, which was a mantra for Kang, Sun Zhongshan, Jiang Jieshi, and Mao Zedong, Liang realized that the datong society aims for all the people and is "absolutely democratic."[42] "Men practiced good faith and lived in harmony" (讲信修睦), which means egalitarianism, mutual trust, solidarity, pacifism, and anti-militarism. Giving priority to the individual rather than tribes or family, datong urges individuals not only to love their kin but to love everybody else under heaven. As a welfare system, datong cares for the vulnerable and disadvantaged and protects the old and disabled. It discourages private ownership of property and frowns on selfish gains. Labor is regarded as sacred, and the individual's service to the common good is an honor.

This datong humanism slides to socialist equalitarianism. With an eye on the inequality of labor processes, worker-capitalist relations, and the concentration of wealth in Europe, Liang rediscovered the ideas of equitable redistribution of goods and public ownership of wealth. A passage from the *Analects* states, "What worries the stateman or chief of a household is not the scarcity of people but inequality; not poverty but instability. Therefore, equality means the absence of scarcity; harmony goes with the absence of poverty, and stability hedges against social collapse." This quote prompted Liang to delve into political economy by citing Han dynasty thinker Dong Zhongshu: "If there is a heavy concentration of wealth and power (*jizhong* 積重), there will be scarcity." Inequality makes the rich arrogant and the poor miserable. Misery and depravation lead to crime; arrogance leads to brutal dominion. The Confucian datong, Liang realized, gestures toward a form of political economy principally geared toward a humanism (人道) and public policy. Its essence consists in the redistribution of wealth in the name of people's livelihood and welfare (*renmin shengji* 人民生計).[43] He made a point of calling such socioeconomic rationality "socialist." Although Confucian harmony maintains a hierarchy of differential socioeconomic status, its emphasis on the fair redistribution of wealth ensures that the rich have enough to show their status without arrogance, and that the poor have enough for living without worry, thus leading to the harmony of the upper and lower classes.

In recapturing the classical motifs as socialist and democratic, Liang was concerned with the proto-socialist ideas of equality, redistribution, and the sharing of resources and power. On the other hand, this reading of equality allowed him to understand the problems of China's disadvantage in the worldwide system of inequality and uneven development between the metropolitan center and the colonized peripherals. Although never a convinced socialist, Liang was drawn to the classical ideas of equality and redistribution redolent of modern socialist principles. Throughout the 1920s and until his death in 1929, Liang's reflection on the labor-capital conflict, his rediscovery of datong, and his valorization of economic redistribution and social harmony—all this anticipated the eddies of socialism and internationalism in decades to come.

World Literature
in the Mountains

IN DECEMBER 1939, after a long journey amid snow blizzards, Zhou Libo arrived in Yan'an, the revolutionary base in Shaanxi province. Zhou had lived and worked in Shanghai as a writer, critic, and translator. As the editor of the League of Left-Wing Writers, he introduced a long list of authors of world literature: Mark Twain; James Joyce and Bernard Shaw of Ireland; Romain Rolland and Henry Barbusse of France; Antonio Machato of Spain; Regino Pedroso of Cuba; and others. Most prominent were Russian and Soviet writers, including Maxim Gorky, Alexander Pushkin, and Leo Tolstoy. Zhou's revolutionary credentials were legendary. He constantly participated in street demonstrations against the Guomindang regime and served time in prison for his activism. His pen name, Libo, stemmed from the English word *liberty*, signaling his devotion to humanist ideas and liberation.[1]

Zhou soon became a professor of literature and the director of the translation department at the Lu Xun Academy of Arts (Luyi 鲁艺). Situated on a hillside not far from Yan'an, the academy was built in 1938 out of old cave dwellings around an old Catholic church. This setting brings to mind the ancient academy nestled in the mountains, but an international atmosphere was in the air. Most faculty, writers, and artists were Western trained and steeped in cosmopolitan culture. A literary society took its name from Walt Whitman's *Leaves of Grass*, and the song for the May Day celebration was "The Internationale." At the academy, Zhou ran a lecture from 1940 to 1942 titled "Selected Readings in Literary Masters." Works by Russian socialist writers Gorky and Alexander Fadeyev as well as those of czarist Russia, such as Pushkin, Mikhail Lermontov, Nikolai Gogol, and Tolstoy, were prominent on the reading list, along with European writers like Johann Wolfgang von Goethe, Honoré de Balzac, Stendhal (Marie-Henri Beyle), Guy de Maupassant, and Prosper Mérimée. Written on coarse paper, Zhou's lecture notes were crammed with Chinese characters, leaving no blank space or margins. In his teaching, Zhou cited long passages of European novelists from memory to explain the texts. The class drew numerous students and cadres from the departments of drama, music, and arts, filling up the front yard of cave dwellings. Captivated by Zhou's lecture, the students took notes and responded to occasional questions. Bombing raids and explosions nearby were frequent, but the class continued uninterrupted. The students later recalled that it was a rare pleasure to sit in this class and hear Zhou speak.[2]

Nicolai Volland's insightful study portrays Zhou Libo as a socialist cosmopolitan writer, whose novel *Hurricane* belongs to the international canon of land reform and socialist reconstruction, resonating with *Virgin Soil* by the Soviet writer Mikhail Sholokhov and *Land* by the Korean novelist Yi Ki-yong.[3] The memory of colonialism and exploitation of the landlords, the vigilance against residual saboteurs, collective reclaims of the land, and the shared destiny generated a crisscrossing of literary motifs across the socialist camp. Building on Volland's findings, I attempt to recover a humanism in Zhou's world literature class. This is a socialist form of humanism, which is the key to the rising revolutionary culture. Initially guided by an abstract humanism, Zhou's lecture evinces a shift from the liberal humanism of European writers to a socialist and class humanism. The dual task of national liberation and class emancipation prompted Zhou to see the importance of the Chinese peasantry as a revolutionary subject ascending to the center stage of history.

The English word *humanism*, translated into *rendao zhuyi* 人道主義 in Chinese, implies human rights, humanity, freedom, and humanitarianism. The term may also mean *renwen zhuyi* 人文主義, referring to educational programs akin to the academic discipline of "the humanities." Both aspects of humanism were at work in the nascent revolutionary culture in Yan'an. But the rural setting of the revolutionary base does not sit well with humanism, which is evocative of "universal," "bourgeois," and "Western." With its central locus in mountainous, rural areas and the peasantry as the constituents, the Chinese Revolution has been seen as rural and nationalist and rooted in the agrarian tradition. Humanism seems an urban affair, and the city figures as the hub of enlightenment and cosmopolitanism. Humanism belongs to the city-based May Fourth modern culture whose protagonists are Western-educated intellectuals, whose cosmopolitanism has little to do with a peasant revolution. Chinese philosopher Li Zehou has elucidated this split in his well-known claim that China's humanist enlightenment was blindsided by the violent rural revolution.[4] By examining Zhou's literature class in the Lu Xun Academy of Arts, I highlight the link between local and global, between rural revolution and internationalism. Zhou's work reflected a shift from an abstract humanism to a class-based humanism, which promoted the cultural transformation of the peasants as political subjects. This class-based subjectivity is both nationalist and international: nationalist in the military struggle in the War against Japanese Aggression; international in the consciousness of the common, working-class pursuit of a socialist future.

Humanism and Political Practice

Defending humanism against the imperialist agenda of "humanitarian intervention," Edward Said defined the "core of humanism" as "the secular notion that the historical world is made by men and women, and not by God." Disputing academic antihumanism that reduces human agency into linguistic performance, Said asserted that humanism is grounded in "human history as made by human action." Indebted to Giambattista Vico, the Italian humanist and author of New Science, humanism claims that the key to understanding history must derive "from the point of view of its human makers."[5]

For all his involvement in the Palestine struggle for human rights, Said taught only the "Western humanities" at Columbia University. But this seeming paradox should not obscure the connections between humanism and political commitment. Rather than a Eurocentric discourse, humanism remains a source of inspiration for worldwide emancipatory movements: "people all over the world," wrote Said, "can be and are moved by the ideals of justice and equality," and "the humanistic ideals of liberty and learning still supply most disadvantaged people with the energy to resist unjust war and military occupation."[6] In the struggle against despotism and tyranny, the ideas of human liberation and global justice are very much alive around the world.

Rooted in the "recognition of the inherent dignity and of the equal and inalienable rights of all members of the human family," humanism constitutes "the foundation of freedom, justice, and peace in the world."[7] In modern history, the concept provides the inner motivation for the struggle against monarchial despotism and for national independence and decolonization, bearing direct links to socialism. Heir to the Enlightenment, socialism challenges the power structure of the few and keeps faith with the world-making capacity of "men and women," regardless of nationality, ethnicity, and regions. Marshall Berman made this clear: "Marx proposes the Enlightenment and its central ideas, universal human rights and political democracy. He presupposes the English, the American, the French revolutions; he sees communism as a way to make good on their broken promises of democratic citizenship and human rights. Among the generations that made the Russian and Chinese Revolutions, there were millions of men and women who imagined the triumph of those revolutions, in 1917 and in 1949, as a chance to fulfill those promises in their own lives."[8]

The discovery of Marxist humanism by Jean-Paul Sartre, Simone de Beauvoir, and Henri Lefebvre in postwar France fueled the debate on "socialism with a human face." But the debate also involves the fraught relations between universal values and political practice, liberal cosmopolitanism and socialist internationalism. Louis Althusser claimed that Marx, while espousing humanism in his early work, departed from it to investigate the materialist history and political economy of capitalism. Initially keeping faith with the humanist values such as rights, autonomy, and freedom, Marx had believed that the human spirit drives historical progress and would culminate in the liberal state as the citadel of freedom. In his essays in *Die Rheinische Zeitung*, young Marx deemed the liberal state "as the great organism in which legal, moral, and political freedom would find realization, and in which the individual citizen, when he obeys the State's laws, is only obeying the natural laws of his own reason, of human reason."[9] Embodied by institutions of civil liberty and free press, humanist politics holds the state accountable to the liberal principles. Vigilance against the state's lapses from justice and freedom constitutes "political action par excellence." But the reality of capitalism fell far short of the ideals. Although the bourgeois state is supposed to embody reason and rights, everywhere it "slides into the contradiction" between its ideals and practice. Capitalist production exploited and alienated workers "in the fantastic forms of money, power, and gods." To make social change, liberal public criticism is far from adequate and revolution becomes necessary. Revolution aims to dismantle and reorganize the state machinery yet appeals to "the lost human essence."[10] Taking issue with Althusser's antihumanism, John Roche claims that while Marx saw working-class emancipation as a movement to overcome capitalist exploitation, the movement "contains universal human emancipation" rather than being confined to one class. At the heart of revolution lies the hope for the realization of human reason and freedom.[11]

Antonio Gramsci's notion of humanism has much to say to the Chinese Revolution.[12] Linking humanism to political practice and emancipation, Gramsci regarded socialism to be more a culture of self-knowledge and egalitarianism than an economic management and redistribution. Quoting the German romantic Novalis (Georg Philipp Friedrich Freiherr von Hardenberg) and Italian humanist Vico, Gramsci saw culture as a matter of "gaining possession of one's transcendent self" requisite for understanding others. Vico transposed the Greek thinker Solon's dictum "Know thyself" to a political consciousness that enables the plebeians to know themselves as equal members of a society. With the ideas of "bestial origin" drummed into them, the masses blindly subordinate themselves to their superiors deemed of divine lineage. But with awakened self-consciousness, the masses would "reflect on themselves and see that they had the same human nature as the nobles and hence should claim to be their equal in civil law."[13]

For Gramsci, culture is an ongoing work toward self-understanding and the consciousness of human equality and dignity. Far from signs of superiority, pedantry, and power, culture is a collective self-education aimed at the "discipline of one's inner self, a coming to terms with one's own personality." It enables individuals and groups to understand their own historical value, their function in life, and their rights and obligations. Demands for equality by disenfranchised classes drive emancipation actions to "throw off the patterns of organization" imposed on society by elite minorities in the past.[14] Critical reflection, first by a few people and then by an entire class, reveals why certain conditions of domination and oppression prevail, and shows "how best to convert the facts of vassalage into the signals of rebellion and social reconstruction." Humanist culture engages in "an intense labor of criticism," and by diffusing knowledge and ideas among the masses, enlightenment lifts class-bound individuals out of their myopic obsession with economic gains and allows people to transcend parochial identities and unite with others.[15]

The Chinese Revolution, by absorbing themes of self-reflection, class equality, and political consciousness, was thus a cultural revolution. Gramsci's insight sheds light on Yan'an's educational program and Zhou Libo's world literature class. Rather than dogmatism and intellectualism, the revolutionary movement took culture as the key driver for national liberation and international alliance.

The Lu Xun Academy of Arts as Cultural Sphere

The Japanese intrusion on July 7, 1937, into Northern China marked the beginning of the War of Resistance against Japanese Aggression. With the United Front newly established between the nationalist government and the communists, and as growing anti-imperialist sentiment swept through the nation, Yan'an, a remote, rural township in the border area of Shaanxi province, quickly became the center of the resistance movement. Urban intellectuals, artists, writers, and students flocked there, hoping to participate in the war efforts and to turn a page in their personal lives. Trained in the West or schooled in cosmopolitan culture in the cities, fluent in foreign languages, and accomplished in arts and letters, this intelligentsia fueled the resistance with intellectual reflection and cultural creativity. They set up theaters, formed study societies and literary associations, published journals and magazines, and built schools and colleges at different levels. The Military and Political University of Anti-Japanese War (Kangri junzheng daxue 抗日軍政 大學), founded in 1937, was the most comprehensive higher education institution in Yan'an. Amid this growing cultural momentum, the Lu Xun Academy was the "humanities and arts" wing of the university. In his statement "The Origin of the Lu Xun Academy," the vice president, Zhou Yang, proclaimed that the academy's mission was to play a role in the nation's survival and liberation by battling Japanese aggressors and contributing to world peace.[16]

The Lu Xun Academy represented a transformation from the bourgeois democratic revolution to what Mao Zedong defined as the "new democratic culture."[17] It carried on the May Fourth legacy, mobilized the energy and talent of Western-educated urban intellectuals, and created artworks under the influence of the Soviet Union and America as well as the European humanist tradition. Historians have shown how theater, literature, music, translation, and cinema in Yan'an incorporated and transmitted "universal values" of democracy, political rights, equality, self-determination, and internationalism.[18]

Far from cutting themselves off from cosmopolitan culture, the writers and students studied and absorbed liberal humanism and turned it in a national-popular and internationalist direction. The Lu Xun Academy tapped into the peasants' hopes for a new society of the people. Its humanist education aimed at raising the people's consciousness, forging revolutionary subjectivity, and mobilizing political alliances. Key to this program were enlightenment and education. As Mao stated in the "Yan'an Talks," illiterate and uneducated peasants "are eagerly demanding enlightenment, education, and works of literature and art." To meet their needs, the cultural workers should create new works that would "heighten their enthusiasm in struggle and confidence in victory, strengthen their unity, and fight the enemy with one heart and one mind."[19] The goal was to build an independent nation-state and align the nation with worldwide working-class movements. Against feudalism and imperialism, the revolutionary culture aimed to achieve national independence by the toiling masses as an integral part of the global socialist movement.

The academy's mission statement emphasized the key term *mobilization*—mobilizing the masses by the enlightened intellectuals so that the rural population could be rallied into a force in revolutionary struggle. The university setting was regarded as the most effective method for recruiting and training new cultural cadres from the uneducated masses. Zhou Yang stated: "Arts—drama, music, visual arts and literature—are the most powerful weapons for mobilizing the vast masses. Art workers are an indispensable force in the war of resistance. Thus, the training of a cadre with artistic expertise is at present the most urgent task."[20]

The "Lu Xun direction" designated by Mao signals the humanistic agenda. As a national-international thinker, a cultural hero, a standard bearer of modern culture, Lu Xun epitomized the tenacity and vitality of the Chinese people as well as a humanist profile admired by cosmopolitan intellectuals. His work inspired the new culture with three components: national, scientific, and popular.[21] Receptive of Western humanism and the May Fourth anti-traditional stance, and ready to reenergize resources of Chinese tradition, Lu Xun sympathized with national liberation by colonized people in Eastern Europe and translated a large amount of their literary works. With a cosmopolitan outlook, he declared that the Chinese should "prevent ourselves from trailing behind the rest of the world in terms of intellectual developments while remaining in touch with the pulse of our cultural heritage."[22] Learning from the West and carrying forward the indigenous tradition was to build up the independent character of a nation: "It will enable people to achieve a more profound understanding of the significance of life and lead them to achieve the self-awareness so critical in the development of the sort of individual potential required for the transformation of this 'country of loose sand' into a nation of human beings."[23]

Since the May Fourth era, modern Chinese universities in the cities grew into a hotbed of political ferment, free and iconoclastic thoughts, and artistic creativity. Far away from the urban centers, Yan'an's University of Resistance signaled that modern enlightenment had now put down roots in mountains and fields. Issues vital to the whole nation and the world found a venue for reflection and discussion in the rural backwater. As a humanities branch, the Lu Xun Academy was a discursive and pedagogic space for cultural and artistic knowledge, covering a wide range of disciplines such as literature, performing arts, visual art, film, sculpture, and theater. Its international wing included readings and translations of European, Russian, and American classics.

Emphasizing critical thinking as the guiding principle in the mission statement, Zhou Yang urged students to pay attention to "the dark sides and weaknesses of the emerging new society" and "constructively criticize and correct them."[24] They should be independent in their thought and judgment and maintain a unique style and the right to criticize. Edgar Snow reported that the educational programs fostered a "spirit of internationalism" and rank-and-file soldiers tried to keep abreast of the news and developments of the Spanish civil war, its relevance to the antifascist resistance in China. "It was quite surprising sometimes to find," he wrote, "even far back in mountains, Red farmers who knew rudimentary facts about such things as the Italian conquest of Abyssinia and the German-Italian invasion of Spain. . . . Despite their geographical isolation, these rustics knew much more about world politics . . . than the rural population anywhere else in China."[25] The academy constituted what David Apter and Tony Saich have called a "discourse community." In this community, people spent their time "poring over the text, interpreting their experience, and expressing themselves in public utterances that bound addresser and addressee."[26] To be sure, doctrinaire imperatives were imposed, and historians have discerned evidence of brainwashing and manipulation.[27] But the blanket view of brainwashing ignores the vibrant discursive atmosphere and dynamics. Making a premature closure, the view reduces political enlightenment to religious orthodoxy and ideological indoctrination. Contrary evidence abounds. For example, the method of *qifa* 啟發 (illumination or inspiration) practiced in the academy ran contrary to indoctrination and thought control. As Jane Price notes, "At Kangda [University of Resistance], the qifa method was contrasted to the traditional lecture format, rote memorization, and simple questions and answers." Following this method of investigation and moving from induction to deduction, the investigator "proceeded from the near to far, from the concrete to abstract, from part to whole."[28]

In such a setting, inherited and prior identities—rural, patriarchal, and traditional—were to be transformed and transcended, and new personalities and aspirations were to be forged. Culture—literature, art, and symbolic representations—became intimately intertwined with political practice. As

Craig Calhoun aptly puts it, culture is conceptualized as "a setting for rational debate and decision making" and for "the development of social solidarity as a matter of choice, rather than necessity." Such choices may be textual and interpretive, but they entail enlightened political judgement and action in world making in Hannah Arendt's formulation.[29]

Zhou Libo and His World Literature Class

At the Lu Xun Academy of Arts, Zhou Libo ran a world literature seminar, lectured on works of European and Russian masters, and discussed themes of humanism. Zhou practiced a mode of interpretation worthy of the humanistic tradition. Along with biographical background for each author, he delved into the social historical contexts from which the work arose, situating personal material in history and politics. Due to the lack of critical resources, he resorted to remarks and observations by literary masters to explain the texts, making frequent connections between texts, writers, and critical works. He also invoked Chinese writers, notably Lu Xun, and referenced Chinese literary classics, citing eloquent and poetic passages. Bringing Western literature to rural revolutionary China, the lectures contributed to the broader cultural program designed to train new writers and artists in Yan'an (see figure 3.1).

3.1 Zhou Libo teaches a class at the Lu Xun Academy of Arts.

Zhou's class was an anomaly in Yan'an's politically charged atmosphere. In a study about Mao's rise to power in Yan'an, Gao Hua notes that there was a "honeymoon period" between Mao and the urban cosmopolitan writers. But as the cultural policy of the Chinese Communist Party (CCP) took hold, tensions arose and cultural autonomy came under fire.[30] I am inclined, however, to see the rectification campaign as endeavors to create a new political culture. While acknowledging May Fourth as the groundwork for the new democracy, Mao guarded against its "bourgeois" and "urban" remnants. Terms such as *human nature, individualism,* and *love* were suspect and deemed dangerous. While historians tend to see in early 1940s Yan'an an ascent of authoritarianism and a sharp break with May Fourth, a closer look reveals that Zhou's lecture incorporated and developed humanistic themes. Standing on the shoulders of May Fourth culture and Western humanism, the new culture took both traditions in a new direction.

Zhou's lectures offer insights into how art fuels politics. Raising the question of "the apprehension of life and the representation of that apprehension" in European fiction, Zhou focused on romantic individualism under the rubric of "human nature" and analyzed the novel's power to articulate historical change and social upheavals.[31] Stendhal, Balzac, and Tolstoy canvas a spectrum of "human nature" embodied by the romantic individual. Love and affection escalate into revolutionary passions, combining romantic imagination and the heartfelt, quixotic plunge into social change. French novelist Stendhal, deeply involved in the Napoleonic War that heralded worldwide political upheavals in Europe, depicted romantic love as his primary passion. In 1821 Stendhal listed on his epitaph the names of six women he had loved, proclaiming that for all his disagreeable complexion, "four or five of these women did indeed love him" (7). In an essay on love written in Milan, Stendhal treated love broadly as a risky yet challenging experience, mixed with joy and sorrow, and consonant with tumultuous historical events. As love shifts to passion, passion becomes an appreciation of power as aesthetic representations. Instead of private feelings, true love spirals into a broad pattern of emotion and sympathy, a spiritual and sublime passion, like "the heat of summer and the freshness of spring" (15). Zhou comments that such love can be fulfilled only by giving others happiness; it is intimate, kind, and altruistic: "In the mutual love of parents and children there is tremendous and beautiful pleasure. . . . This pure love may be enhanced by sexual feelings and made sweeter, but it can work independently." Respect and gratitude are the right motivation for love, just as youth and beauty are legitimate cause for desire. Old age will reduce the latter but will keep the former (15–16).

To Zhou, narrative fiction thrived on the cusp between fiction and reality. Realistic fiction zeroed in on the tension between imagination and reality. This chimes in with the romantic tenor of May Fourth fiction, with idealistic aspirations interwoven with realistic portrayals. Western realistic authors, as Leo Ou-fan Lee notes, were "received romantically" by Chinese writers. Yet the "romantically inclined" Chinese novelists were also drawn to the realistic aspect of European romanticism and ignored its transcendent, mystical element "in favor of a humanistic, sociopolitical interpretation."[32] This injection of ideals into reality foreshadowed socialist realism, which is characterized by realistic portrayals of actual conditions informed by visions of utopia. After Mao's "Yan'an Talks" in 1942, the balance between the real and the ideal tipped toward the latter, as official socialist realism became the order of the day.

In Stendhal, Balzac, and Tolstoy, Zhou discovered a theory of the novel that places "social man in natural history." Wedded to the evolving social manners and customs, fictional characters are products of their specific time and place. The novelists excel at depicting the layouts of a city and the complexity and myriad details of urban life. Stendhal supplements this naturalist realism with romantic charms of legend and fantasy. No stranger to exaggeration and ahistorical fantasy, he weaves the fanciful and extraordinary into realistic narrative. Blending melodramatic motifs such as passion, jealousy, power, women, sex, and murder into realistic depictions, Stendhal turns his work into a crucible between fiction and reality.

Influenced by Walter Scott's Waverly novels, Stendhal's fiction moved away from the romantic storyline to chart an epic insurgence of popular movements. Balzac, on the other hand, was the real master of a mature realism. Balzac's novels reflected a tendentious stance toward the historical upheavals from 1816 to 1848 in the wake of the French Revolution. This turbulent era witnessed the decline of the ancien régime as the new bourgeoisie was coming onto the world stage. Though a staunch conservative, Balzac was quick to see the changes that swept away the old strata in political and social conflict. His work rolled fantasy and reality, imagination and epic into one, mixing poetry and vernacular, drama and portraits (28).

Zhou's perspective on Stendhal, Scott, and Balzac attested to a new understanding of art in history. Art not only depicts reality but also projects world visions. Viewing the historical novel from the lens of Hegelian historical philosophy, György Lukács saw Scott's fiction as inaugurating a sense of history, germane to both German nationalism and the French Revolution. Rooted in Johann Gottfried von Herder's notion of the folk, German nationalism awakened Germans to national consciousness and the desire of a sovereign people.³³ National art and culture reasserted national identity and contributed to the nation's birth. The French Revolution, on the other hand, transcended the nation and made history a worldwide mass experience. The upsurge of the masses among European nations "inevitably conveyed a sense and experience of history to broad masses." Under the international impulse to transform domestic societies, "more and more people become aware of the connection between national and world history."³⁴

This emergent consciousness departs from romantic, cultural nationalism embedded in the organic *longue durée* and in time-honored language, ethnicity, tradition, and mythology. The old historical novel, with its nostalgia of the frozen landscape, amounts to mere costume history, mired in exotic curiosities of a museum milieu of "blood and soil." In contrast, the world historical novel portrays the epochal transformations seething in the depths of lives of men and women across the European continent. Social changes reach into everyday life, economy, and the psychology of average people, signaling that the people are involved and become a driving force in overturning the status quo and making history.

The new historical consciousness radically challenged the abstract humanistic concept of reason and the "conception of man's unalterable nature," recasting world history as an upswing narrative of popular movement.³⁵ Echoing Lukács, Zhou Libo drew attention to a historical narrative that underscores popular action in mass democratic movements. Stendhal's novels attach great importance to the narrative layout. A great plan coheres around a series of moving actions, which remain unperturbed by desultory conversations and psychological self-indulgence. In contrast, the modernist novel is keen on capturing the fleeting moods and delving into elusive sentiments. In its probes into the inner recess of the mind, the modernist novel delves into the subtlety and vagary of the psyche and sits uneasily with the overall plan of collective action. Eschewing the modernist, self-indulgent narrative, Zhou leaned toward an action-packed, popular, and transformative realism.

The talk of human nature and universal love put Zhou at risk, as Mao's "Yan'an Talks" targeted precisely the ideas of human love. But Mao attempted to historicize rather than deny universal love. "Is there such a thing as human nature? Of course there is," Mao responded. "But there is only human nature in the concrete, no human nature in the abstract." With regard to love, what is questioned is the timeless, ahistorical notion of love: "There will be genuine love of humanity—after classes are eliminated all over the world."³⁶

Zhou does not shy away from humanist universals in Tolstoy, Gorky, and Fadeyev. Tolstoy shows religious love for Russian peasants and following

Rousseau, advocates love for nature and female beauty against the artificial and fashionable society. Tolstoy celebrates starlit night, the sky resonant with songs, full-blooded and innocent love, and the breasts of Corsican girls. His art brings humans into communion with love and affection. Instead of expressions of God or aesthetic play rooted in biology, art is "a form of social communication essential to human life and humans' propensity for happiness, allowing mankind to be linked on the basis of reciprocity and sympathy" (120). Gorky evinces a "proactive humanism that encourages people to move toward a better life" (123). Fadeyev, whose novel *Debacle* was translated by Lu Xun and mentioned by Mao, celebrates love of mankind and of comradeship by calling for a new morality and emotional elevation. Seeking this new human spirit through his art, Fadeyev remarks (Zhou quotes him in English): "A lonely sower of Liberty, I left my dwelling early, before the rising of the stars and with my clean, unsullied hands, I scattered life giving seeds among the enslaved furrows" (129).

Zhou's "love talk" evinced a shift from romantic love to class sympathy, manifest in compassion for the peasants, factory workers, and disadvantaged people in Gorky and Tolstoy. Romanticism, a form of sentimentalism, suggests that "the sense of the beautiful lags behind questions of reality. The consciousness of the progressive class is still unclear, vague, and defuse." The related sense of beauty can only be a "confused, undefined sense of pleasure and anticipation, as well as a loud call for change" (122). Citing Marx, Zhou adds that from the inchoate anticipation of the proletariat for social change arises the dream of a future society. Romanticism paints extravagant pictures and is "composed of thick, strong colors. It is subjective and dreamy. Brought to full relief, upstaged, and elegant, it is more powerful in arousing strong passion, but it is not profound as real life" (122).

"Real life," canvased in Tolstoy's "clear-headed realism," sets itself off from sentimentality in Gorky as well as Charles Dickens, who were famed for their tear-jerking stories of the poor and helpless. Going beyond Dickensian sentimentalism, Tolstoy exposes the structural injustices inherent in the Russian rural order and land ownership. *Anna Karenina*, for example, attests to a sober realism and exposes the prerogatives of the corrupt nobility aligned with the emergent bourgeois class, the wage labor system, and the exploitation of peasants. Penetrating through the superior veneer of the aristocracy, Tolstoy "perceived the real cause of all forms of injustice, and tensions among social classes."[37] Stressing the centrality to the ownership of land by peasants, Tolstoy debunked the privileges enjoyed by the aristocrats. This insight resonated the collective action to reclaim land ownership under land reform. Like Levin in *Anna Karenina*, Tolstoy in his later years engaged in a socialist experiment by distributing land to the peasants and building farming collectives based on public ownership and mutual assistance. The shift from abstract humanism to the concern for the peasantry is reminiscent of Liang Qichao's reading of the tianxia credo as an economic agenda of fair redistribution and equality, underscoring the deep bond between humanism and socialism.

Zhou's novel *Great Changes in a Mountain Village* (*Shanxiang jubian* 山鄉巨變) exemplifies the shift from abstract humanism to class compassion for the downtrodden. Although the novel depicts rural transformations under the Communist Party's collectivization policy, the land reform activity unfolds as a tentative experiment in a village. The mission is to meet the peasants' needs and to appeal to the inherited mental habit and custom while changing them. Individual peasants have different motives in joining the cooperative. A protagonist, the literati of the village, intends to serve the times and submits his house deed to the authorities, only to have it returned. On hearing that the cooperative cares for the old, he remarks that this is indeed socialism with ancient roots: "As Mencius said, 'Treat the elders of others as you would treat your own.' Our ancestors long ago wanted to establish socialism."[38] This paradoxical comment resonates well with the agenda of mutual assistance and universal care for all promised by the rural reform.

Zhou's novel depicts the wide-ranging and multifaceted texture of rural life, custom, and personalities under the land reform. Its immersion in the tenacious residues of backwardness, inertia, self-interest, ignorance, narrow-mindedness, and fatalism invites the term *realism*. But the realistic groundwork heralds socialist and mental change. The novel entails a mild and compassionate form of the mass-line social practice. Instead of overhauling rural culture overnight drastically, land reform activities seem to be a cultural revolution that works through the meticulously textured lifeworld of entrenched ancient customs and habits.

National Form and World Literature

Capitalist expansion spread the bourgeois mode of production and remade the world in its own image. Driven by the need for trade and communication, wrote Marx, "the intellectual creations of individual nations become common property. National one-sidedness and narrow-mindedness become more and more impossible, and from the numerous national and local literatures, there arises a world literature."[39]

For all its humanist programs and internationalist atmosphere, Yan'an witnessed a turn toward issues of nationality and national culture between the late 1930s and the early 1940s. As Japanese forces encroached deeper into North China, the communists were forced to act more as nationalists and to focus on national politics under the mandate of national defense and unity.

National concerns, however, had not been the priority of Chinese socialist internationalism. Aimed at the worldwide emancipation of working classes, socialism is inherently internationalist and opposed to the bourgeois nation-state. A certain strand of Marxism disengaged nationality from worldwide class emancipation and expressed the distrust of nationality exemplified by the bourgeois nation.[40] In this light, the refocus on the national question by Chinese communists seemed to be a paradox. Addressing this paradox in his speech "On the Role Communist Party in the National War," Mao asked, "Can a Communist, who is an internationalist, at the same time be a patriot? We hold that he not only can be but must be." The Chinese communists must "fight to defend the motherland against the aggressors" and patriotism was an "inescapable duty" for achieving "national liberation." This claim was, interestingly, uttered in the same breath of internationalism: Chinese communists are both "internationalists and patriots," and patriotism for national defense against Japanese aggression was "applied internationalism." It is so because "only by achieving national liberation will it be possible for the proletariat and other working people to achieve their own emancipation."[41]

Issues of nationalism and nationality were closely linked to the heated debate on national form. Mao first raised the question of national form in the essay "Oppose Stereotype Party Writing." Against the empty and dull style of party propaganda and the stilted and arrogant discourse of the educated elite, the chairman called for a "national style of propaganda: "Foreign stereotypes must be abolished, there must be less singing of empty, abstract tunes, and dogmatism must be laid to rest; they must be replaced by the fresh, lively Chinese style and spirit that the common people of China love."[42] Under the nationalist imperative, the University of Resistance was designed to train cultural workers for the national defense against the Japanese invasion. Together with Zhou Yang, Zhou Libo championed and discussed "national defense literature." Although national defense literature was apparently anchored to "national one-sidedness," the debate shed light on how nationalism is linked to internationalism.[43] As the Japanese invasion of North China threatened the country's survival, advocates of defense literature called on writers to depict the crises and traumatic experience of war in order to rally patriotic passion. Zhou Libo traced national defense literature to the Literature Association of the Red Army and Navy in the Soviet Union. Founded in 1930, the group used literature as a means of promoting patriotism in the war of self-defense against foreign invasion. As a voice for toiling multitudes (*qinlao dazhong* 勤劳大众) ravaged by the war, national defense literature was to describe the masses' plight and suffering, raise their anti-imperialist sentiment, and elevate them from passive victimhood to active resistance. Distinguishing it from the parochial cultural identity, Zhou asserted that national defense literature was bound up with internationalism, but not with the kind rooted in "national nihilism." Only by driving out the invaders and achieving national independence could China fulfill internationalist goals.[44] Similarly, rejecting the parochial, narrow sense of natural culture, Zhou Yang wrote that all people and nations being robbed of their own country and land should have patriotism. A broad patriotism had international implications and encouraged people to understand and sympathize with other people across national lines: "patriotism is naturally compatible with internationalism."[45] Class analysis, however, split Lu Xun and the advocates of national defense literature. The class question turned on the social constituencies of national literature: Who is the main subject matter: the toiling masses or all segments of the national population in a united front? Lu Xun's phrase "the mass literature of national revolutionary war," by intertwining class with nationality, was eventually accepted by Yan'an theorists, who reasserted that working-class emancipation went hand in hand with national defense.[46]

Discussions of national defense literature went with the intense debate on national form. In Yan'an's cultural and educational sphere, a disconnect between the demand for a new national culture and residual local subnational forms was striking and self-evident. When Western-educated urban intellectuals migrated to the revolutionary base, they were entrusted with the mission of educating and mobilizing the rural masses in order to build a culture of a modern nation. But they did not know whom to speak to and whom to serve with their talent and knowledge. They possessed no language to communicate with peasants, soldiers, and workers. The need of communication raised the question of the relation between national form and subnational forms. The subnational forms included diverse local, grassroots, and multiethnic motifs and practices—age-old cultural residues of multicultural landscapes of imperial China. Chen Boda designated local forms as *minjian xingshi* 民間形式 (folk and grassroots forms) and distinguished them from the national forms that the revolutionary culture aspired to. Minjian xingshi includes "specific properties of local songs, stage performances, dances, and literary works in each locality."[47] As specific aesthetic forms, minor traditions, and folk cultural survivals from the past, these were still alive and well in rural communities and populations. To Chen and other debaters, folk and local forms were potentials to be used and to be enfolded into national forms, but they were not there yet. Chen's view challenges the presumed "authentic" link between local folk forms and national forms.

Writers of nationalism have theorized an authentic national form rooted in the entrenched tradition premised on a continuous lineage between premodern traditions and cultural identity of the modern nation-state. Levenson reminded us that this view implies a primordialist, ethnonationalist definition of a people, *minzu* 民族. The term denotes "a people in organic synthesis," who embody a cultural essence constituted by ethnic and kinship ties, history, custom, religion, and tradition.[48] Mortgaged to romantic nationalism by Herder, the organic concept of national form valorizes the essence of literature as uniquely national and antithetical to cosmopolitanism.[49] National literature embodies the soul, genius, and heritage of a nation, which "possesses its own special character and so must be judged according to its own value, independent of the place and value of others."[50] Unabashedly one-sided and parochial, this concept prides itself on the age-old, organic tradition and a long history. For Levenson, this is how the Guomindang's Nationalist regime defined the Chinese nation. As a minzu, China presented "an integral nationalist organic community" and "implied a national essence, transcending individuals but an individual itself, a folk, in its resistance to cosmopolitanism."[51] Incidentally, *minzu* in Levenson's sense should be fine-tuned as *zuyi* 族裔 to highlight its ethnic and blood lineages.

The national form debate, however, did not fall into the ethnonationalist trap and refused to return to a primordial depository of "Chinese-ness" embedded in grassroots or authentic traditions. Socialist culture was to articulate the emancipatory goal of the oppressed nation and its people. This marks the radical difference between ethnonationalist views and the socialist internationalist culture, which cuts across all regions, ethnicities, and nationalities. Although the emergent revolutionary culture called on writers not to lose sight of local and indigenous forms, it also urged them to create new meanings and forms. In his Yan'an Talks, Mao urged cultural workers to move out of the ivory tower and go to the people and study the local and folk forms, such as "the raw materials found in the life of the people" and "the wall newspapers, songs of the masses, the dramatic troupes in villages."[52] Immersion in traditional and local forms, however, was by no means a cycling of the past and the residual. Rather, the search for the national form was a creative project. The local, age-old forms are the pregivens, a culture *in itself*; they are to be elevated into a culture for the socialist nation. As Mao stated, "The literary and artistic works of the past are not a source but a stream; they were created by our predecessors and the foreigners out of the literary and artistic raw materials they found in the life of the people of their time and place. We must take over all the fine things in our literary and artistic heritage."[53]

The discussion of national form projects a literature created out of cultural specificity and indigenous resources. Thus, national form and subnational forms are related in a process of creation. Besides the preexisting forms, Western culture was regarded as another rich resource flowing into national culture. This is why Zhou Yang saw the emergent national form as inseparable from "Europeanization" (*ouhua* 欧化). Rather than the mere learning, translation, and teaching of "world literature" of the Euro-American canons—a May Fourth tradition—Europeanization is also a reinvention that contributes to the formation of national culture. Zhou's provocative claim that "Europeanization and nationalization" (*minzu hua* 民族化) are "by no means contradictory concepts" spells out the inseparable and underlying link between the national and the international. The national form emerges not by insulating China from the world but through appropriation of foreign resources. Spurred by Europeanization, May Fourth culture was an enlightenment project encompassing both humanist values and national consciousness. The influx of Western vocabulary, styles, motifs, and aesthetics spurred Chinese writers to appropriate European imports to meet China's own needs and address the nation's specific conditions. As "things imported from foreign countries to meet our real needs" and "applied concretely in China's peculiar environment," the Western forms "cease to be the way they were in foreign countries and become an organic part of the Chinese nation's blood and flesh."[54]

Views by Zhou Libo and Zhou Yang pointed to the socialist international dimension in the national-international nexus. Revolutionary thinkers were indeed cognizant of aesthetic values of folk arts, opera, dance, and drama forms. But the premium on national and regional traditions did not lead to a primordial sense of Chineseness but to democratic and popular expressions of ordinary people's lives, experiences, and lifeworlds over the centuries. It is this disavowal of national uniqueness that prompted Zhou Yang to say that the "old forms are not national forms." They contain feudal vestiges, values, and emotional structures—barriers rather than resources for the new socialist culture. Although rich in aesthetic value, local color, history, and artistry, these indigenous elements can only be a temporary means to an end.[55] They should be appropriated to propagate new ideologies and values. Instead of pouring new wine in the old bottle, both old forms and contents must be renewed.

A new idea of national culture emerged from the debate and redefined the revolutionary culture as a self-conscious invention. Nation and culture are part of this process of reconfiguration and re-creation. The new culture strategically appropriates indigenous as well as cosmopolitan resources and renders them into the service of building up a new nation-state. The national form arises not from the nostalgic unearthing of native treasures and ancient traditions but from an endeavor of political and cultural construction. Building a new culture requires making enlightened choice and engaging in reflection. Steering clear of the entrenched "feudal" tradition as well as imperialist, comprador culture, the revolutionary writers absorbed, deployed, and reconfigured resources from all quarters. Political invention involves judgments and choices with the goal of refounding culture and politics altogether on a new ground. This is what Calhoun has called, following Arendt, "world-making."[56] World making does not work in the shadows of inherited cultural traditions trying to exhibit and flaunt the "Chinese difference" or ancient glory, nor is it a freewheeling cosmopolitan game of individual freedom and aesthetic pleasure.

It is the people's nation that undergirds the link between a national people and the international outlook. Levenson's coinage "communist cosmopolitanism" alludes to the image of a world that encompasses people, working classes, and international alliance across nations. Speaking of a 1952 Chinese translation of the American playwright Albert Maltz, Levenson saw the playwright's joy in being a bridge between American and Chinese socialists. Maltz's perception of China as "a liberating force for the whole world today" brought to the fore the national and internationalist aspects of the translated work. In this case, the concept of the national people breaks away from the logic of ethnic and cultural identity rooted in an organic lineage of blood and soil. The new people are both "nationalist and internationalist at the same time."[57] Such people are capable of understanding each other, not because they are individuals with cosmopolitan empathy but because they belong to the same international class. Levenson wrote: "Cultural cosmopolitanism, *on a class basis*, seemed to pair with nationalism, not to impair it. For the *jenmin* of all nations were supposed to have a common cause, while the *jenmin* of each nation (especially China) was supposed virtually to constitute the nation. If the local bourgeois failed to make the common cause with 'the people' (*jen-min*), they are denationalized, as imperialists or running dogs of imperialists, disqualified for the *min-tzu* (*minzu*) variant of 'people.'"[58]

In other words, when the nationalist regime failed to respond to the will and concerns of the Chinese people, it lost legitimacy as national leadership and became a comprador under the imperialists and colonialists. Moreover, a nation constituted by its people is able to identify with another national people, and this opens the door to international affinity and solidarity. People-to-people relations are the foundation of mutual support and sympathy on an international scale and underlie the translation and teaching of world literature. Later in socialist China, this national-international nexus accounts for large amounts of translations of literature from all parts of the world and the dissemination of world literature outside the circuit of capital.

To conclude, Zhou Libo's lecture and the national form debate project an image of a people who are both national and internationalist. Internationalism means the alliance of people with the shared experience of victimhood and oppression, an awareness of the common fate of the working class of different nations, and the need for their mutual understanding and sympathy. The people, though embedded in different cultures and ethnic backgrounds, are ready to identify with the similar endeavors of other people in forging affinity and solidarity. So cultural infusions from European humanism are "to pair with nationalism, not to impair it."[59] People of diverse nationalities are peer groups whose separate pursuits of independence made a common cause.

In her interview with Mao in Yan'an, the American journalist Agnes Smedley raised concerns that the nationalist thrust of the United Front might obscure class-based internationalism. To her question "if the policy of a United Front implied that the Chinese communists had abandoned the class struggle and turned into simply nationalists," Mao replied: "The Communists absolutely do not tie their viewpoint to the interests of a single class at a single time but are most passionately concerned with the fate of Chinese nation. . . . The Chinese communists are internationalists. They are in favor of the world communist movement. But at the same time they are patriots who defend their native land. . . . This patriotism and internationalism are by no means in conflict, for only China's independence and liberation will make it possible to participate in the world communist movement."[60]

Mao's last line recalls Sun Zhongshan's insight about nationalism as a way station to cosmopolitanism: "we must restore our nation to the status of equality and freedom with other nations before we discuss cosmopolitanism."[61] In the note to this passage, Stuart Schram points out that the word *communist* was interchangeable with *datong*. Defining the new People's Republic of China (PRC) in 1949, Mao reminded the audience that Kang Youwei wrote *Datong shu* to advance the idea of world harmony but "did not find and could not find the way to achieve Great Harmony." Yet the datong dream now had a chance to be put into practice. Chinese communists found an effective way—by building a people's nation: "There are bourgeois republics in foreign lands, but China cannot have a bourgeois republic because she is a country suffering under imperialist oppression." The only way to reach the great world community was "through a people's republic led by the working class."[62] The way to internationalism was a new nation-state capable of reaching out to other nations constituted by working people.

Art, Politics, and Internationalism in Korean War Films

Four

STRIVING TO LIBERATE THE CHINESE PEOPLE from colonial domination and the domestic ruling class, the Chinese Revolution was primarily a national independence movement. But with the founding of the PRC in 1949, China was poised to wade into the world, and its international agenda confirmed Mao's remark that "only China's independence and liberation will make it possible to participate in the world communist movement."[1] To promote alliance and mutual support among colonized nations, socialist China engaged with nations in Asia, Africa, and Latin America in a new united front, breaking through the vicious circle of interstate geopolitics and colonialism.

The Cold War era saw a new round of imperialist rivalry over former colonies and spheres of influence by two hegemonic powers. Socialist internationalism sought to battle this power structure. The battle lines were drawn between the geopolitical confrontation between the United States and

the Soviet Union but also on cultural fronts.[2] The United States committed large resources to propaganda in the name of free information. Carried
by the Congress for Cultural Freedom, the American outreach had offices
in thirty-five countries, published some twenty magazines, and organized
high-profile arts and academic events around the world. On the other hand,
China embarked on the mission of nation building and forging diplomatic
and international allies.[3] In a clash of culture, images, and propaganda, the
antagonist camps deployed aesthetic media—film, imagery, ideologies, and
arts—as weapons of geopolitics. In this chapter, I turn to films of the Korean
War as a venue for understanding political culture, internationalist imagi-
naries, and revolutionary ideology during the Cold War.

Rooted in the realpolitik tradition, the Cold War lens sees international
relations in terms of bloody Darwinian struggle for self-preservation and
domination. Ironically, this perspective has become widely accepted in the
post–Cold War and globalization era, when the Hobbesian "war of all against
all" prevailed in global outlooks and geopolitics. What is lost is memories of
mass-based emancipatory movements: anti-colonialism, pursuits of equality and social justice, national independence, Third World movements, and
international cooperation. The Cold War perspective has also affected the
perception and representation of the Korean War. Focusing on interstate
antagonism and geopolitical rivalry, historians and critics have looked at the
Korean War as a war between two nation-states in pursuit of self-interest,
national security, and power. What is elided is the ideological difference between revolutionary and imperialist war, between socialist internationalism
and interstate antagonism.

The US intervention in the Korean conflict in June 1950 posed a threat to
China's territorial security and industrial base in the northeast region, disrupting the plan to liberate Taiwan. But China's decision to enter the war entails
nationalist and internationalist dimensions often obscured by the realpolitik
analysis. The naming of the war reflects these two aspects. The "Korean War,"
a neutral term in reference to an interstate conflict, obscures the implications
of social revolution, national liberation, and internationalism. By contrast, in
Mao's designation "The War of Resisting US Aggression and Assisting Korea"
(*kangmei yuanchao* 抗美援朝), resistance highlights decolonization and national
liberation; assistance underscores the concerted effort and mutual support
between one revolutionary nation and another. Distinct from interstate geopolitics, kangmei yuanchao, paired with "defending our home and country"
(*baojia weiguo* 保家衛國), put the stress on the national as well as international
aspects of China's military involvement beyond its territory.

Chen Jian has shown that the Chinese leadership believed that by firmly confronting US imperialist aggression in Korea, the new Chinese nation "would be able to translate the tremendous pressure from without into dynamics that would help enhance the Chinese people's revolutionary momentum while legitimizing the CCP's authority as China's new ruler."[4] Having founded a new state, the Chinese revolutionaries were poised to consolidate state power but also to expand revolutionary momentum to East Asia. What is the "revolutionary momentum" in this apparently interstate conflict? Bruce Cummings's influential work has defined the nature of the Korean War by situating it in the context of anti-imperialism, anti-colonialism, and revolution. At stake was the conflict of two socioeconomic systems. As a forgotten and unknown war in American consciousness, the Korean War, more than a conflict between North and South, was in its nature a civil war fought between two different futures of modern Korea and by two different socioeconomic forces. The nation-building project was entangled with the expanding US domination in East Asia. The occupation and division of Korea through the 38th parallel decision in 1945 taken unilaterally by Americans, the popping up of the privileged ruling class, the "spread of democracy," the continued colonization through a dependent economy and open markets, and the exploitation of the peasantry—all these factors created the same colonial patterns that were as true of semicolonized China as Third World peripherals. The division split Korea into two classes: a population with a vast majority of poor peasants, and a tiny minority of landowners who held most of the wealth and formed the base of the elite Korea Democratic Party. These social and class tensions were volcanoes ready to irrupt into conflict—into the revolt of the revolutionary masses against the ruling elite. The United States intervened on behalf of the smallest Korean elite group and aimed to perpetuate its power and privileges. The socioeconomic inequality and class oppression account for China's assistance to North Koreans in expanding the "revolutionary" momentum.[5]

As US intervention in the Korean peninsula threatened the industrial infrastructure in Manchuria and the new state's territory, China's entry into the war constituted a self-defense: one leg of the war effort was "defending our home and country." The other leg was battles fought by the Chinese volunteer army in the spirit of internationalism. Premised on the "Eastern Camp and international solidarity between the people's democracies," the internationalist dimension made the war a precursor to China's subsequent agenda for supporting Third World decolonization and international assistance to developing countries.[6]

One deflection from the political analysis of war narrative is the emphasis on individual trauma and suffering. In recent decades, war narrative has turned away from the broad questions of why fight a war in favor of an individual's vicissitudes, romance, trauma, and the "human spirit." The Korean film *Brotherhood of War* (*Taegukgi*, dir. Kang Ju-gyu, 2004) and the Chinese film *Assembly* (*Jijie hao* 集結號, dir. Feng Xiaogang, 2007) exemplify this trend. War films and stories no longer tell us anything about ideological and systematic antagonisms between socialism and capitalism, colonialism and national liberation; between oppressors and oppressed, violence and counterviolence. Under the neoliberalist culture industry, war films tend to picture belligerent circumstances as a grim, incomprehensible backdrop for a personal story. Never mind that war is imperialist or anti-imperialist, fascist or anti-fascist, invasion or resistance: all war wears the same dark color of terror, violence, slaughter, and apocalypse. In the murky pools of bloodbath, there is no difference between just and unjust wars. All military campaigns crush individuals in indiscriminate slaughter and bloodshed. Bloody and fatal events engineered by the juggernauts of the modern state fall from the sky and steamroll over mutilated bodies, unmotivated by reason and purpose. Granting primacy to individual survival, camaraderie or family ties over collective and historical context, and advocating a form of survivalist individualism against death, the "war" genre focuses on traumatic blows to "cosmopolitan," "human" rights and obscures political conflict and ideological divides in the past and present. By reexamining Chinese films about the Korean War, I intend to bring a political perspective back to our interpretation of war in the history of the Cold War.

By examining two films, this chapter takes a look at the national and internationalist aspects of China's international agenda. The film *Shanggann Ridge* (*Shanggan ling* 上甘嶺, dir. Shameng, 1956), a product of the early days of the PRC, addresses the national and patriotic theme. On the other hand, *Heroic Sons and Daughters* (*Yingxion ernü* 英雄兒女, dir. Wu Zhaodi, 1964), released on the eve of the Cultural Revolution, takes national concerns into the ideological climate of decolonization and Third World movements. The film extols the internationalist ethos of volunteer soldiers and the power of the human spirit, compressing art, politics, and war into a compelling spectacle.

Realism, Patriotism, and Technology

As a medium of national politics, the Chinese war film propagates national unity, strength, and patriotic sentiments by means of audiovisual effects, images, and symbols. The canon of Chinese cinema from 1949 to 1966 was the film of "revolutionary history"—a history of wars and armed struggle. Marked by crucial campaigns and fierce battles, this genre depicts the military action by revolutionaries to combat foreign invasions and wrest state power from the domestic ruling regime. The war film serves an educational function in regard to the history, struggle, and buildup of the PRC. Mao's famous statement "Political power grows out of the barrel of a gun" captures the experience of armed struggle against overwhelming odds and affirms the belligerent nature of state building.[7] Traversing several stages, the war film covers the War of the Northern Expedition (*beifa zhanzheng* 北伐戰爭, 1926–28) and dramatizes the campaigns against the warlords and the corrupt government. The second period, 1927 to 1937, witnessed the wars of land revolution, the birth of the Red Army, and the Long March. The next stage, from 1937 through 1945, covers the Anti-Japanese War, which includes some memorable productions such as *Landmine Warfare* (*Dilei zhan* 地雷戰, dir. Tang Yingqi, 1962) and *Tunnel Warfare* (*Didao zhan* 地道戰, dir. Ren Xudong, 1965). The fourth stage, the War of Liberation against the Guomindang, is reflected in the iconic film *Battles across the Land* (*Nanzheng beizhan* 南征北戰, dir. Cheng Yin and Tang Xiaodan, 1952). The Korean War broke out shortly after communists took state power, and *Shanggan Ridge* and *Heroic Sons and Daughters* have figured as the most iconic representations.

The typical war film in China performs a number of functions. It asserts the centrality of a strong army for class and national struggle in the revolutionary era and for territorial security under the geopolitical threat in the Cold War. As Mao said, "Without a people's army the people have nothing."[8] The genre's educational role is to present exemplary heroes for the moral edification of the masses, foregrounding the themes of self-sacrifice and martyrdom. Combining instruction and entertainment in a realistic and romantic style, the war film exerts audiovisual impact and proffers excitement, pleasure, and catharsis for mass audiences. Embedded in a cultural tradition boasting works such as Sun Zi's *Art of War* and the novel *Romance of Three Kingdoms*, the Chinese audience had long been fascinated with the tour de force in strategy and tactics. The ingenuity of strategists and the maneuvers of the rank-and-file soldiers are a popular attraction. Bravery in combat has everything to do with calculated choice and tricky ploys and little to do with foolhardiness. All these features make a typical war film, combining pleasurable spectacles with ideological edification.

Released in 1956, three years after the cease-fire of the Korean War, *Shanggan Ridge* became an instant classic. The film's success stemmed from a growing sense of nationalism and pride in a David against Goliath win. The PRC, barely on its feet as a state and mired in dire economic straits, surprised the world by intervening in the war in late November 1950. Taking an enormous risk by clashing with a superpower, the poorly equipped Chinese voluntary army, allied with North Koreans, nevertheless managed to defeat the well-armed US/UN troops and bring them to the negotiating table.

The film is based on a real battle. In the fall of 1952, during the break of the cease-fire negotiations at Panmunjorn, the US/UN troops suddenly launched a massive attack on the area close to the 38th parallel, seeking to overtake the strategically important Shanggan Ridge on Mount Wusheng. In the film's story line, a company of the Chinese volunteer soldiers is charged with the task of holding the ground against enemy advances. Although they have fended off thirty-eight attacks in a single day, they are far outnumbered and suffer heavy casualties as enemy reinforcements close in. Ordered to retreat into tunnels and caves and hunker down in the belly of the ridge taken by enemy troops, the soldiers attack the enemy's flanks and drag down their advance. Fighting under nearly impossible conditions for twenty-four days, they endure enormous hardship and exhibit courage and perseverance, until the Chinese and North Korean forces launch a counteroffensive, eventually forcing the US/UN forces back to the negotiating table.

While the war film generally adopts an aesthetic of realism mixed with romanticism, the balance between the two varies according to the ideological climate of production. For all its nationalist and heroic flair, *Shanggan Ridge* tips toward a gritty realism rarely found in other war narratives of the socialist era. The hand-to-hand combat, the piles of wounded and dead soldiers, the raining bombardment, and finally the excruciating details of day-to-day survival in the dark bunker with constant water shortage—all point to an impulse to register the traumatic experience of war. These realistic details constitute what one critic calls "new realism" (新寫實主義) and stand in stark contrast with the romantic style of *Heroic Sons and Daughters*.[9]

This gritty realism is not incompatible with the rising national pride in the wake of the Korean War. While the war boosted national confidence, the heavy tolls had to be remembered to make the victory seem all the more hard-won and significant. An immediate personal experience for the population, the war meant a huge sacrifice of Chinese lives in a foreign land and economic hardship at home. The burden of realism seemed to be on the director, Sha Meng, who tilted the balance of realism and romanticism toward a starker realism. While recognizing the importance of elevating combat experience to a higher inspirational level, Sha believed that a work of art should be faithful to the actualities and that realism should not give way to ideological messages.[10]

In addition to the frontal portrayal of combats and casualties, the film depicts a range of idiosyncratic characters. Absent from this gallery is the familiar image of the sublime hero who is "tall, grand, and perfect" (高大全). The company commander Zhang Zhongfa appears uncouth, awkward, and rustic. He needs a drink in the middle of intense fighting, behaves erratically at times, and is undisciplined and quick to run afoul of rules and authority. In one episode, when the soldiers are thirsty and parched from lack of water, the political instructor recounts a story by the ancient warlord Cao Cao from the novel *Romance of Three Kingdoms*. To quench the marching soldiers' thirst, Cao Cao tricks them into looking forward to a berry orchard. That this "feudal" and backward story comes from the ideological director is paradoxical yet a proof of realism. The film does not flinch from a straightforward depiction of brutality and gore in the combat sequences. When Zhang's company is sent to replace another company, for instance, we are told that the Chinese troops have been nearly crushed and that the airstrike bombardments and artillery shelling have swept several feet of the ridge. The Chinese war film often features at the climax a heroic soldier triumphantly delivering a death-defying message in the last gasp. But *Shanggan Ridge* offers a disturbing and sobering image. In the last episode, a soldier throws himself onto the bunker to block a shooting machine gun—a reenactment of the legendary death of the hero Huang Jiguang 黃繼光. But this gloried death occurs only after a stream of soldiers attacking the bunker has already been mowed down.

The gritty realism enhances rather than undermines heroism. Highlighting the soldiers' plebeian but admirable courage and perseverance, the film's general tenor remains positive and upbeat. At a significant moment, heroism is fueled by patriotism. At the lowest ebb, when mere survival is in doubt, the female nurse Wang Lan, a typical figure in the rank and file, sings "My Motherland" ("Wode zuguo" 我的祖國). With its beautiful melody and patriotic sentiment, this song has registered *Shanggan Ridge* deep in the memory of generations of the Chinese audience. Beginning with a close-up of Wang Lan, the camera slowly pans over the soldiers' smeared faces, as they listen to the song and visualize their homeland. The singing resembles the soundtrack of an MTV-like montage ranging from the Yellow River to the industrializing cities, from booming factories to thriving crops in the fields. Significant in this montage are the emblems of industrialization and modernization, manifest in towering chimneys, gigantic dams, and monumental construction sites. There are beautiful girls and broad-minded boys who are born and raised in the motherland. The soldiers' mission is to protect this land, so that "when friends visit we treat them with good wine; but when wolves come we meet them with rifles."

In addition to national pride and strength, the film depicts how heroism is wedded to a judicious use of military strategy. Patriotic ardor may drive the volunteers and propel them to fight. But the spirit alone does not win a war. Modern weaponry, backed by industrial might and economic power sought after by the newly minted PRC, is also an important motif. Much of the drama hinges on a mismatch between the technologically advanced US/UN troops and an ill-equipped Chinese volunteer army. With poor supplies and transportation lines constantly under air raid, the Chinese and North Koreans need time and transportation to move ammunition, supplies, and troops to the front. In tactical terms, therefore, the battle of *Shanggan Ridge* is a delaying move. From his underground command center, the army commander strategizes for small groups to halt a full-scale enemy offensive, confirming the past guerrilla tactics of deploying few to defeat many and of the weak prevailing over the strong.

Modern hardware is as decisive as the spirit of valor and self-sacrifice in this asymmetrical conflict. A myth of the Korean War paints the Chinese volunteers as undifferentiated and faceless hordes, overrunning American troops like swarms of locusts. In a polemical jab at this caricature, the film lavishes attention on the effectiveness of technology and weaponry. A few Korean War films highlight this factor through a focus on the struggle to keep the supply line open. In *Train through War Flame* (*Fenghuo lieche* 烽火列車, dir. Zhu Wenxun,1960) and *Railroad Guards* (*Tiedao weishi* 鐵道衛士 dir. Fang Ying, 1960), for example, the railroads and bridges are constantly under attack, and the narratives evolve around the urgency of repairing the broken railroads, so that supplies and reinforcements will transfer from the northeast industrial rear to the battlefront.

Technology, weaponry, and strategy are crucial to winning the war. The division commander who directs the campaign proves to be a military expert well versed in strategy and weaponry. Company leader Zhang, a sharpshooter with an advanced machine gun, is portrayed as a professional soldier, not exactly as a romantic hero. To him, war seems to be a dangerous job that he has to do. Martial virtue, in the words of Ross Etherton, consists in "finding the most efficient way of doing the job, not in the *beau geste* of a bayonet charge."[11] The counteroffensive of the final episode bombards the viewer with a massive display of advanced weapons. As row after row of heavy artillery and Soviet bazookas fire brilliantly into the night sky and savagely pound their targets, the film stages a spectacular display of firepower, aestheticizing military technology. The strategically savvy commander contrasts sharply with the political director in *Heroic Sons and Daughters*.

The Politics of Spirit

Compared with *Shanggan Ridge*, *Heroic Sons and Daughters* is less realistic in its portrayal of warfare and more romantic in its cinematic effect. *Romantic* not only entails the intense, extravagant expression of emotion and imagination but also invokes what Stuart Schram has called Mao's "military romanticism." Born out of the experience of years of revolutionary wars, military romanticism views war not as a contest of weapons and strategies, but as the "highest manifestation of 'conscious action' and the supreme test of the human spirit."[12] Shuguang Zhang has shown that military romanticism in the Korean War lies in the ardent belief that subjective factors constitute a military capability and a form of political power. Buttressed by ideology and spirit, such romantic fervor drives the army to victory.[13] *Heroic Sons and Daughters* is less concerned with battle scenes than with ideology and propaganda. The film conveys Mao's exhortation to "put politics in command" and places people over machines by promoting the spiritual qualities of heroism, self-sacrifice, and idealism. The imbrication of politics with spirituality culminates in what I call a "politics of spirit."

Adapted from Ba Jin's 巴金 1961 story "Reunion" ("Tuanyuan" 团圆), *Heroic Sons and Daughters* stemmed from the author's field trip and experience in the Korean War. Accompanied by a group of well-known writers, including Wei Wei, whose essay "Who Is the Most Lovable People" celebrated patriotism of the volunteer soldiers, Ba Jin went to the war front to observe battle scenes up close. Focusing on family relation, the story describes how Wang Wenqing, the political director of a volunteer army, hides from the female soldier Wang Fang that he is her biological father. Wang Wenqing and his wife have worked in preliberation Shanghai as underground activists, and after his wife was arrested and killed by Guomindang police, he entrusted the care of his daughter to his neighbor Wang Fubiao. During the Korean War, Wang Fubiao visits the volunteer army and reveals to his foster daughter that Wang Wenqing is her biological father. Hence the reunion.

The film version develops the themes of family separation and mistaken identity in the turbulent battlefield ambience. The film begins as Wang

Wenqing meets a familiar-looking female soldier and immediately realizes that she is his daughter. Soldier Wang Cheng encounters his stepsister Wang Fang on the battlefield and then goes on to a critical battle and sacrifices his life. After the victory, Wang Wenqing tells Wang Fang that he knows her brother, admires his heroism, and encourages her and the artistic team to launch a campaign to extol her brother's heroic deeds. When her foster father, Wang Fubiao, comes to visit the volunteer army with a delegation of civilians, he meets and reveals to his foster daughter that Wang Wenqing is her biological father.

Wang Wenqing carries the mantle of "politics in command." Though a military commander, he cuts a prominent figure as political director and ideological propagandist, signaling the crucial role of consciousness as the lifeline of the army. An army general recalled in 2011 that the film "accurately reflects the wartime political work and method."[14] Owing to this political priority, *Heroic Sons and Daughters* has been widely adopted as a visual textbook for routine ideological training in the Chinese army. Instead of seeking power, status, and ranks, "political work" aims at raising political consciousness as a spiritual quality translatable to military capability. In Mao's military romanticism, politics is less combative power than moral virtue, less technical matter than inner strength, less institution than culture. Unlike *Shanggan Ridge*, which places a strategist as commander in chief, *Heroic Sons and Daughters* depicts a leader who is in fact a political director. Wang heads off to the frontline on the eve of a battle not to supervise battle plans but to exhort the soldiers with ideological messages and boost their morale, delivering an inspirational speech in a ritual of precombat mobilization. During the battle, he never issues any order of military importance but instead offers moral encouragement, as if spirit alone would empower combatants and propel them to victory. This ideological role falls on the propaganda of Wang Cheng's heroism in the postcampaign celebration, rallies, and artistic performances. With gentle bearing and soft-spoken manner, he appears paternalistic and cultured, a far cry from the commandeering officer. With him at the helm, the battleground amounts to an ideological and political theater. This war film, remarkably cleansed of violence, bloodshed, and gore, is indeed a propaganda campaign for spreading heroism and internationalism.

The campaign to extol Wang Cheng's sublime image transfers the politics of spirit into the realm of art, creating a well-sung legend widely circulated in Chinese and North Korean armies. A composite figure composed of traits from many, Wang Cheng's image was mainly inspired by Yang Gensi 楊根思, a voluntary solider. While holding a high ground to fend off advancing enemy troops, Yang called upon the Chinese artillery to shell closer and closer around him. Similarly, Wang Cheng holds out against an enemy outnumbering him by the thousands yet beats back wave after wave of attack. Surrounded by enemy troops closing in, he phones and calls on the Chinese artillery to "fire on me." This call becomes the signature of the ultimate self-sacrifice of the Chinese volunteer soldier.

For all its intense battle scenes, *Heroic Sons and Daughters* departs from the realism of *Shanggan Ridge* and rises to romantic exuberance, staging combat actions in a highly operatic and theatrical fashion. The prominent role of music has been noted, especially in the combat scene where Wang Cheng holds the ground against enemy advances. When the enemy troops are about to overtake the hill and descend on him, Wang is poised to plunge into the crowd with an explosive. At this moment, all battle noises are suddenly muted.[15] A magnificent music suffuses the soundtrack, and a booming voice-over launches into a recital extolling his valor and heroism. Choral singing accompanies the fighting acts, and orchestral music elevates the battlefield into a grand theater and an edifying morality play.

Wang stands on the hilltop, explosive in hand. A low-angle shot reveals his robust upper body. Taking up the entire screen, the image dramatizes the stock phrase expressive of a godlike human shouldering heaven while firmly planted on earth (*dingtian lidi* 頂天立地). A defuse backlight breaks through the clouds and imbues the statuesque figure with a saintly halo, bathing a towering body in a divine aura. A medium close-up reveals the hero's resolve as he faces death as the ultimate triumph. This sequence of shots creates an extravagant operatic impact and choreographs Wang's sacrifice into a sublime musical poem.

Such combat episodes, however, take up only a fifth of the film. The center of gravity falls instead on the aesthetic campaign to celebrate and memorialize Wang's heroism. In the aftermath of the battle, the film depicts how Wang Cheng's stepsister Wang Fang sings, performs, and propagates her brother's heroism throughout the army camps (see figure 4.1). Why does a war film give such short shrift to combat while focusing profuse attention on artistic performance? The answer can be found in the role of art in relation to the politics of spirit.

Composed of singing, poetry, and performance, the art program taps into a long tradition in the Chinese army. Granting great importance to the politics of spirit through the medium of art, this tradition, instituted in the political department, engages in ideological propaganda. Every army unit has a political department that manages a propaganda team composed of profes-

青天响雷敲金鼓,大海扬波作和声

4.1 An art campaign to extol heroism in the military in *Heroic Sons and Daughters* (1964).

sional artists and writers. Thus, Wang Wenqing, the political director, issues an order right after the battle to launch a campaign to extol Wang Cheng's heroism. Entertainment, such as performances of Korean folk dance and songs, blends into uplifting ideological and political messages.

The campaign's lead performer, Wang Fang, is an exemplary member of a cultural troupe (*wengongtuan* 文工團), ubiquitous in the Chinese military. Versatile and talented, she excels in Korean drum dance and solo singing, and is good at composing song lyrics, doing "clapper talks," and performing the folk art of "drum song" from North China. Her effort to glorify her brother proves to be a story of self-transformation. The first draft of lyrics she writes is drenched in tears as she mourns his death and is deemed to be too soft and sentimental. In revising, she manages to overcome her sisterly sorrow, and the new lyrics take her brother's heroic deeds to a higher political conscious-ness and artistic pitch. Her singing and performance spread Wang Cheng's heroism in the heart and mind of each soldier. The crowning moment comes when she sings and performs the "Song of the Hero," whose lyrics and melody have gone down in history as a best-loved work of the red classics of Mao's era.

Imbued with a cosmic magnitude, Wang Cheng becomes "a man made of special material," a gigantic figure capable of saving the world: "Stopping the collapsing earth with his own body, raising a single arm to hold up the falling sky" (*di xian xiaqu du shen dang, tian ta xialai zhi shou qing* 地陷下去獨身擋, 天塌下來只手擎).

> In the winds and flames of war we sing of the hero.
> The green mountains around prick up their ears to listen.
> Thunderous claps resonate with the beating of golden drums,
> Wave after wave of the ocean surges to keep harmony.
> The people's soldiers are driving away tigers and wolves,
> Sacrificing their lives to preserve the peace.

> 烽煙滾滾唱英雄
> 四面青山側耳聽
> 晴天響雷敲金鼓
> 大海揚波作和聲
> 人民戰士驅虎豹
> 捨身忘死保和平

As the singing continues, the camera slowly pans over the audience, followed by a series of long shots of landscape, the sky, and pine trees, bringing forth the immortality of the spirit. Images of diverse combat units of the Chinese and North Korean military—tanks, artillery, fighter jets, and foot soldiers—are all enveloped in the aura of heroism. The popularity of this performance prompts the art group to travel far and wide in the front lines to stage more shows.

The Cold War and the People's War

Made in 1964, about a decade after the Korean War and on the eve of the Cultural Revolution, *Heroic Sons and Daughters* speaks more to the Third World than to the Korean War per se. The combination of propaganda and military harks back to a legacy of the Chinese Revolution. In his talks at the Yan'an forum, Mao stated that literature and art are essential to the Anti-Japanese War. As "a component part" of the revolutionary machine, literature and art "operate as powerful weapons for uniting and educating the people and for attacking and destroying the enemy." Art and literature "help the people fight the enemy with one heart and one mind."[16] Refuting the fetishism of weaponry during the Anti-Japanese War, Mao observed that "weapons are an important factor in war, but not the decisive factor; it is people, not things, that are decisive. The contest of strength is not only a contest of military and economic power, but also a contest of human spirit and morale. Military and economic power is necessarily wielded by people."[17]

The spiritually empowered people will prevail over superior military technology. That captures the essence of the politics of spirit. In Wendy Larson's account, this fierce spirit, evolving from Liang Qichao to Mao, upholds the decisive power of human consciousness and agency in overcoming the odds and making political change. The spirit "encourages people to devote to a cause and to sacrifice their comfort and their wellbeing, and even their lives in times of intense struggle."[18] Placing this spiritual power in the context of Cold War confrontation between colonized people and imperialist war machines, Alexander Cook compares the spirit's explosive outburst to the atomic fission. By splitting the atom from the inside, the spirit releases "vast amounts of internal energy." The people's war against imperialist hegemony opposes this "spiritual atom bomb" against the actual atom bomb. The revolutionary people will triumph over the weapons of mass destruction wielded by the imperialist powers.[19]

The revolutionary spirit was urgently needed in the Cold War context marked by the asymmetrical power relation between the center and the peripheral, an extension of the past discrepancy between Chinese revolutionaries and their oversize enemy. In the early 1960s, China's split with the Soviet Union deprived the country of much-needed expertise and technology. The US embargo barred China's trade relations with developed countries. To bridge the gap in material, technology, and arms, the politics of spirit called for a revival of revolutionary belief in subjective willpower. By rendering ideological attitudes into material strength, the project aimed to make up for the lack of technology and resources. By forging subjectivity and common purpose and unifying different interests, it aimed to bolster a massive solidarity and united front. Through dramatic performance and appeals to emotion, the artistic propaganda strove to mobilize the masses and inspire them into combat readiness. This campaign turned the Chinese army into as much a political and cultural institution as a military unit. Disciplined, inspired, and selfless, the soldiers became a model for emulation and transformation of the moral ethos of Chinese society at large. Inseparable from the people, the army was fish to the ocean. The military was a school, a production unit, a university, and a powerhouse of art and performance.

Heroic Sons and Daughters presents an allegory of cultural mobilization on the eve of the Cultural Revolution. The emphasis on artistic propaganda, the nationwide campaign to learn from the People's Liberation Army, the injunction to emulate Lei Feng and exemplary soldiers—all this revamped a form of spiritualized politics. What Schwartz termed the "reign of virtue" prevailed as a countervailing force of the social body against the bureaucratic machine.[20]

The primacy of the people's power over machines speaks to the power relations between state and society in the Cold War. The era witnessed a growing administrative and bureaucratic tendency in the Chinese party-state. From the 1950s up to the Cultural Revolution, a divergence between a "hard" and a "soft" approach to modernization was taking hold. The former favored a statist, administrative, and "capitalist" project by the technocratic elite, modeled on the "universal" path of modernization adopted by the Soviets and the United States. The cultural and spiritual counteract, by contrast, strove to keep the socialist ethos alive by revamping revolutionary drives and passion. Socialism, this approach claimed, involves not only the mastery of machines but also the creation of new human relations based on revolutionary consciousness. This divergence intensified as the CCP launched ideological polemics against the Soviet Union over its technocratic orientation and against US involvement in Southeast Asia. The ideological split reinforced the vision of popular classes in the Third World as a new "united front." As a counterforce against colonialism and imperialism, people seeking national independence and laborers fighting capitalist exploitation had a ready example from the Chinese Revolution. China doubled down on forging alliances and solidarity with newly independent nations in Asia, Africa, and Latin America. The moral virtue of the new socialist human was part of the "export" of internationalism.

Unlike the top-down statist internationalism by the Soviet Union, Third World internationalism stressed bottom-up rebellion and independence movements. The revisionist Soviet Union sought to make peace with US imperialism by means of détente and was on the slippery slope to a bureaucratic and technocratic party-state. The concentrated state power over working people put the world's first socialist country in the same league as its Cold War rival. The widening abyss between state and society during the Cold War, observed Franz Schumann, indicated that the modern world was leading toward the bureaucratic state buttressed by the military-industrial complex. The liberal ideology in America accepted much of the de facto ideology of the Soviet Union, both tending toward an imperialist and military-industrial state dominated by corporate monopoly and technocratic elites: "there is thus not only a systematic convergence between the United States and the Soviet Union, but also an ideological convergence."[21] Against this top-heavy bureaucratization between two superpowers, Mao warned, "Any alienation between state and society will lead either to tyranny or a revolt of the masses."[22] Thus it fell to the decolonizing people to keep alive the anti-systemic grassroots momentum. Afro-American uprisings in the inner cities, dissident youth and counterculture in the West, and decolonizing and independent people in emerging nations shared solidarity and aspirations. Relying on the broadest swaths of masses as a world class, Third World internationalism stressed "the role of the united front, guerrilla warfare, and the creation of revolutionary base areas." During the 1960s and the Cultural Revolution, China encouraged organization of revolutionary movements; supported antirevisionist, anti-state communist parties; and built alliances with Third World nations.[23]

The language of the people's war, integral to Third World internationalism, received a clear expression in Lin Biao's 1965 essay "Long Live the People's War." Commemorating the twentieth anniversary of the victory of the Anti-Japanese War, Lin situates the war in the context of decolonization and national liberation. The Anti-Japanese War dismantled imperialism's East Asian front and shook up the power relations in East Asia, becoming a source of inspiration for worldwide national liberation movements in Asia, Africa, and Latin America. As US interventions in Southeast Asia perpetuated the prior colonial policy of the Japanese empire, the Vietnamese people continued their fight as part of the worldwide decolonization movement.[24]

The Chinese Revolution had lessons to offer in this movement. Armed struggle and a highly disciplined army under the command of the party was the key to winning victory. Lin's text alludes to the debate within the CCP between politics and morality, between the bureaucratic apparatus and spirited mobilization. The statist and bureaucratic tendency in the Soviet Union and the United States and within the CCP—the so-called capitalist roaders—represented a growing distance between the party-state and the people. Wary of the revisionist tendencies, Mao turned on the party by resorting to the military.[25] Imbued with revolutionary virtue and a bulwark of spiritual politics, the army challenged the party bureaucracy from outside and could reverse it from the technocratic path. Despite the mismatch between impoverished China and the mighty US/UN army in the Korean War, the poorly equipped volunteer soldiers prevailed over the technological "tiger." The politics of spirit believes in the power of human spirit over machines, of revolutionary virtue over technological fetishism. Victory requires not just weapons but spirit—the unified strength of an organization driven by moral imperatives and focus of purpose. "The people's army surely should constantly improve weapons and equipment and enhance military technology," Lin wrote, "but winning a battle does not only depend on weapons and technology. More importantly it depends on politics, on commanders and soldiers' proletarian revolutionary consciousness and bravery." Mao's program of building the army, Lin continues, will heighten the political morality of the soldiers, raise their morale, and enable them to stand tightly united based on deep hatred against the enemy. This spiritual power translates into fighting power: "fearing no hardship and death, the soldiers can advance and hold their ground. One person can match dozens, even hundreds. . . . This can create unimaginable miracles in the world of humans."[26]

This well-known image of the "spiritual atomic bomb" identifies moral virtue with military power. If war is politics by other means, nonmilitary power stems from political power, driven and amplified morally and spiritually. An increase of power hinges on a heightened state of morality.

Family, Class, and Internationalism

The Chinese Revolution coincided with those of working classes in other nations for national self-determination. All working classes of the world share, as Levenson put it, "a common plane of victimization and a common destiny."[27] Early in the war of resistance against Japanese invasion, Mao noted that revolutionaries are both patriots and internationalists, because different national people could form an international class based on common interests and endeavors.[28] Not only did the experience of the Chinese people under foreign and domestic class rule resonate with that of other Asian nations; it also provided an example of throwing off the yoke of colonialism and imperialism.

From the late 1950s through the Cultural Revolution, China's increasing alliance with movements of decolonization and independence in the Third World challenged the bipolar Cold War structure maintained by the Soviet Union and the United States. The 1960s witnessed a high tide of decolonization, non-aligned, and independence movements. In response, Mao revised his earlier notion of the three worlds. The initial idea arose in the revolutionary era as the broad zone of colonized, peripheral regions between the United States and the Soviets. These non-Western regions would unite and aid each other in national and international struggle.[29] In the Cold War era, the Third World evolved into a more radical vision regarding concerted struggles of Asian, African, and Lain American nations against colonialism and imperialism. Mao's Third World theory includes these key elements: the opposition to the ideological convergence of Soviet revisionism and US imperialism, the armed struggle to rally the world's undeveloped country-side to encircle the metropolitan centers, and mutual assistance and support among these nations in self-reliant development.[30]

Heroic Sons and Daughters casts the Korean War as an anti-imperialist war of resistance by the Chinese and Korean people in taking control of their own destiny and defending their territories. The film illustrates the con-nection between the Chinese Revolution and internationalism through the interlinked theme of class and nation. As an underground revolutionary in Shanghai, Wang Wenqing entrusts Wang Fubiao's family with his daughter. As workers in an auto factory owned by foreign capitalists, the family bears the brunt of colonial capital and imperialist invasion, as the Japanese bomb-ing of Shanghai forced them to flee the devastated neighborhood. Exploited in a foreign factory under colonial capitalism, both father and son clash with their foreign bosses. Wang Wenqing, on the other hand, is a revolutionary leader, but without support from the worker's family, he is unable even to care for his daughter. The two Wangs belong to the same revolutionary class, the working class aligned with a revolutionary identity.

The family/class relation extends to relations between Koreans and Chi-nese. A Korean family, a father and a daughter, dote on Wang Fang as if she were their own. Wang Fang learns Korean folk dance from her Korean sister and addresses the elder man as *abeoji* 아버지 (father). In one episode, the Korean father and daughter brave icy water and raging bullets from American planes to carry the wounded Wang Fang across a river. The film's repeated highlighting of war-torn landscapes also suggests that Korean mountains and rivers are to be defended by the joint forces of the Korean army and Chinese volunteers, and that the Chinese volunteers readily sacrifice their lives in defense of the Korean homeland.

The family relation is manifest in cultural exchange and mutuality be-tween Koreans and Chinese. The film gravitates toward scenes of everyday life and activities in logistics, transportation, infrastructure repair, civic as-sociations, artistic performance, and cultural sharing between Chinese and Koreans. If China's intervention in Korea had been for the sake of national defense, there would have been no good reason in this drama for extensive portrayal of cultural ties. If patriotism were the priority, why do friendship, mutual aid, and cultural relations between the two nations figure so promi-nently? The absence of such exchange and friendship in *Shanggan Ridge* makes this point clear. Extolling the bravery and endurance of the volun-teer soldiers, *Shanggan Ridge* links their heroism to a full-blooded patriotism rooted in the love of China's beautiful land and rivers. National defense and security also inform the film *Railroad Guards,* in which patriotic, vigilant protagonists thwart US- and Japan-sponsored domestic sabotages. In contrast, *Heroic Sons and Daughters* speaks to a broader horizon of nationalism with an internationalist dimension.

Internationalism envisages an intersocietal relation based on an imagined international coalition of people in the drive for independence and development. Interstate, intercultural relations mark historical relations between China and Korea in trade, commerce, and tributary relations. Traces of the empire, the premodern relations were taken over by interactions of internationalism in the Anti-Japanese War. Cummings sees the Japanese occupation of Manchuria from 1931 to 1932 as the beginning of the Korean War. The Japanese invaders faced a formidable Chinese resistance force, whose majority was Koreans led by Kim Il-sung. The total number of Korean troops who fought in China and filtered back to the Korean War was somewhere between 75,000 and 100,000.[31] In the Korean War, the past experience of cooperation enhanced teamwork between two armies, and some commanders from both countries used to be comrades in arms in the anti-Japanese resistance.

Cultural and military cooperation between Koreans and Chinese takes on new significance in the context of Third World internationalism. In the 1950s, China's foreign policy leaned toward the Soviet Union, even though the Chinese leaders sought in vain to build trade and diplomatic relations with the United States. With the Sino-Soviet split in the early 1960s, China began to regard the Soviet Union as a superpower like the United States, bent on dominating the world at the expense of Third World nations. A reassertion of national independence, economic self-reliance, and regional non-aligned movements came as the answer, but this movement also urged a continuous revolution of oppressed classes. In the Third World concept, the United States and industrialized countries of Western Europe make up the First World, the USSR and Eastern Europe constitute the Second World, and developing nations in Asia, Africa, and Latin America belong to the Third World. As China's natural allies, the poor and developing nations were also the recipient of China's extensive foreign aid, which often came in amounts disproportionate to the nation's impoverished conditions and capacity. Although Third World countries rewarded China by voting it into the United Nations in 1971, the vision of international alliance went beyond national interests. What sealed the ties between developing countries was the ideology of internationalism predicated on the solidarity of the world's working people.[32]

Ties between societies and people put the accent on the general term *people* as a class. *Heroic Sons and Daughters* dramatizes this insight. Speaking of socialist cosmopolitanism and nationalism, Levenson wrote that "peoples"—be they from the Third or First World—"could be nationalist and internationalist at the same time." Based on the notion of oppressed classes of different people, internationalism is "to pair with nationalism, not to impair it."[33] This is because people of all nations are supposed to share a common cause. Within a bounded territory, a particular national people constitute the nation. Inwardly, oppressed people as the revolutionary class make a genuine nation with its broad popular constituency and with a claim to national sovereignty. Outwardly, people of oppressed classes around the world make for outreaching internationalists in their common cause. If a certain class within a country claims to be the nation while serving as lackeys of colonialism, this class does not deserve to be considered national, for it fails to represent the will of the people.

Premised on international class solidarity, this concept of "the people" resonates with Mao's Third World theory and Gramsci's notion of the national-popular.[34] Third World internationalism combines far-reaching international affinities with historically endowed national, cultural identity. This encourages the appreciation of a unique national cultural endowment as being both national and international, turning both inward and outward, both provincial and cosmopolitan. Instead of being guarded jealously as inherited treasures, a national culture becomes open public assets sharable by other nations.

The class line defines socialist realism. To Levenson, realism pertains to "real life," majority life, not the artificial existences of an effete, self-styled elite.[35] Levenson noted that Chinese translations of Western masterpieces operated on class consciousness and favored the narratives about ordinary people in European nations in democratic revolt against the aristocratic regime. The use of language further affirms the style of the popular masses. The popular national style is internationalist without essentialist, canonical exclusiveness. The realistic language is embedded in the everyday, inherited lifeworlds and styles of everyday people or *laobaixing* 老百姓—literally the "old hundred names."[36] Since this unique national style is the cultural achievement of each nation, it follows that one particular national style may join and exchange with another unique style, based on the sharing of cultural accomplishments by different people. One can understand Italian people or English people, despite or precisely because they create something very different on their own, just as Chinese people have created their own culture independently.

The combination of nationalism and internationalism accounts for the salience of family relations in *Heroic Sons and Daughters*. This family relation bonds Koreans and Chinese—in cultural exchange and nonmilitary cooperation—into an international revolutionary family. Wang Fang excels in the Chinese popular art form of drum singing as well as Korean folk arts. Her most stunning performance is a Korean drum dance she has learned from her Korean sister. With the camera intercutting between her performance and the mixed audience of Koreans and Chinese, it is difficult to tell if the performers are Korean or Chinese. "Defending our homeland and nation" pairs with "resisting America and assisting Korea," and Chinese volunteers are willing to sacrifice their lives for protecting both Korean people and Chinese homeland.

To conclude, in the context of the Cold War and Mao's military romanticism, *Heroic Sons and Daughters* brings art and propaganda into military life and dramatizes the politics of spirit in the campaign to popularize heroism. The politics of spirit gained prominence for Chinese society at large on the eve of the Cultural Revolution. Rather than battle scenes and military actions, the film celebrates heroic subjectivity and moral character. This subjectivity has both national and international implications, fueling cultural exchange based on Third World internationalism.

National Unity, Ethnicity, and Socialist Utopia in *Five Golden Flowers*

Five

SOCIALIST INTERNATIONALISM IS DISTINCT from liberal cosmopolitanism by engaging both nation and class. As we saw in the previous two chapters, Zhou Libo taught world literature based on the notion of international affinity of working classes while promoting national forms. The concept of class nation underlies mutual aid between Chinese and Koreans in the Korean War. As this chapter will show, class also trumps the issues of ethnicity and plays a part in socialist China's domestic policy toward ethnic minorities.

Socialist China strove to integrate its diverse ethnic minorities into a national community. International alliance with the Third World and domestic integration are two sides of one coin. As Lin Chun writes, just as socialist internationalism aspired to a world of equality and peaceful coexistence, its domestic wing promoted ethnic equality and cooperation by combatting majority chauvinism.[1] The ideal of ethnic equality and harmony militates against the logic of ethnonationalism, underwritten by a mode of racist thinking endemic to the capitalist system as well as the clash of civilization thesis. These discourses operate by differentiating people along racial lines and polarizing societies into unequal and competing groups: colonizer and colonized, superior and inferior, and master and slave. Directed at this ethnonationalism, Marx's credo "Workers of the world, unite" appeals to the world-historical and international working classes and is consistent with the aspiration for ethnic equality in the national domain. Just as class analysis was meant to unite workers around the world into an international community, so China's ethnicity policy ran a class line through multiethnic differences in pursuit of an inclusive national family.

Jie Chen has described how class cuts across ethnic divides in films about ethnic minorities.[2] Tensions within ethnic groups and without were seen as a matter of class oppression and exploitation rather than cultural clash and ethnic divide. Aiming to overthrow the oppressive class nationwide, the revolutionaries dismantle the autocratic local regime in ethnic communities and regions. In the Marxist trajectory of progress, China's socialist modernization required the inclusion of ethnic minorities in a teleological path through socioeconomic developmental stages, going from the primitive to feudal modes of production to reach the socialist stage, culminating in a utopian society of universal equality and prosperity.

The temptation is strong to see the socialist minority agenda as a form of colonialism. With the perspective of ethnonationalism, critics have tended to see China's policy toward minorities as a replay of the civilizing mission in the West. Under this aegis, the Han majority at the center attempts to assimilate peripheral minorities into a homogeneous Han culture, thereby maintaining a structure of domination and cultural imperialism akin to colonialism and orientalism. Centered on issues of ethnicity, Han chauvinism, nationalism, colonialism, and orientalism, the debate on China's minority policy brings us back to the focus of this book: Was socialist China a copy of the Western nation-state or a socialist state with residues of the tianxia legacy?

This chapter addresses the legacy of tianxia and empire manifest in China's minority agenda in the socialist era. By taking a look at *Five Golden Flowers* (*Wuduo jinhua* 五朵金花, dir. Wang Jiayi, 1959), a canonical minority film, I explore the controversy on minority issues and the socialist state's aspiration for national unity in ethnic diversity. As a romantic comedy, the film deploys an aesthetic of laughter, eulogizes intimacy and harmony between ethnic groups, and expresses an ethic of commitment to collective labor.

The ethnonational lens sees the empire as a premodern structure whose diverse ethnic groups inevitably grow into discrete pieces called "nation." This view ignores the tenacious hold of the tianxia legacy: modern China has endeavored to preserve the territory and demography inherited from the imperial past. Whether China is a nation understood in primordialist terms of ethnicity, language, and history or a civilizational state has preoccupied thinkers since the late nineteenth century. When the Qing dynasty faced off with Western nation-states, Liang Qichao devoted much thought to the idea of nation in ethnonationalist terms of ethnicity, lineage, language, customs, and biological traits. But emerging out of an empire composed of myriad mixed ethnic groups over millennia, modern China could hardly fit into this Western concept. As we saw earlier, fearful of the Qing empire's fragmentation under colonial encroachment and regional separatism, Kang Youwei and Liang Qichao "called for saving the country by uniting the people." "The people" was not only a national people but also a multiethnic society that included the Han, Manchus, Muslims, Mongols, and Tibetans. The five ethnicities, a symbol for many other groups, had long amalgamated across the land and should form themselves into a people, striving to "fuse all of China's ethnicities into a Chinese nation."[3]

The asymmetrical power relations between the Han majority and ethnic minorities have always existed in the past and the present. Works by Dru Gladney on the Hui, Stevan Harrell on the Yi, and Thomas Mullaney on ethnic classification have addressed how ethnic minorities engage their own heritages while resisting the state's control and assimilation.[4] Based on postcolonial assumptions, they have viewed China's minority policy as domination and subjugation. The minorities, in Harrell's view, "have been subjected over the last few centuries to a series of attempts by dominant powers to transform them."[5] This "civilizing mission" has sought to transform ethnic cultures and assimilate them to the standards of Confucian order or statist imperatives. Presuming the inferiority of minorities versus superiority of the center, the Han-centric regime's domination has met with constant resistance. In cultural and visual representation, this domination sets up a self over and above the other, a patriarchal subject that objectifies female bodies of minorities as erotic objects. Most visible cinematic images belong to a trope of eroticization and feminization whereby minority women are subjected to the male gaze and consumption.[6]

This view of Han-centric domination has been challenged and belied by historical perspectives. In her recent book *Communist Multiculturalism,*

Susan McCarthy has identified the socialist minority legacy in the continuing minority cooperation and engagement with the Han majority, between multiethnic populations and the central government, and between ethnic differences and national unity. Focusing on the Dai, Bai, and Hui in Yunnan province, McCarthy examines rich and vibrant activities of ethnic mingling and mixing as signs of interactive engagement in forging multiethnic identities. Cultural revivals of recent decades among ethnic minorities testify to the lingering socialist legacy of national unity in ethnic diversity. In a conversation with an interviewee during her fieldwork, McCarthy came to see the ethnic complexity in China. Knowing that the interviewee's mother is Yi and her father Han, McCarthy said, without thinking, "So you are half-Yi and half-Chinese." The girl snapped back, "I am half-Yi, half-Han, and I am all Chinese!" Taken aback by the response, McCarthy embarked on research on multiculturalism.[7]

McCarthy's shock derives from the habit of treating "Chinese" as synonym for "Han." But the interviewee's reply entails the inclusiveness of "Chinese" as a political and multicultural rather than ethnonational category. Cultural revival in recent decades by minorities expresses a renewed sense of ethnic cultural identity but "can be as much about being Chinese as it is about being minority." Instead of identity politics, minorities were bolstering their differences in such a way as to articulate "concepts of citizenship and Chinese national identity more generally, including the discourses on minority autonomy and on China's post-1949 modernization." They participate in socialist modernization and see this process as "a means of asserting citizenship and membership in the national body politic."[8]

The awareness of national unity in diverse ethnic groups dates back well before 1949. Early in the twentieth century, Liang Qichao took a close look at mutual engagement and coexistence among ethnic groups. As we saw in the introduction, Liang invested Qing China with a cosmopolitan dream and mapped out a trajectory from provincial to global. In this ascent, the individual cultivates the ability to fulfill multiple obligations as a modern person, ranging from an upright family member through a citizen of a nation to cosmopolitan ethics. The cosmopolitan ethic should transcend not just family but also ethnicity. In a 1921 essay, Liang grouped many ethnicities into a common framework by modeling the Chinese republic on the cosmopolitan state. The principle of tianxia incorporates all ethnicities into "one family under heaven" (*tianxia yijia* 天下一家). The way to achieve this was the civilizational transformation of *jiaohua* 教化. Rather than imposing the normative standards on others, the transformation (*hua* 化) sought not to indoctrinate but to attract ethnic minorities through the inner appeals of the civilizational norms. Through consent and learning, the minority recipients took over and internalized the civilizational norms. The motto "Treat kindly different groups so that they would come join you" (*huai rou yuan ren* 懷柔遠人) marked a long tradition of inclusion and diversity. Unlike nationalist separatism that broke up European empires, Liang noted, China, for two thousand years, had effectively gathered myriad and diverse ethnic groups, tribes, and regions under one imperial roof. Under the Republic of China (Zhonghua mingguo 中華民國), the mixed, multiethnic conditions held steady and continued to enable different groups to live and coexist under one national community despite occasional tension and conflict.[9]

If Liang's image presents a domestic variant of the cosmopolitan state, Wang Hui's analysis of the empire-to-nation transition articulates a socialist dimension. Although the Chinese Revolution built a socialist nation-state on the ruins of the empire, new China carried over certain residues of the ancient infrastructure and evolved into a three-pronged synthesis of "imperial legacy, the nation-state, and socialist values."[10] The imperial legacy retains elements of the empire's administrative mode of governance as well as the territories, landmass, population, transethnic linkages, and cross-cultural networks. A recognizable modern multiethnic mainstream and a uniform linguistic system highlight the persistence of the past. Preserving and keeping these heritages alive makes modern China unique and distinct from the Western nation-state. On its international face, the Chinese nation attests to the fact that the People's Republic of China has become a modern polity recognizable by the international system.

The concept of "socialist values," the third piece of the triad, refers to the recognition of the minorities' cultural differences, their equality with all other groups, and their rights and autonomy. Designed to bring diverse ethnic groups into the common project of socioeconomic development, these principles place national unity at the center in order to avoid the tendencies of separatism. In the revolutionary era, ethnic tensions remained and divided the majority and the minorities. But revolutionaries tried to build partnership and friendship with minorities to fight the ruling class in a multiethnic landscape. The Red Army on the Long March forged bonds with the Tibetans, Hui, and other minorities, who were alienated by the Han chauvinism of the nationalist government. Numerous films depict how the soldiers receive assistance from and resolve misunderstandings with minorities in wars and the postwar cleanup in frontier areas, where the nationalist remnants estranged ethnic groups from the liberation army. The socialist state arranged a system of autonomous regions in order to facilitate common progress and economic development. The major challenge was to combat Han chauvinism and prejudice. As Wang Hui writes, "The goal of regional ethnic autonomy was to allow different ethnicities to progress together, not to isolate them from one another; expanding the autonomous regions and encouraging interethnic cooperation became the means by which different ethnicities could share the fruits of progress."[11] The prominent anthropologist Fei Xiaotong explains, "This unity in diversity was formed through a process by which innumerous separate and distinct ethnic unities came into contact, mingled, united and amalgamated even as they sometimes split and vanished, eventually forming a body containing much individual character, a good deal of coming and going and in which parts of me were in you and parts of you were in me. This is perhaps the common process by which all nationalities in the world were formed."[12]

Fei seems to imply that the formation of the multiethnic nation is not unique to China but somehow common to "all nationalities," an insight that may be read as a projection of Liang Qichao's notion of cosmopolitan state as opposed to ethnonationalism. It is the ethnonationalist lens that fuels the charge against the orientalist gaze and colonialist domination. Based on the doctrine of the nation-state as a colonizing power lording it over ethnic minorities, skeptics see a statist repressive agenda, as China seems to be taking an ethnonationalist path and wading deeper into global capitalism. Han chauvinism did exist in socialist China but was fiercely curbed and combatted. Four decades since the start of market reform and integration into global capitalism, we have witnessed escalating tensions and resistance from minorities and a tightening of state control. One wonders if this testifies to the aggressive tendency of a rising capitalist ethnonational state. It is beyond the scope of this book to discuss whether China is abandoning its inclusive agenda concerning ethnic minorities of the past. I want to stress here that domination and engagements are two aspects of China's minority policy, and that socialism, premised on internationalism of associated working classes of all nationalities, offers a more inclusive perspective on ethnic diversity.

The Han-centric domination did not go uncontested in the socialist era. China's minority agenda in the 1950s and 1960s strove to meet the challenge of how to include ethnic minorities as citizens and members of the socialist nation. This was a subject of long and intense debates in policy and academic circles. Prime Minister Zhou Enlai and other leaders made numerous speeches warning Han cadres and administrators against the propensity to marginalize the ethnic minorities they were working with. The most significant challenge was to resist and combat what Zhou called "Han chauvinism" (*da hanzu zhuyi* 大漢族主義) and bring diverse ethnic groups into a harmonious society.[13]

National Unity in Diversity in *Five Golden Flowers*

Ethnic interaction and engagement find a beautiful expression in *Five Golden Flowers*, a film about relations between Han majority and Bai minority in Yunnan province in Southwest China. A comedy of errors, the film tells the story of Ah Peng's romantic quest for Jinhua, which means golden flower, a common name among Bai women. On a horseback ride to a country fair, Ah Peng, a young farmworker of the Bai, stops to repair a broken cart managed by Jinhua. Love blossoms and at the legendary Butterfly Spring, the couple pledges to meet again a year later, without exchanging contact information. The following year, Ah Peng returns to Cang Mountains, looking up and down for Jinhua. Two artists, apparently of Han background and looking to learn folk culture, cross paths with him and offer help in his love pilgrimage. As Golden Flower is a common female name, the youth chases one mistaken Golden Flower after another, trailing a laughable series of comic errors. But this romantic quest also presents a gallery of five female model workers who participate proudly in socialist work. Resolving misunderstandings in the end, Ah Peng and his Jinhua finally unite and pledge love at Butterfly Spring amid cheers from friends and villagers.

A tribute commemorating the tenth anniversary of the PRC, the film affirms the energy, bravado, and passion of female workers in social and economic production. Beautiful and well crafted, it displays attractive women, exotic sceneries, ethnic music and dance, romantic love, and warm relations among ethnic groups in Southwest China. An instant hit on its release, the film charmed the world: it was screened to sold-out audiences in Hong Kong and exported to forty-six countries—a record of Chinese cinema's international appeal in the Third World. At the Second Asian and African Film Festival at Cairo in 1960, the film won both Best Director and Best Leading Actress awards.[14]

Critics, however, question the spectacle of interethnic sympathy and conviviality and discern orientalism and racial tensions in colorful performances by Bai minority women and men. From a top-down ethnographic perspective, the alleged Han subject—a privileged, orientalist self—keeps ethnic minorities at arm's length as exotic objects. Rather than celebratory and joyous in its own right, the ethnic lifeworld and custom are "staged for Han viewers," and the "Han gaze" is revealed to be a mirror image for the socialist state, which seeks to maintain Han hegemony at the expense of ethnic minorities. Thus, the spectacle of ethnic minorities is contrived and disingenuous.[15]

The Han-centric argument takes a postcolonial approach to majority-minority relations. Unhappy with that view, Bao Ying contends that *Five Golden Flowers* offers room to release private desire and love, which makes a universal appeal and transcends ethnic boundaries. The exotic gaze of Han outsiders—the musician and painter from the Changchun film studio—is offset by interactive and reconciliatory relations. The two Han cultural workers act as pupils ever ready and eager to marvel and learn arts, folkways, and wisdom from the Bai minority. Their ignorance, clumsiness, and over-zealousness frequently cause blundering and errors, rendering them into buds of comic laughter. Instead of looking down, their looking reciprocates with the returning look from minority characters.[16]

But this attempt to smooth over the Han-minority divide reconfirms rather than resolves the antagonistic, colonial relations between Han and minorities and obscures socialist China's policy toward ethnic minorities. Based on the ethnonationalist lens, the critique of Han dominance sees China as an exact copy of the classical Western nation-state.

Jie Chen's analysis of *Five Golden Flowers* and other minority films in Mao's era offers a broader reading in the context of ethnicity, nation, and internationalism. Stressing the theme of national unity in diversity, Chen contends that ethnic representation "reveals the symbiotic development of the concepts of 'nation' and 'ethnicity,'" and these two categorical identities conflate and merge in modern China. "The symbolic importance of the ethnic minorities is one of the legacies of the agonizing process through which China was born as a nation—the entry of an old empire into a modern world of nations."[17]

Confronted with a hostile Cold War situation, China was far from secure as a regular nation-state. The ethnonational perspective demands that a qualified nation tap into its tradition, lineage, history, and cultural capital to shore up its identity in the eyes of the international system. But the traditional cultural repertoire had been under fire and all but discredited in the wake of the half century of May Fourth new culture and communist anti-traditionalism. Modern Chinese culture arose by negating China's long feudal traditions. Confucianism and related "Han" culture were viewed with suspicion and could hardly be deployed to showcase a deep-seated "Chinese difference." But not all is lost. Ethnic resources, fortunately, came to pick up the slack and serve as a unique sign of new Chinese national difference, providing cultural specificity and historical depth to China's international self-image. This makes eminent sense, for ethnic cultures for millennium have been an integral part of the fabric of the empire. Ethnic cultural traditions and lifeworlds, complete with colorful performances, dances, folkways, and rituals, become the "constitutive outside" of the national image. Far from detached and separate from the mainstream, ethnic markers are crucial to the transethnic image that socialist China wished to present to the world.[18]

In writing her dissertation on minority films, Chen interviewed a veteran dancer of Miao ethnicity, a member of the Central Troupe of Ethnic Song and Dance (Zhongyang minzu gewu tuan 中央民族歌舞團). An agency of China's minority policy, the troupe's mission is to raise national awareness of ethnic minorities by performing and disseminating their arts and cultures. With pride and confidence, the dancer told Chen that as professionals they were trained to perform dances not only of his own Miao group but also a broad repertoire of choreographic forms belonging to other minorities. When Chen voiced concerns about authenticity, the dancer explained that as a dancer of a national center, he should be able to represent a variety of ethnic dance forms. Then he threw the question back: "Could you expect a state institution to focus on a selected number of ethnic groups?" He and his colleagues traveled the country to showcase the diverse ethnic cultural forms to the whole population. Now, can you expect a national institution to recruit a set of actors from each of the fifty-six ethnic groups to perform their own dances? This response reveals the poverty of the essentialist concept of ethnicity rooted in parochial identity as well as the impoverished concept of authenticity embedded in the ethnic body and primordial tribe.

The Western media voiced a similar concern about the use of nonethnic children dressed in ethnic costume singing and dancing under the national flag in the 2008 Olympics opening ceremony. As the children turned out to be of Han ethnicity, the media pronounced the show fake and inauthentic. This view misses the long historical condition of ethnic intermingling and the socialist minority agenda that have forged strong overlapping bonds between ethnic groups. Representations of ethnicity, though diverse and different, are folded within the Chinese multiethnic identity and staged on a nationwide platform. Whether the performer belongs, by blood or skin or lineage, to a certain group and "authentically" performs his or her own culture is irrelevant. If we put a "Han" performer to the test of blood and lineage, it would be extremely difficult to trace a biological essence of "Han-ness."

Throughout history, "Han," or rather "Chinese," has been a wide river into which have flowed myriad streams of ethnicities, cultures, traditions, and lifeworlds. Authenticity is not a fact of nature, biology, lineage, and least of all blood ties but has trailed a long politically constructive trajectory—a history of integrating all ethnic groups into the Chinese people. Rather than a withdrawal into an essentialist closet, an ethnic performance participates in the representation of a transethnic national framework, interacting with different groups and bringing diversity into unity.

Lü Xinyu reminds us that there was no clear demarcation of "minority film" in film criticism before the 1980s. References to films like *Five Golden Flowers* in socialist China fall into a category that addresses "brotherly ethnic groups or their struggle." The idea of the "Chinese people" encompasses both ethnic minorities and the majority. If the minority film has to be sui generis, it is defined, without clear ethnic markers, as the "People's Film."[19] The people as a universal designation is also true of literature written by ethnic minorities. Literature about and by minorities had no ethnic markers; it was referred to as *minjian wenxue* 民間文學, which could be translated as "literature by folks and people." This understanding calls into question the colonialist and orientalist perspective that sees the mixing of minorities and "Chinese" as paradoxical and discriminating. In socialist China, the general aesthetic attitude was to treat ethnic difference as fascinating and refreshing rather than as signs of otherness, because ethnic difference is integral to and constitutive of the transethnic and unified People's Republic of China.

Transethnic Music and Interaction

Instead of a superficial comic narrative, *Five Golden Flowers* attests to a form of joy and laughter evocative of socialist China's minority agenda. The film's exotic spectacle of ethnic culture, rather than serving to identify "us" versus "them," is shared and enjoyed by all ethnicities in the celebration of an interethnic lifeworld. Such films, writes Ling Zhang, "supplant ethnic difference and hierarchy" with socialist "class identification" and joy of liberated people. Resolutely anti-assimilationist, they uphold equal rights of ethnic groups and promote their distinct culture and folkways.[20]

The film opens with the blowing of a long horn that launches the March Fair, a tradition in the Dali region in Yunnan province. The ensuing events draw the viewer into a crowded and joyful milieu of festivity and sociality. Horse racing, prize-winning games, and antiphonal singing and dancing by minority girls and boys mark the festival as a coming-out party for young men and women for romantic love. Long and panning shots survey the vibrant market scenes, crowds, and activities. But instead of demarcating separate borders between ethnicities and people from a vantage point, the establishing shots thrust the viewer right into the thick of action through immersive editing and camera work. While occasional "ethnic" distinctions such as the white pagodas are visible, exotic distancing is absent; the intent of "othering" is out of place. Ethnic minorities and Han people are included in the mise-en-scène: they mingle and converge into a streaming, fun-seeking crowd. We witness a display of ethnic differences evocative of intimate fascination, mutual exchange, and pleasurable appreciation.

More than a traditional celebration of the arrival of spring, the March Fair is an actual market for commerce and trade. Raw materials, consumer goods, and artifacts are changing hands, bought and sold in lively fashion. The vibrant market brings together diverse ethnic groups who have long lived in and beyond the Dali area. As the festival song goes:

> March Festival every year,
> From everywhere people come and gather.
> All ethnic groups [*gezu renmin* 各族人民] sing and dance.
> We horse race, sing, buy and sell.[21]

A few state-run department stores set up retail stands, which are surrounded by sprawling private merchants and peddlers. A man in Tibetan dress demonstrates a deer antler sample to a Bai minority person, and two girls of the Tujia 土家族 ethnicity get excited over "modern" goods and ethnic decorations. Bao Ying complains that the festival music edits out the "natural" and everyday noises of the market, locals, and crowds, and channels them into a simulacrum of political integration.[22] It is true that the music structures and reorganizes, but it is not homogenizing and not designed to erase the ethnic differences. The music and songs are to highlight a common space for each ethnic group to share, exchange, and enjoy. The name for this integration is socialist utopia.

The sprawling scenes, complete with music, conviviality, and laughter, as well as exchange of commodities, are not a fantastic illusion. They allude to the dreamscape of social and economic progress. The busy buying and selling, rather than signs of consumerism, express the desire to enjoy material goods and improved living standards accessible to all citizens and ethnic minorities in less-developed areas. This attests to the socialist minority policy calling for all groups to enjoy the fruits of modernity. The thriving market also reflects the decentered production as part of the Great Leap Forward economic plan, which gave rural areas more control in the production of consumer goods, utensils, and tools independently of the urban industrial centers. The collective enjoyment of socialist modernity constitutes a source of laughter and conviviality.

The joyous laughter is associated with the music resounding through the whole film. Ling Zhang notes that the group singing and dance sequence in the March Fair, while highlighting the distinct art and romantic rendezvous of the Bai minority, blends into the mundane activities of consumers, trading, and prize-winning games of horse racing. The film's soundtrack features melodious Bai folk songs, with the theme song "By the Butterfly Spring" as the centerpiece that bookends the narrative. The eight songs in the narrative are "musical numbers, sung as solos, duets, or in chorus," and are accompanied by group dances. Although the songs are embedded in the story as the main source of joy and laughter, they are not specifically marked as artistic expressions unique to the Bai minority.[23] At the end, the ethnic minorities as well as the musician and painter from the Changchun film studio all enjoy the antiphonal singing of "By the Butterfly Spring" at Butterfly Lake.

The "Han" painter and musician, hailing from the urban center, appreciate and absorb rich ethic culture and arts as humble pupils. Their learning on the field trip suggests how ethnic music is elevated to the national status. The musician, who jots down every folk tune and collects songs by asking minority singers to sing all night, could have Lei Zhenbang 雷震邦 as a prototype. A composer of the film's theme music and many other popular songs derived from ethnic melodies, Lei has been celebrated as the master of folk music. Although of the Manchu stock and a student of music in Japan, he collected and re-created folk songs from a large number of minorities, such as the Bai, the Uyghur in Xinjiang, Zhuang, and others. Lei traveled widely in China, lived together with minority folks, and created many "hits" that remain popular to this day. Not contented with simply registering authentic folk tunes and formats in composing for *Five Golden Flowers*, Lei turned duet love songs into the Bai-style antiphonal singing but toned down the high-pitched tunes traditionally sung across vast open space by making them more mellow and melodious.[24]

Lei's work offers a glimpse of how the artist creates "authentic" artworks in the context of the relationship between the mainstream and the minorities, national and ethnic. Although the painter and musician of the Changchun film studio come from the national center, there is little evidence of a superior Han gaze looking down at minorities. In their interaction with minority characters (Lei is himself a minority person), the two cultural workers act as humble pupils eager to learn and as passionate fans of folk culture. In their first meeting and conversation with Ah Peng in a boat, they are curious about the technique of collecting fertilizer from the bottom of the lake and admire the artistic design of the handcrafted pouch that Jinhua has given Ah Peng. Along the way, they constantly marvel at the beautiful music, sceneries, and the minority people's robust personality. When they meet Jinhua's grandpa, who is gathering herbal medicine high in the mountain, they hear him singing off screen, express admiration and delight, jot down the tunes, and then an old man emerges. In spite of his age, Grandpa works hard while singing joyfully, proud of being able to contribute to socialist construction. In the second March Fair, the two cultural workers are submerged in the audience, harvesting every precious new find and reveling in an atmosphere of music and dance.

The scouting of folk and ethnic music corresponds to the New Folk Poetry movement (Xin minge yundong 新民歌運動), a remarkable phenomenon in the Great Leap Forward. In response to the efflorescence of poems and songs by farmers engaged in productive activity, the movement sought to collect poems and lyrics from rural minority regions and publish them for readers nationwide. Brimming with vitality and virtue, the new poetry was deployed to fuel passions and drive economic production.[25] This practice draws on the ancient tradition of song collecting called *caifeng* 采風 in Chinese antiquity. Court-sponsored musicians would travel widely across the empire and collect folk tunes from the peripheral regions. Collected music and tunes, regarded as lively and "naive" yet unpolished and vulgar, were modified and elevated into elegant styles and canons. Revolutionary art workers inherited this practice. The 1984 film *Yellow Earth* (*Huang tudi* 黃土地, dir. Chen Kaige) illustrates how the collector of folk songs, an army officer, runs into a farm boy's vulgar ditty about bedwetting and pissing with the Dragon King. In socialist China, the practice continued, and in the Great Leap Forward, the New Folk Poetry movement made a great leap into a mass-based cultural movement. In the film, the re-created songs and art maintain the authentic flavor of specific minorities but also get elevated with a universal appeal to all listeners across the country.

Laughter, Labor, and Socialist Utopia

Brimming with laughter and joy, *Five Golden Flowers* has been regarded as a classic of eulogistic comedy films (*gesong xiju* 歌頌喜劇) between 1949 and 1966. A product of the CCP's relaxation of control over film production, the film manages to produce light-hearted laughter derived, writes Zhuoyi Wang, from "coincidences and innocent misunderstandings" surrounding five girls named Golden Flower. What keeps this comedy in line is the devotion of five Golden Flowers to the socialist project. Departing from the comic genre with the satirical attack against corruptions of the status quo, the film deploys "laughter as a way to affirm and praise."[26]

The "eulogistic comedy" runs counter to most Western theories of comedy, which gravitate toward the satirical and the subversive. Comedy thinkers have identified three key sources of laughter. Laughter could stem from a superior position mocking the weakness of others (superiority theory); from a discrepancy between high and low, grandeur and baseness, and knowledge and ignorance (incongruity theory); and from the unleashing of pent-up energy from stressful cognitive activity (relief theory). A less-studied theory claims that laughter is an invitation to social interaction by providing amusement and pleasant social sociality, which resonates with my analysis of interethnic connections and shared joy.[27] Christopher Rea's engaging study of comedy in republican China follows the mainstream Western emphasis on satire and debunking with an irreverent spirit. Faced with social and ideological crises, Chinese comedic artists mocked the moribund cultural habits and authority, attacked oppressors, and made jokes to cope with misery.[28] At the risk of generalization, one could say that comic laughter entails a stance toward laughing down.

Examining the filmmaker Lü Ban's work, Bao Ying also privileges satirical over eulogistic comedy. The loosening of control during the Hundred Flowers Bloom campaign allowed some room for artists "to vent their frustration and anger at an ideologically rigid, brutal and corrupt system."[29] Satirizing the official lines represented by stern figures of authority, the film *An Unfinished Comedy* by Lü Ban targets Comrade Yi Bangzi, a censorious party official, by portraying him as a cultural commissar dead set against humor and comedy. So fixated is Yi on the artwork's soul-engineering function that he appears tone deaf to all three comic shorts. His inability to laugh induces our laughter at his miserable absence of humor.

Comedy with satirical intent has been the favorite among critics of a liberal bent, who claim Lu Xun as the exemplary of stringent satire. Lu Xun's sardonic humor rests on the artist's autonomy and ability to hurl "daggers and spears" at received ideas and authoritarian decrees. The Anti-Rightist movement in 1957 closed the door to satirical comedy, which was taken over in the Great Leap Forward by new comedy. Dubbed eulogistic comedy, the genre's mission was to eulogize the positive aspects of the new socialist order, a propaganda form laced with laughter. This is distasteful to most critics. To them, rather than genuine laughter, eulogistic comedy does little more than search for ways of releasing alternative "comic energy" erupting within cracks of the official parameters. *Five Golden Flowers* offers a utopian space that departs "from the conventional view of Chinese filmmakers' compliance with the state and ideological apparatus" by raising the possibility of "filmmakers' agency" and artistic innovations. For all "the heavy-handed political control," the artists looked for alternative comic forms and were "able to create a utopian space addressing everyday desires and fantasies, therefore providing a psychological outlet in an intensified political climate."[30] While eulogistic film comedy from the 1950s to the early 1960s offered a vision of "what an ideal society should be," its utopian longings speak instead to individuals' desire for a happy romantic life.[31]

This analysis attempts to rescue a bit of utopia of personal freedom from the collective utopia. The distrust of eulogistic comedy stems from a Western influence that pits comic laughter against order and authority. The Judeo-Christian tradition has viewed laughter as being silly and as irrational behavior of fools. By contrast, wise men are stern and rational, equipped with the wisdom and ability to be guardians of society. The mainstream discourse of comedy in the West, from Aristotle and Plato to modern theories, has viewed the comic as dangerous and subversive to the political order.[32] The authoritarianism of religion or state tolerates comedy only as harmless jests and entertainment and always frowns on its penchant to hurl ridicule and laughter against the powers that be. Against this tradition, comedy theorists, schooled in liberalism, have favored the biting satire that harbors malicious and subversive intent, reacting with suspicion against the eulogistic form of comedy aligned with collective politics and ideology.

This approach obscures the importance of laughter to mass social movements and the importance of comedic aesthetics to the emergence of a new culture and society. Cutting propaganda off from pleasures and laughter, this view severs didacticism from comedy, politics from utopian desire. But comic laughter is no stranger to the Chinese Revolution and collective art making. Early in the revolutionary era, writers and critics put comedy on cultural agenda. Mao Zedong and intellectuals distinguished the Lu Xun–style satire from the eulogistic form.[33] In "Talks on Yan'an Forum on Literature and Art," Mao, while recognizing the value of Lu Xun's satire in mocking the enemy, called for eulogistic works. He seemed to anticipate future skeptics when he asked, "Why should we not eulogize the people, the creators of the history of mankind?"[34] Aimed at educating and raising the consciousness among the masses, eulogistic artworks should take precedence over satire against social ills. Eulogistic laughter was essential to advance forward-looking visions for the peasants, and as part of revolutionary propaganda, it was meant to educate self-interested individual peasants into a modern people. It was designed to make the masses aware of their conditions, raise their consciousness, and enable them to grow into active players in national and social revolution.

The American journalist Edgar Snow noted the importance of laughter to propaganda and the formation of revolutionary subjectivity. Laughter and humor worked to transform the masses in order to forge the "reign of the people." In the chapter "Red Theater" in his influential *Red Star over China*, Snow reflects on humor, laughter, and propaganda enacted in one of numerous theaters in the revolutionary area. One Saturday he was invited to attend an open-air theater set in an old temple in the township of Bao-an in the Yan'an area. Top leaders, clerks, peasants, workers, soldiers, and villagers with infants gathered on the grassy open space by the river. Without tickets and a privileged "dress circle," an audience from all walks of life converged and formed a "democratic gathering."[35] The three-hour performance comprised a variety show or vaudeville, a series of playlets, dancing, singing, and slapstick comedies. Highlighted in these shows were political themes of anti-Japanese war and revolution. While performances lampooned the burlesque and absurd behavior of Japanese soldiers bullying and exploiting local citizens in Manchuria, the shows were also sprinkled with sparkling humor, robust vitality, and local idiom. The satire against Japanese atrocity blended into contemptuous laughter at Japanese absurdity and savagery, and the harvest dance and pantomimes produced the aesthetic effects of joy, hope, and humor among the audience. In a "dance of red machines," little dancers mimicked the thrust and drive of pistons and the mechanical turn of cogs and wheels, offering a vision of China's industrial future (112). The props, costumes, and material were primitive and crude, and most players were untrained women and children aided by "professionals" from dramatic schools of the Lu Xun Academy of Arts. In spite of or because of the amateurism, the performance set itself apart from the moribund convention of "cymbal-crashing, falsetto-singing . . . and meaningless historical court intrigues that are the concern of the decadent Chinese opera" (109).

Rather than a mere exercise in theatrical convention and entertainment, the performance goes right to the heart of the "living material": the war, the nation's survival, the plight of the people, and their hopes. The red theater offered information and enlightenment, like newspapers and topical news, and the current events were rendered into dramas that are humorous and accessible to the peasant audience. Against the bourgeois refusal "to drag art into politics," Snow floats the radical notion of "propaganda in art": "Yet in its broadest meaning it is art, for it conveys for its spectators the illusions of life, and if it is a naïve art it is because the living material with which it is made and the living men to whom it appeals are in their approach to life's problems also naïve. For the masses of China there is no fine partition between art and propaganda. There is only a distinction between what is understandable in human experience and what is not" (116).

Snow's use of *naïve* alludes to Friedrich Schiller's theory of naive poetry.[36] The naive relation of art to nature and the world is concerned with the authentic unity of an individual's growth in tune with changing society and history. In the naive state of affairs, feeling and rationality, imagination and reality are of one piece, entailing a symbiotic, organic relation, which is eroded by the onset of the modern "disassociation of sensibility" in T. S Eliot's famous phrase. Naive art is not immature or unsophisticated but is free from conventional constraints and rules, and is intimately interwoven with lived experiences of folks, the soil, and nature. It does not recognize, as Snow puts it, a "partition between art and propaganda," because art propaganda assumes that ideas and feelings rise from the day-to-day living and work.

Naive points to a different understanding of revolutionary propaganda. Dance and singing are collectively a performative act driven by a political imagination to advance revolutionary culture. Their mission is to put utopian visions into practice. Snow saw the importance of the performances to the audience because the people knew that they were building a new life and working for themselves.

In a chapter titled "They Sing Too Much," Snow captured workers' pride and joy as he interviewed them in the factories in the township of Wuqi. Mostly young women from the rural areas, the workers had little to warrant smiling and laughter: their pay was very low and living conditions primitive. Their meals consisted of millet and vegetables, and their dormitory was the cave house with earthen floors. But working under the socialist principle of equal pay for equal labor, they appeared to be the happiest and proudest people Snow had ever encountered. Lacking in cultural resources, the workers treasured the scant opportunity of learning and education. They valued their "two hours of daily reading and writing, their political lectures, their dramatic groups" (274), and everybody competed vigorously for the small prizes in contests in sports, literacy, writing, and productivity. Puzzled by the incongruity between material squalor and mental happiness, Snow searched for an answer by recalling hundreds of female workers toiling for long hours in foreign factories in Guomindang-ruled China. An engineer in the factory expressed similar bewilderment. Western educated, polyglot, and a "red expert" who quit his foreign firm in Shanghai to come to Yan'an, the engineer was shocked to find in his plant so much "horse-play going on and everybody apparently happy" (276). Due to his obsession with productivity and efficiency, the engineer complained that "these people spend entirely too much time singing" (276).

Constant singing, commented Snow, sums up "a great deal about the youthful bravado of these young women workers" (276). For they felt they were working for themselves and nobody was exploiting them. Compared with their past servitude, the revolutionary life was one "of good health, exercise, clean mountain air, freedom, dignity, and hope" (274). It is no wonder that singing, joy, and laughter are the natural and spontaneous expression of this spirit. The revolutionary propagandists "aim to shake, to arouse, the millions of rural China to their responsibilities in society; to awaken them to a belief in human rights, to combat the timidity, passiveness and static faiths of Taoism and Confucianism." Revolutionary dramatists and performers encouraged the people to fight for the "reign of the people," a society of justice, equality, freedom, and human dignity (117).

This utopian laughter receives a new incarnation in *Five Golden Flowers*. Set in the context of the Great Leap Forward, the film projects the dream of speeding up economic production and meeting citizens' everyday needs. As we follow Ah Peng in his love quest, we find all five Golden Flowers to be model workers and leaders of productive teams. Ah Peng's beloved Jinhua serves as the deputy head of a big commune. The young women are extremely busy and are racing against time. Yet they are also singers of happy songs. The beautiful and productive women seem the daughters of Snow's female workers' singing joyfully at work in Yan'an, illustrating the link between dignity of labor and eulogistic comedy.

Distinct from satirical laughter, eulogistic comedy grounds itself in the socialist moral imagination. The success of comic films like *Five Golden Flowers* and *My Day Off* (*Jintian wo xiuxi* 今天我休憩, dir. Lu Ren, 1959) inspired the Association of Film Workers and the magazine *Film Art* to run a forum in April 1960. Prominent filmmakers, writers, and critics participated and explored the new form of laughter.[37] They raised the possibility of eulogizing positive values purged off biting satire and "laughing down." Li Zehou, already a well-known aesthetic thinker, drew on insights of the participants to formulate a comic aesthetic. In his essay "On the Sublime and the Comic"

("Lun chonggao yu huaji" 論崇高與滑稽), Li claims that eulogistic comedy uses humor and laughter to highlight positive qualities. It thrusts a good character into an awkward situation and makes him blunder and suffer from mishaps, subjecting him to humorous laughter. But this laughter only sharpens our perception of his admirable moral quality in tune with a healthy social climate. In *My Day Off*, a comic film discussed in the same breath with *Five Golden Flowers*, a policeman devotes all his leisure time to helping others yet blunders and errs, missing time and again his dates with his girlfriend and ignoring his own needs. Similarly, Li Kui, a hero in the classic novel *Water Margins*, is laughable yet admirable. The image of rude, crude, boorish, and amusing Li Kui does not stop the character from cutting a figure of courage and virtue.[38] Instead of moral deficiency and flaws, eulogistic laughter arises from an embarrassment and distortion of the norm and through an excessive display of noble qualities at the expense of personal well-being and interests. In the film, Ah Peng and Jinhua are often carried away by their commitment and passion in productive work, which make the lovers blunder and err at the expense of their love interest, leading to humor and laughter. But laughing at their mistakes and missed opportunities, we look up to them as exemplary characters with noble qualities.

Comic laughter thus stems from the imbalance between selfless devotion to the common good and private desire, between libidinal expressions of happiness and self-fulfillment through public commitment. Instead of covert libidinal release from politics, the film celebrates the mutual enrichment of personal happiness and collective welfare. What eulogizes is the idealistic virtues of overzealous characters like Ah Peng and Jinhua, who are so devoted to the public good and communal affairs as to constantly get derailed from their own legitimate self-interest and private life. They "suffer" from excesses of their moral quality. Rather than looking down on them as comic objects, however, our laughter makes us look up to them and admire their idealism.

The very first comic episode arises from Ah Peng's trip to the horse race. Asked by a group of girls to repair their broken carriage, Ah Peng gets so absorbed in repair that he forgets the time. On hearing the start signal, he races to join and eventually wins the race. Comedy plays on this false alarm and the episode plays out with comic relief. In their first rendezvous at Butterfly Lake, the lovers' antiphonal singing follows the standard folk ritual of romantic exchange and flirtation, but the test of love is firmly premised on Ah Peng's dual working-class status: a blacksmith family and expertise in steel production. His knowledge of iron ores and production techniques evokes the motto of "red and expert" as well as a faith in the moral purity of rural peasants capable of updating traditional handicrafts by modern technology.

Ah Peng's technical expertise, combined with his altruistic and generous personality, induces a comedy of errors. At the first rendezvous, Jinhua's proposal that he return the following year to find her—without giving her address in a large area of Cang Mountain—sounds incredible and funny. But this is a test premised on the firm conviction of his moral integrity and unwavering love. As the narrative unfolds, both Ah Peng and Jinhua blunder and err in trying to balance love and work. While driving the carriage in the company of the two cultural workers, Ah Peng suddenly quits to help search for workers lost in the depth of mountains, leaving two visitors to clumsily manage the carriage on their own. The carriage runs into a telephone pole, disrupting an eagerly awaited phone call between Ah Peng and Jinhua. Meanwhile, Ah Peng locates another Golden Flower, the model worker of the iron plant, trapped in the cave with her colleagues. As the director of the iron plant, this young woman often argues with her husband over the quality of ores and productive technology. But her husband takes the argument personally and sees it as a sign of her waning love. Detecting his wife and Ah Peng's tête-à-tête at the cave, bending over and examining the quality of ores, the chagrined husband sees signs of her growing infidelity.

As a structural device, the man's jealousy of his wife is more than a lack of communication. The comedy plays on the tension between the female worker's public commitment and male possessiveness. The husband-wife quarrel escalates into an impending divorce and threatens Ah Peng's relationship with his love. Mistaking Jinhua for the bride in a wedding, he suppresses his broken heart and decides to return home. At the request of Golden Flower of the iron plant, however, he agrees to help her and plunges into steel production. The mise-en-scène and camera work present numerous signs of their intimacy and growing "affection," all seen in the eyes of the husband plagued by growing jealousy. When the impending divorce comes to the attention of Jinhua, it almost throws her off balance. But she keeps a tight upper lip and applies herself diligently to her duty. Her grandpa, unhappy about her inaction, goes to the plant to ascertain the "truth" of the alleged intimacy between Ah Peng and the female director at the steel plant, only to find her looking after the exhausted Ah Peng sleeping in bed. As Grandpa confirms his "change of heart," we are at the last straw of this playful game of misreading. Our heart goes out to the "agony" piercing through Jinhua, but we also see how firmly she holds on to her duty and responsibility as the leader of the community.

This split between female workers' public commitment and male possessiveness sheds light on a feature of eulogistic comedy. By subjecting male jealousy to laughter and mockery, this form changes humor by a sleight of hand into an admiration of women's dedication to the common good. In one telling episode, Ah Peng traces, wrongly again, a Golden Flower working in the stock farm through tips given by the latter's husband. The man then sneaks behind and spies on Ah Peng and the two cultural workers. As Ah Peng is serenading the female worker with the music instrument outside the cowshed, the husband, through a medium shot, slowly and sneakily emerges from behind a low wall, his facial expression anguished and green with jealousy. When the mistake is revealed in the end, he smiles with a sigh of relief. But when his wife asks why he has come to the stock farm in the midst of a busy workday, he answers that he suspects a secret liaison between her and the stranger out of town. What he gets in return is a quick, contemptuous "Phoo" from his wife.

It is by no accident that *Five Golden Flowers* was a product of the Great Leap Forward. The campaign strove to make a great leap in the transformation of human consciousness. Although the movement turned out to have disastrous consequences, its utopian aspirations remain relevant for understanding socialist China. Rather than a crash program to achieve rapid economic growth, as Maurice Meisner averred, the Great Leap Forward embodied the voluntarist belief in the decisive role of moral quality and political consciousness in advancing social change. Going hand in hand with the imperative of material production was an initiative for the development of an "ever higher level of consciousness and economic progress, each stimulating the progressive movement of the other." An ideal society hinges on "the emergence of a spiritually transformed people." The campaign's most significant guidelines were "man is the decisive factor" and "men are more important than machines." The politics of spirit in the Korean War was now transferred to the economic realm. Taking moral virtues of the peasantry as an engine to bolster productivity and social change, the politics of spirit viewed rural producers as the principal agency to eliminate the differences between town and country, agriculture and industry, and mental and manual labor.[39] In opposition to the urban centers marred with bourgeois lifestyle, bureaucrats, and technocrats, the peasants in the countryside could make a great leap forward in social, moral transformation. The emphasis on rural culture and virtue extends to ethnic minorities, and the Bai minority heroes epitomize a rich reservoir of morality, productivity, and creativity.

To conclude, *Five Golden Flowers* engages profusely in singing and dancing and stages dazzling and charming spectacles of ethnic minorities. The film propagates the principle of national unity in ethnic diversity, offering a glimpse of the minority policy and practice of socialist China. The principle of unity in diversity aims to bring all ethnic groups into a common project of economic, social, and moral progress. The film's laughter expresses the heartfelt joy of workers and farmers in working for themselves, for the community, and for the socialist future. The overzealous heroines and hero put themselves in a laughable position as they err and blunder, but we laugh and look up to them with admiration.

The Third World, Alternative Development, and Global Maoism

Six

FROM 1970 TO 1975, China assisted and underwrote the construction of the Tanzania and Zambia Railway in Africa. As its largest overseas project at the time, the railway linked the copper belt in Zambia with Tanzania's port city Dar es Salaam. China agreed to support this 1,060-mile-long project after the World Bank and the Soviet Union rejected repeated requests of assistance by presidents Julius Nyererer and Kenneth Kaunda.[1] When premier Zhou Enlai visited Dar es Salaam in June 1965, he recalled, in a speech to a large audience in the national stadium, China's historical contact with Africa. Between 1405 and 1433, Zheng He 鄭和, a Ming dynasty official, commanded huge fleets loaded with commodities and gifts, traversed the Indian Ocean, and landed on the East African coast, including Zanzibar in Tanzania. Zheng "did not come to Africa," said Zhou, "with the intention of colonization but rather sought to trade and interact with the African people as equals."[2] China's relation with Africans was to "help African nations to build self-reliance and to avoid dependence." Proclaimed as the "Freedom Railway," the Tanzania-Zambia Railway sought to free Zambia from its "dependence on Rhodesian, Angolan, and South African rails and ports." It was, as Jamie Monson writes, "an anti-apartheid railway," "a symbol of revolutionary solidarity and resistance to forces of colonialism, neocolonialism, and imperialism."[3]

Zheng He's voyages operated under the aegis of the tributary system and Silk Road trade route—extensions of tianxia beyond the Middle Kingdom proper. But the PRC's involvement with Africa from the 1960s to the 1970s was to assist decolonization and postindependence development. Separated by three hundred years, the two events seemed to have little to do with one another. In light of China's rise as a global power and increasing influence in Africa, however, studies in the past few decades have showed that memories of the ancient trade routes are being recalled as the deep background for China's world vision. Henry Kissinger has written a volume about how tianxia and the tributary system shaped China's perennial worldview and foreign policy.[4] David Kang has examined five centuries of premodern East Asian relations of trade, tribute, and cultural exchange modeled on tianxia until the encounter with the West.[5] The Tanzania-Zambia Railway project was underway during the Cultural Revolution, when Levenson saw global Maoism as a substitute for tianxia. Despite the break with the imperial tradition, he wrote, Mao harbored the unfulfilled aspiration to restore China's greatness, which "depends on an international premise."[6] The wounded pride of the tianxia order at the hand of colonialism and imperialism "was healed with a Marxist salve."[7] The salve was none other than Marxism Sinicized into Maoism. By substituting the Mandate of Heaven with Third World movements, Maoism represented "a world-view that compensates for Confucianism lost."[8]

The Maoist worldview mapped history onto a teleological timeline where China could recover its past preeminence through a universal sequence of progress and modernization, restoring the Middle Kingdom's ancient mantle. But the Chinese Revolution taught Mao to question the Marxist faith in the potential of urban industrial modernity. Based on the experience of an agrarian revolution, Maoism evolved into a radical theory of rural modernity. Anticipating revolutionary potentials in the peasantry and rebellions from rural peripherals, Mao's Third World theory arose in the 1940s as an analysis of geopolitical dynamics of colonized, intermediate regions between the United States and the Soviet Union. The theory forecast that the colonized agrarian people would unite and aid each other in national liberation and decolonization.[9] In the Cold War era, this vision evolved into a strategy exported to Asian, African, and Lain American nations in struggles against colonialism and the pursuit of postcolonial development. The nucleus of Maoism includes the opposition to the ideological convergence of Soviet revisionism and US imperialism, the strategy of armed struggle waged by the undeveloped countryside to encircle the metropolitan centers, mutual support between decolonizing nations, and self-reliance in economic development.[10] During the global sixties, Mao's ideas exerted powerful appeal to national independence movements and socialist reconstruction in the Third World. It also inspired anti-hegemonic movements in countries from France to the United States, leading to protests such as anti-war movements, civil rights activism, feminism, and anti-racism. Alain Badiou and many others of the French Left, for instance, turned to Maoism and the Third World to revamp the people's power and critique dogmatic Marxism.

In the mood of farewell to revolution, historians have remained reticent about China's Third World involvement. The post–Cold War era witnessed the retreat and amnesia of social movements, ideological debate, and collective mobilization. Neoliberalists cast China as getting on track with global capitalism and realists raised alarm at its menace and hegemony. But hegemony was precisely what Mao's China was combatting in its alliance with Third World nations. As an anti-hegemonic, grassroots movement among the world's poor, the Third World marked a global protest against neo-imperialist hegemons. The movement sought to build a sovereign nation-state and create independent space for economic reconstruction and institutional transformation.[11] China played a large role in its vigorous support and promotion of Asia, Africa, and Latin America. Revolutionary politics and programs from Bandung to Vietnam and Tanzania marked a mobilization of popular energy, a mass-based campaign against the entrenched state power and military-industrial complex.

This chapter addresses China's connections with the Third World. Rather than a hermitic nation isolated from the world during the Cold War, China reached out to connect with the part of the world that has come to be known as the Global South. A continuation from the revolutionary goal of challenging uneven development and colonial rule, the Third World alliance searched for a socialist model of development rooted in the Maoist mass-line and self-reliance strategy—a faith in the virtue and power of the rural masses as political subjects. Combining economic development with social progress, the socialist development strove to close the divide between city and country, industry and agriculture, and mental and manual labor.

China's investment in the Tanzania-Zambia railway stemmed from the empathy and solidarity born of a shared history of oppression under colonialism. Defined as a case of "the poor helping the poor," the railway project affirmed Mao's insight that "only China's independence and liberation will make it possible to participate in the world communist movement."[12] The claim that an emancipated and sovereign people are able to help others is a precondition for internationalism: only when the Chinese people have stood up could they support other independence-seeking nations. This internationalist ethos was enacted in Cultural Revolution dramas. In *Song of the Dragon River*, as Xiaomei Chen has shown, a village leader urges the peasants to help the drought-stricken neighbors but also to look beyond the mountains to empathize with "the sufferings of the poor 'brothers and sisters' in Third World countries." An "imagined international community" links oppressed people from Asia, Latin America, and Africa.[13] The ethos accounts for the refrain of the "Internationale" at the critical moment of altruism in five Cultural Revolution model plays, including *Red Lantern* (*Hongdeng ji*), *Azalea Mountain* (*Dujuan shan*), *Raid on White Tiger Division* (*Qixi baihu tuan*), *Red Detachment of Women* (*Hongse niangzi jun*), and *Haigang* (*On the Harbor*).

"The people who have achieved the victory of revolution should assist the on-going struggle by other people for liberation. This is our international duty." This quotation by Mao sets the tone of *On the Harbor* (*Haigang* 海港, 1973), one of the eight Cultural Revolution model plays. The story centers on the assistance to an African country through a shipment of rice seeds in support of its national independence and economic self-reliance. Driven by political urgency, the dockworkers must beat the deadline by uploading rice seeds to an ocean liner. Qian Shouwei, a class enemy, attempts to sabotage the shipment by dropping glass fiber on the ground and having it mixed with the rice package. A young dockworker, Han Xiaoqiang, unwittingly gets glass fiber into a bag of loose wheat and rice seeds, endangering the whole project. Discovering the danger, the leader, Fang Haizhen, mobilizes all dockworkers to inspect eight thousand rice bags overnight in order to identify the wrong one. Meanwhile, making Han realize his error, Fang reveals Qian's subterfuge. Workers capture Qian as he escapes.

Set in the Shanghai harbor, the drama evokes a locus fraught with memories of colonialism and imperialism. Since the late nineteenth century, Shanghai grew into a treaty port with busy international trade and commerce, acquiring the aura of "Paris in the Orient"—a crown jewel of colonial modernity. *The East Is Red*, a song-and-dance epic made on the eve of the Cultural Revolution, illustrates the treaty port's colonial character. It is a place where colonialists, capitalists, and Chinese compradors operate hand in hand. The international commerce deals exclusively in exports of Chinese silk—a symbol of oriental luxury. In cargo boxes marked with "Made in China," silk is headed to the Euro-American metropolises and consumers. Anchored in the nearby waters is an array of warships that fly the British, US, and Japanese flags against the low-hanging, gloomy sky. Under this "cosmopolitan" atmosphere, the warships safeguard the freedom and safety of colonial trade on behalf of capitalist expansion. A lanky white man, in suit and tie, dominates the scene. His Chinese assistants scrutinize every move of the dockworkers, who toil like beasts of burden and have lashings rain on them if they slow down.

Haigang turns this scene upside down. The former dock slaves have taken over the harbor and are presiding over the work process. "Made in China" on the cargo is renamed "Made in the People's Republic of China." Bustling scenes of loading and shipping teem with images of international assistance and trade, with cargos bound for the vast continents in the Global South. Fang sings, "The Shanghai harbor is linked to China's southern areas and north frontiers; connected to countries of vast nature and palm trees [莽原椰林]; we support domestic construction and aid world people." The motif of international support, writes Xiaomei Chen, links "the sufferings of the Chinese workers in the old society" to "that of their black brothers and sisters in present-day Africa."[14] The rice seeds shipment is intended to assist a newly decolonized African country and to free it from dependence on the neocolonial development of agribusiness under the World Bank. Western financiers have imposed unequal terms of capital investment and economists have predicted that African rice growing is doomed. Thus, the stakes are high in the rice shipment for Africa's national independence and economic self-reliance. The Chinese dockworkers are tasked with the urgent political task of delivering on time to honor the African nation's independence day.

As a member of the Chinese comprador class, Qian the saboteur has worked as an accountant in the service of foreign firms before 1949. He has remained a sleeper agent bent on undermining economic production. By mixing glass fiber with grains, he seeks to endanger the African shipment and hence China's international image. The glass fiber shipment, on the other hand, represents foreign exports to a Scandinavian country of the First World. Contrasting high-tech glass fiber with basic foodstuff, the film portrays the former as a dangerous material. Elusive and overrefined, it is likely to jeopardize the grains if not handled properly. Glass fiber earns foreign currency, whereas the African aid symbolizes the international spirit and moral duty.

Qian tricks Han Xiaoqiang, a young dockworker, into an unwitting act of sabotage. Though from a family of dockworkers, Han detests his job and dreams of becoming a sailor and roaming the world. Egged on by Qian, he comes to despise fellow dockworkers and calls them "stinking coolie," a slur from former colonialists. Han constantly intones a sailor's wanderlust for "crossing the oceans and traveling around the world" (*piaoyang guohai, zhouyou shijie* 飄洋過海，周遊世界). This pipe dream renders him close to the venture capitalist or globe-trotting entrepreneur—the privileged inhabitants of old Shanghai's "ten miles of foreign realm and settlement" (*shili yangchang* 十里洋場). Signaling a stylistic and superficial cosmopolitanism, Han's desire reflects a sensory exposure to a garden variety of geography, custom, and culture. This globe-trotting cosmopolitanism derives from a canonic structure of feelings in romantic seafaring fiction, such as *Lord Jim* by Joseph Conrad. Steeped in colonialism and orientalism, the desired experience is hostile to the pursuit of national independence and sovereignty. Han's cosmopolitanism mirrors the privileges of the colonialists, characterized by an "open-minded," catholic taste for possession and appreciation of commodities from around the world.

The sailor's dream is so enticing and dock work so disappointing that Han throws away his identity card. This signals a forgetfulness of the memory of colonial oppression. In the past, Han's parents labored like slaves for colonial trading firms. The founding of the new nation freed dockworkers from oppression and exploitation and granted them the right to work. Recognized as masters of the Shanghai harbor, the workers take pride in working for themselves and for the nation. The job ID symbolizes the dignity of labor, decolonization, and emancipation.

It is by revisiting the colonial history of the Shanghai harbor that Han realizes his mistake and sees through Qian's plot. Fang Haizhen and veteran dockworkers take him to an exhibition displaying records and relics from the colonial past. Japanese, Americans, and Chinese compradors used to rule the dock. The exhibition hall, previously the office of an American trade firm, signals the dominance of a taipan or trade executive. Colonial capitalism, hand in hand with Chinese compradors, constituted a regime of exploitation and oppression. Qian stands revealed as a lackey to American and Japanese colonial capitalists, having been handsomely rewarded for his service and loyalty. Reclaiming the Shanghai harbor for working people, the Chinese

Revolution dismantled the exploitive relation between labor and capital, sidelined the capitalists, and drove out colonialists. The outgoing American executive predicted, like all colonialists fleeing China, that the Chinese coolies were too stupid and backward to manage a modern harbor and doomed to failure in running the economy.

Han's change of consciousness comes about through the remembrance of the past, resulting in the uncovering of Qian's sabotage. The investigation traces Qian's counterrevolutionary plot to his previous subversive acts during the Korean War and espionage for the Guomindang regime in Taiwan in the early 1960s. In addition to a class enemy within China, Qian represents an international enemy in the service of neocolonialism. The Cold War climate, fraught with espionage, subversion, and intrigue, necessitates a continuous revolution and anti-colonialism in postindependent Third World nations.

Socialist Development

Maoism, wrote Maurice Meisner, represents "a global vision of a worldwide revolutionary process." It proclaimed that the revolutionary countryside of economically backward lands would triumph over the urban capitalist centers of Europe and North America.[15] Derived from Mao's utopianism, the strategy of the rural Third World besieging the First World was grounded in a belief in the spontaneous capacity of the peasantry to overturn the unequal structure between the urban centers and rural peripherals. Colonial powers' encroachment into peripheral regions, Rosa Luxemburg wrote, gave rise to global inequality. Instead of free and equal exchange, colonial capital shows "how commodity exchange turns into exploitation and equality becomes class-rule."[16] This explains why China needed a rural revolution, not simply because its population was largely rural and economy agrarian. As Lin Chun points out, "Modernization by imitating the West to achieve a homegrown, robust national capitalism was only an illusion" because colonial capital "violently dismantled" rural communities. Western capitalists perpetuated the semicolonial conditions and hampered peripheral development. It was only after achieving national sovereignty in 1949 that China was able to pursue its own development as a socialist developmental state.[17]

The rural-urban divide was the bone of contention between two contrary paths of China's modern development. As Arif Dirlik has shown, Western capitalists had no interest in developing far-flung regions for the benefit of local communities. On the contrary, they preyed on the colonies for raw materials, cheap labor, and markets. The Chinese bourgeoisie was weak and dependent—an appendage of global capital. The Chinese capitalists were unable to respond to the needs of their fellow countrymen and remained at the mercy of foreign capitalists. Colonialism widened the chasm between the haves and the have-nots and the division between the urban centers and vast rural areas. Before 1949, the Chinese economy was split into one section dependent on global capital in the coastal treaty ports, and the other section a vast rural hinterland mired in poverty, deprivation, and decay. This situation gave rise to an unholy alliance of colonial capital, a domestic comprador class, and a traditional oligarchy—the proverbial "three mountains" of imperialism, feudalism, and bureaucratic capitalism in Mao's phrase.[18]

The colonial order epitomizes uneven development in the Global South, making it necessary to search for alternatives. Genuine development must await the rise of the sovereign nation along with social revolution. The Chinese Revolution built a socialist state and lay the groundwork for a new model of development. The slogan "Serve the People," as American scholars argued, captured the essence of socialist development, which aimed at "improving the lives of almost everyone." The new government "did not represent and work on behalf of a small group of merchants or traders," or "a class of landed proprietors," or "foreign interests allied with domestic entrepreneurs," but was aimed at the interests of the masses of poor people.[19] Resorting to a self-reliant economy, socialist development was committed to providing benefits to the working people of the entire society.

Scholars have focused on the thesis of rural development as a distinct feature of Chinese modernity. A long-term process, China's rural development, as Yu Zhang has shown, addresses "the vast gap between the city and the countryside."[20] The rural development evinces socialist features not only in political economy but also in subjectivity, representation, and sociality. In constant crossings between cities and the countryside, the rural project "opens up new possibilities to imagine alternative human subjectivities and experience."[21] Mao's vision of development envisaged the countryside as a reservoir of revolutionary virtue and potential, where the peasants were mobilized into self-conscious political subjects. On the other hand, Mao's utopianism, linking the cities in North America and Europe with capitalist modernity, represented, as Meisner wrote, a refusal to "accept the consequences of 'modernity' as the necessary price of historical progress."[22] The socialist development path challenged the Cold War global structure dominated by the two superpowers. Vigilant against the widening gulf between state and society as endemic to technocratic modernization, Maoism evinced "the antipathy to large and centralized form of political and economic organization, the deep aversion to all manifestations of bureaucracy, and the distrust of formal higher education."[23] Breaking with the Soviet model of heavy industry, centralized administration, and official hierarchy, Mao warned against the growing ills of urban institutional ossification and social inequality. The growth of an oppressive bureaucracy, social inequality, and the entrenchment of a privileged elite fueled the controversy over development within the CCP. The debate arose during the First Five-Year Plan (1953–57) and persisted through the Great Leap Forward (1958–62), reaching a crescendo in the Cultural Revolution (1966–76). The debate continued during Deng Xiaoping's reform and today, when the mantra "development is the ironclad logic" is being contested amid social and environmental crises. These questions are central: Should China pursue wealth and power and go on track with capitalism, or should it pursue a sustainable growth in the name of political unity, socioeconomic equality, and community?

In the Mao era, the question was whether China could achieve an all-around development of egalitarianism and equality by overcoming the divisions between the city and the countryside, industry and agriculture, and intellectual and manual work. Socialist development challenged the modernization paradigm steeped in technocratic rationality and ideology. Touted as a program to improve living standards in underdeveloped countries, West-sponsored development was, in Sigrid Schmalzer's words, "a strategy for preventing ideologies opposed by the US."[24] It sought to neutralize revolutionary movements and replace socialist experiments with a "technocratic vision," relying on "technical experts to provide technological fixes for social and political problems."[25] To be sure, China's modernization did not escape the technocratic trap, which was manifested in the rise of a technocratic class, inequality, and the urban-rural divide. In the deepening bureaucratization of state and society in the First Five-Year Plan, "the cadres of a revolutionary party became administrators and bureaucratic functionaries," and the ideal image of the red-and-expert cadres turned to mere experts and administrators, governing the masses from their office desks.[26] The Soviet model fostered a new fetish in the expertise and power of technological specialists, engendering a pattern of inequality and hierarchy at the expense of the revolutionary spirit and the socialist ethos of equality and well-being for all.

To counter the trend, the socialist approach sought to integrate technological advances, social progress, and political mobilization. Derived from the Yan'an tradition, the project rearticulated "a heavy reliance on the creativity of the Chinese people, particularly the peasantry," and a "rejection of domination by an administrative or technical elite operating through a centralized bureaucracy," giving primacy to "popular participation, decentralization and community power."[27] Mao reinvoked this approach in the 1950s as three parallel movements: "class struggle, the struggle for production, and scientific experiment." These movements would ensure that China is "free from bureaucracy and immune against revisionism and dogmatism."[28] Class struggle, frequently understood as the cynical and abusive estrangement, classification, and persecution of innocent people, means different things and serves different purposes in different periods. But in light of development controversy, the term has a specific goal: to combat the bureaucratic administrators and a rising technocratic elite. The class divide worsened, in Carl Riskin's analysis, as "administrative state planning had combined political and economic power in the hands of a bureaucracy aloof from the masses." This tendency went beyond class and "favored the cities over the countryside, workers over peasants."[29] The socialist development challenged it "through administrative decentralization and mass mobilization."[30] Mass mobilization strove to resolve the confrontation between an all-around development and the elitist tendencies and to battle the growing restratification and social cleavages. The strategy of decentralization sought to energize the masses in the grassroots, give full play to their initiatives, and bring them into political and economic processes. The ultimate goal of socialist modernity was to serve the people by closing the three gaps between the town and country, industry and agriculture, and menial and intellectual labor, combining social progress with material advances.

The development controversy finds poignant and dramatic expression in three films made in the Cultural Revolution. *Spring Shoots* (*Chunmiao* 春苗, dir. Xie Jin, 1975), *Breaking with Old Ideas* (*Juelie* 决裂, dir. Li Wenhua, 1975), and *The Pioneers* (*Chuangye* 創業, dir. Yu Yanfu, 1974) all revolved around the controversies of social progress versus economic development, mass mobilization versus technocratic elitism, and self-reliance versus dependence. Detractors tend to see these films as little more than weapons of faction fight in the Cultural Revolution and ideological polemics as cover for personal intrigues and jockeying for power. Turning a blind eye to the systemic issues, this dismissive view obscures the long enduring and alternative visions of modernity underlying the different narratives in Chinese and world history. For all their strident tones and expression, these films actively engage the public debate of development paths—something that is sorely missing in commercial cinema in China's film industry. Although Mao-era films might be a handmaiden of politics and ideology, I read these films not as propagating false consciousness but as an articulation of visions that challenge the dominant modernization paradigm.

Focusing on education reform—a top priority of the Cultural Revolution—*Breaking with Old Ideas* stages a scathing critique of the educational system evolving over a decade since 1949. Aping the Soviet and Western models, the system trains scientists and experts who are obsessed with personal careerist advancement, status, and privilege. The fetish of book learning and professionalism breeds a technological elite aloof from and unconcerned with public goods and productive practice. Previously a cowherd boy, soldier, and student in the University of Resistance in Yan'an, the protagonist Long is tasked to build a new agriculture university, with the goal of transforming the elitist higher education system. On arrival, Long overturns the admission protocol that bars peasant applicants and begins to recruit them through a consultation with peasant representatives and professors. The admission is made on the basis of work experience, moral character, and dedication to public goods rather than academic preparation. Guided by the open-door principle, peasant students build an agriculture university at the foot of the mountain—right "at the doorstep of the peasants." But the old curriculum continues, and a professor lectures on the anatomy of the horse's tail (*ma weiba de gongneng* 马尾巴的功能) in this southern area where horses are rare. The traditional curriculum pretends to "grow trees in the classroom and do farming on the blackboard," and the professor assigns heavy volumes of agricultural science by foreign authorities that have nothing to do with local livestock, soil, and crops. To change the system, the students take initiatives in collective teaching and learning. They redesign the curriculum and adapt book knowledge to suit the local climate, ecology, and farming conditions. They help each other with guidance from progressive professors, who practice Mao's notion that the educator should learn from the educated. Rather than anti-intellectualism, this down-to-earth approach allows students to acquire rudiments of science and become competent technicians—a testament to the Maoist unity of theory and practice and knowledge integrated with production and community needs.

These initiatives meet stiff resistance from the university administration headed by the vice president with the credentials of an education expert. He maneuvers to get Mr. Long out of the way by offering him a tour to inspect the technoscientific rigor of the nation's top universities. Meanwhile, the administration clamps down on student activities. When forced to prepare for an exam amid a raging pest pandemic in the villages, the students break out en masse and have a field day helping the peasants cope with pesticides. The administration seeks to penalize the revolt and punish the female student leader Li. At the struggle meeting against her, Mr. Long, now back on campus, defers to the peasants for counsel and judgment, which deem Li an exemplary student. Frustrated, the administration, backed with a higher authority, plans to disband the university. But Mao's endorsement of this grassroots creative program arrives in the nick of time and scores the victory of the educational revolution.

Spring Shoots targets the public health system, which is skewed in favor of elites and urbanites. Although the PRC developed socialized health care, hospitals and clinics increasingly became the privileged enclave for bureaucrats, cadres, and city dwellers. The top-rate doctors "were divorced from proletarian politics, from workers, peasants, and soldiers" and focused attention on the treatment of rare disease and difficult cases, oblivious to common diseases affecting ordinary working people.[31]

Inequality in health care marks the film's opening scene. A doctor of the county hospital, busily chatting on the phone with an official, delays urgent care to a critically ill girl, causing the latter's death. It is instructive to note that in China today, denial of treatment to poor, rural patients is not unusual yet barely registers public outrage, which makes this 1975 film all the more poignant and compelling. Outraged by this incident, the protagonist Tian Chunmiao, a peasant girl, teaches herself medical knowledge and dedicates herself to serving rural patients (see figure 6.1). Against obstruction from the professionals preoccupied solely with the health and longevity of officials, and with the help of a doctor committed to the well-being of peasants, she eventually completes her self-education and becomes a barefoot doctor—a symbol of health-care reform. The dramatic conflict builds toward the confrontation of two diametrically opposed lines in health care, raising the questions: What is a public health-care system that refuses to deliver medical care to ordinary people? Public health for what public?

The barefoot doctor emerged as a grassroots and low-cost initiative of public health care decades before it became a *cause célèbre* during the Cultural Revolution. The image refers to a peasant or factory worker who, having acquired basic medical knowledge and skills, is able to treat coworkers with common ailments without leaving the post. The barefoot doctors, reported Victor Li in 1975, represented the "most innovative and far-reaching efforts to provide better health care for the entire population." A campaign to train a large cadre of paramedical workers, the initiative began in the Great Leap Forward and, in response to Mao's June 25, 1965, directive "in medical and health work, put stress on the rural area." The movement climaxed during the Cultural Revolution.[32] Departing from the Western model centered around highly trained professionals, sophisticated technology, complex equipment, and expensive drugs,

6.1 Chunmiao, a barefoot doctor, treats rural patients in *Spring Shoots* (1975).

barefoot medicine signaled an alternative health care that was inexpensive, mass-based, egalitarian, ecological, and beneficial to the rural communities.

The barefoot doctor became a flash point for alternative development, when the World Health Organization promoted it as a model for developing countries in the 1970s.[33] In this decade, convulsed by worldwide critiques of capitalism, medical technocracy, exorbitant health insurance, and profit-driven overmedication, the barefoot doctor epitomized a revolutionary mass medicine. Guided by the principle "serve the people," the practice resonated with an intellectual trend in North America and the Third World. In his widely influential book *Medical Nemesis*, published in London in 1975, the year *Spring Shoots* was released, Ivan Illich critiqued the American technocratic and monopolistic health system and turned to the barefoot doctor as an alternative. Upholding autonomy, community, and freedom from the manipulation of the technocratic and capitalist apparatus, Illich appreciated the way millions of people in China learned and applied simple remedies to common diseases and maintained health care without resorting to expensive drugs and services. In his *Écologie et politique*, published in France in the same year, the French philosopher André Gorz saw in the barefoot doctor the ecological implications of a cheap, homemade medicine, whose grassroots practices fascinated Ralph Nader and Jerry Brown, then governor of California.[34] Barefoot medicine was also adopted in Chile by the proponents of a health practice based on community needs rather than imported drugs. The Chilean reformers "mobilized the poor to identify their own health needs" and "compelled the medical profession to serve basic rather than profitable needs."[35] Illich, however, was aware of the challenges faced by the barefoot doctor in terms of the official bias toward technological expertise and centralization. In the film, this bias was "reflected in the professional reaches of health care." Toward the end of the Cultural Revolution, Illich warned, "barefoot medicine was losing its grassroots semi-independent character" to a new health technocracy.[36]

The Pioneers dramatizes the life story of Wang Jinxi 王进喜, an exemplary worker of the petroleum industry. The oil workers, under the party leadership and guided by geologists and engineers, discovered the Daqing oil field in Northeast China, which became the symbol of socialist industrialization. In addition to serving as a crucial resource for industrialization, oil has been a critical factor in national security and a bone of geopolitical contention. China's search for oil, as Hou Li has shown, trails a long story of the drive for independence and industrialization amid the colonial scrambles to plunder the native resources. The Standard Oil Company began its operation in China shortly after it was founded by John Rockefeller in 1870. Intense conflict and competition arose in the prerevolutionary era among British, Japanese, and American companies, and between the Nationalist government and the Red Army in taking control of oil resources.[37] In 1938 the geologist of Standard Oil declared that China was poor in oil deposits.[38] During the 1950s, China depended on the Soviets for its energy needs, and the split with the Soviet Union cut off the oil supply.

The film depicts the heroic effort of oil workers in developing oil fields. In 1959 they discovered large oil deposits in Daqing and drilled the first oil well. A boost to the young nation, Daqing broke China's dependence on the Soviets and dispelled the myth of oil poverty. Distinct from the Soviet model of urban development and heavy industry, Daqing was elevated into a symbol of socialist development. Defying the Western prognosis and "scientific methods," the oil workers in the film, hailing from the peasantry, collaborate closely with "red engineers." A culture of equality, participation, and power sharing prevails in the work process, as the leaders, engineers, and workers hold brainstorming sessions to solve technical and ideological problems. Participation and self-management boost confidence as the workers take charge of work and community. Their intelligence and consciousness enable a vibrant workplace culture, and the convergence of ideas and creativity trumps technical elitism. The workers' extraordinary deeds and endurance of hardship epitomize the Yugong spirit, exalted by Mao in the speech "Yugong yishan" 愚公移山 (The Foolish Old Man Who Removed the Mountains).

Daqing represented, writes Hou, a "place where the socialist utopia and the people's spirit sought to conquer reality. It was a model that Chinese leaders hoped would propel the entire country to the longed-for industrialized future and to a society built on equality, productivity, and revolutionary progress."[39] Intwining personal commitments with collective endeavors, Daqing strove to achieve a self-sufficient lifeworld and urban-rural integration.

Socialist rural development also figures prominently in films from countries of the socialist camp, such as North Korea, Vietnam, Romania, Yugoslavia, and the Soviet Union. These films regaled the Chinese audience with exotic spectacles and entertainment, filling the entertainment lacuna of the Cultural Revolution with melodramatic excitement, real-life experience, and pleasure. North Korean films of rural reconstruction offered pictures of economic production in the service of people and community, dramatizing local self-management, political subjectivity, and attachment to the land. Dubbed in Chinese, they delineate textures of family life, the fabric of community, and a lifestyle close to that of Northern China. *The Season of Apple Harvest* (*Zhai pingguo de shihou* 摘蘋果的時候, 1971) describes the way a production team in a hilly North Korean village harvests and manages an overabundant crop of apples. A symbol of the success of collective labor, the harvest points to the actual economic growth of North Korea in the postwar period up to the late 1970s. The cinematography of rural landscape exudes a warm feeling of confidence, community, cooperation, and self-reliance. The opening shots of the rural scenes at dawn reveal the farming fields bathed in bright sunshine, and close-ups of beautiful apples impress a sense of appreciation of nature, land, and farmwork. Instead of a preindustrial idyll of nature and happy peasants, the film evokes a modern village in the making and an aspiration for a utopia of socioeconomic prosperity.

Due to continuing Cold War and East Asian geopolitics, few historians have the patience to inquire into the notable achievement of North Korea in the aftermath of the Korean War. The economic fruits stemmed from a combination of factors: self-reliance, international aid from the Soviet Union and China, and the national resolve to avoid developmental pitfalls of the Soviet Union. In the 1950s and into the 1960s, North Korea was well ahead of many socialist countries and certainly ahead of South Korea in several aspects of economic and social development until the 1970s.[40]

In *The Season of Apple Harvest*, the bumper harvest of apples presents a challenge to the farmers: they have to sell apples or preserve them for future use. To sell, they need to make deals with urban distribution centers, rendering the village economy vulnerable to the vicissitudes of the market. To preserve, they must learn new technology and build processing facilities. Although both methods may meet the needs of the local population rather than making a profit, selling large amounts to the distribution centers is the easier way out and prone to competition, market mechanism, and corruption. These two approaches in handling apples lead to a divergence in management style. The bureaucratic style by the team leader is contrasted with the democratic self-management by young people. While the leader scrambles day after day in town to get sales orders and beat the competitors, the young villagers use modern technology to make apple preserves. As the narrative unfolds, economic decision-making gradually shifts from the "market-savvy" leader to the hands of the youth. Pooling their ideas, energy, and creativity, the young villagers, mostly women, learn advanced technology and make connections with urban engineers to implement their projects.

As the leader gradually delegates more responsibility and authority to the female workers, the film presents a dynamic process of self-reliance and self-management in a diffuse network of responsibility and participation. Significantly, the female workers are most active and creative and quick to challenge and educate the patriarchal leader. Participation in communal affairs underlies the conflict between active and passive characters, illustrated by the episodes involving two sisters. The younger sister, Jin-ok, presents an example of what a member of the rural community can accomplish when she draws on local resources, learns technology, rallies group support, and participates vigorously in production. Pretty, smart, educated, and enterprising, Jin-ok, like the women in *Five Golden Flowers*, epitomizes the model worker and a new personality in the socialist countryside. Her elder sister, Sun-ok, is the opposite. Obsessed with the trivialities of private life, she is fixated on marrying her fiancé, a city-based engineer, looking forward to a life of ease and comfort and leaving the countryside for urban amenities. Pursuing a "bourgeois" lifestyle, she drifts away from her peers and their political and cultural activities, and finally withdraws from the day-to-day production process. Engrossed in becoming a model housewife, she neglects her work and causes a near-disaster. What turns Sun-ok around at the end of the story is education and persuasion, which bring her back to much-needed political consciousness and commitment to public goods. The story of her family suffering under colonial rule, told by her father, enables her to realize how important it is to participate in collective efforts.

All these films project scenarios of socioeconomic development on behalf of the people and in service of community. Inspired with the idea of self-reliance and mass mobilization, the development model, according to

Dirlik, expressed "the sense of empowerment" of the people and appealed strongly to Third World agrarian societies.[41] Self-reliance sought to avoid the traps of material dependence on the outside world and to attain independence from the technocratic elite in matters of science and technology. Socialist development called for active participation of the marginalized people in the process of development and recognized the working people "as both the motive force and the end of development."[42] No longer in the hands of experts or bureaucrats and emancipated from technological fetishism, the socialist project brings the people into the center of decision-making and opens up possibilities for grassroots participation in social and productive life. Disillusioned with the modernization paradigm, Rhoads Murphey describes the aspiration for alternatives: "many in the West cherish the hope that somehow the Chinese can produce a form of development which avoids the worst mistakes of the Western model and leads the way to a better world for all of us, as the Maoist vision indeed promises."[43]

The films discussed here shed light on the nature of socialism and keep alive the vision for alternative development, encompassing values of community, the egalitarian spirit, mass participation in politics and production, and, above all, the effort to forge a people-centered economy and culture. These forgotten questions are becoming newly relevant today, as the capitalist mode of production is proving to be ecologically unsustainable, socially destructive, and globally divisive. For all its errors and disasters, the socialist experiment offers valuable lessons for projecting a different path for an alternative future.

Mao's Cult of the People according to Alain Badiou

The socialist model resonated with aspirations and efforts of Third World nations. The Naxalite movement in India, the peasant insurgence under Sendero Luminoso (Shining Path) in Peru, the ujamaa (family) program led by Julius Nyererer in Tanzania, and other movements adopted a similar approach. "Based on collective hard work, popular agrarian transformation, and a resolutely anti-colonial stance," the socialist approach, premised on a Maoist vision of rural transformation, envisaged a future for developing nations seeking to find their ways outside the capitalist orbit.[44]

Richard Wolin writes that Maoism sparked "intoxication of third worldism" among the French Left in the heady days of 1968 amid the raging fervor of the global sixties.[45] For French Marxists, Mao's China provided a model of revolution and social change based on the mobilized power and political consciousness of the peasantry. Turning the Marxist faith in urban working-class leadership on its head, the socialist experiment relied on the peasant masses as a reservoir of virtue and the countryside as the locus for economic development. Mass mobilization empowered and energized the rural masses into a self-conscious force for political change and technological practice, offering an exemplar to the agrarian nations in an era of anti-colonial struggle and postindependence reconstruction. Mao's peasant-based theory and practice were amplified through Fidel Castro's seizure of powers in Cuba and Vietnam's heroic effort to throw off the yoke of imperialism.[46]

Two motifs in Maoism attracted the French Left and affected their interpretation of the Cultural Revolution. One is the mass line, which holds that truth and wisdom come from the people, especially from the peasantry. The mass line presumes a close tie between the leader and the led, between theory and practice. The other is the faith in the peasantry as a source of moral virtue, political subjectivity, and transformative power. Mass mobilization is a consciousness-raising project: it taps into the masses' revolutionary potentials and inspires people to take to the streets to protest the military-industrial complex and the bureaucratic state. The French Marxists, drawing on Mao's faith in the virtue of "the noble peasant" and their spontaneous energy, deployed this down-to-earth stance in their critique of Stalinism and the bureaucratic decay of Marxism.

Alain Badiou is a case in point. A student and then a faculty member in L'École normale supérieure—France's most prestigious university for social thinkers—Badiou studied under Althusser but departed from his teacher and formed his own Maoist group in May 1968. His work arose in a context of widespread Maoism and Third Worldism. Frustrated by capitalist modernity mired in social disintegration, racism, spiritual hollowness, and rampant consumerism, the French leftists looked to the socialist model as well as the Third World as an alternative future. They launched radical critiques of dogmatic Marxism, Soviet revisionism, and French authoritarianism. Although many French Maoists have since grown out of Maoist radicalism, Badiou remains unrepentant and his work has been noted and welcomed by China's New Left.[47]

Badiou and his group engaged the people, working classes, and marginalized groups. By keeping with Mao's credo of "Going to the people" and mass-line method, they worked and studied with immigrants in the shantytowns on the outskirts of Paris. They lived with and mobilized workers on the factory floors and organized grassroots revolutionary councils. Mao's 1927 "Report on an Investigation of the Peasant Movement in Hunan" encouraged them to conduct close investigations of the living and working conditions of French farmers, with the goal of unleashing "the great revolts of poor peasants."[48]

On the theoretical front, Badiou broke with Althusser's structural Marxism. Approaching the state as a watertight and totalitarian apparatus, Althusser advanced the theory of "history without a subject," negating "the role of political subjectivity" and the transformative power of mass politics. Taking issue with this dogma, Badiou adhered to the Maoist emphasis on the revolutionary virtue and political subjectivity of the peasant masses. Viewing the Cultural Revolution and May 1968 student movement as testament to grassroots rebellion, he advocated an emerging political subjectivity against the French bureaucracy and the military-industrial complex. The outcry of grassroots political subjects, surging into tidal waves in the global sixties, was directed against the phenomenon of "depoliticization."[49] A penetrating diagnosis of political decay and atrophy in the top-heavy military-industrial-academic complex in the Cold War era, the term *depoliticization* exposes liberal democracy in deep crisis. The capitalist modernization paradigm gave rise to political paralysis, and governments in the East and West degenerated into arbitrary state power.

By reenergizing political subjectivity among mobilized masses, the French Maoists sought to jumpstart mass politics by making common cause with Third World revolts against the global superpowers. By reviving dynamic energy and transformative potential from below—from societies, communities, villages, streets, factories, and above all the insurgent people—they challenged the Euro-American Cold War hegemony.

Badiou's reading of the Maoist belief in the dynamism and energy of the revolutionary masses shed a different light on the Mao cult, the most maligned feature of Cultural Revolution Maoism. Badiou views the veneration of Mao not as a sign of authoritarianism and emperor worship but as a faith in the people's power and popular democracy, a rearticulation of mass-line interaction between leaders and led. Rather than quasi-religious activities, Mao's cult signals the groundswell of mass movement and an upsurge of revolutionary subjectivity. Faulting liberal democracy for its depoliticization and bureaucratic tendencies, he conceives personal charisma as a flash point for rebooting mass movements.

In the Cultural Revolution, Mao's cult included a textual dimension centered on Mao's *Little Red Book*. An intense religious atmosphere surrounded the activities and rituals of Mao's images and words. Everyday life was immersed in the study sessions, discussions, lectures, public performances of Mao's poems and quotations, ritualistic confessions of one's errant thoughts, and diary writing for self-criticism. The ubiquitous study session seemed to be a form of text-based indoctrination similar to religious catechism, designed not to disseminate knowledge but to foster faith and loyalty. Far from being a new thing, the practice was firmly in China's revolutionary tradition. Treating Yan'an as a discourse community, David Apter and Tony Saich have noted that such text-centered activities contain "certain proto-religious characteristics intertwined in a secular theory of politics that identified logos with power."[50]

Taking issue with this view, Badiou penetrates through the religious mist to discover a political dynamic under the sign of charismatic politics. Andreas Kalyvas's account of charisma in the contemporary crisis of liberal democracy is helpful for understanding this charismatic religious politics. Charismatic politics addresses "religious movements striving to control their communities by challenging the existing dominant beliefs, symbolic significations, and institutions."[51] Charisma-inspired movements seek to forge a new collective will in order to transform the existing structure of political power while affecting the moral orientation of human behavior. Religious leaders inspired groups that scatter in a "plural and contested terrain" where different spiritual and ideological agents compete for the control of symbolic power and sense making. "By virtue of a personal call and of some charismatic qualities," the charismatic leader will "proclaim a new set of values and a new substantive vision of the world, seeking to respond to the growing fears and distress of the masses and to capitalize on their shaky but gradually increasing disillusionment vis-à-vis the established authority."[52]

While the ritual and study sessions surrounding Mao's *Little Red Book* evinced a top-down authority, a deeper analysis reveals an unpredictable and ambivalent process of reading and interpretation. The Red Guards groups would deploy Mao's words in debates and demonstrations. In constantly mulling over the "true" meaning of Mao's texts, readers decentered and fragmented the authoritative words into heterogeneous readings and responses. Textual authority was embroiled in a war of words and split apart through contradictory interpretations, plunging sense making into "a state of constant flux."[53] Instead of condemning the ritual of reading Mao's words, Badiou reconsiders the similar interpretive fluidity and multiplicity in religious practice in the West.

Linking hero worship to personality cult, Badiou discovers the romantic, creative, and transformative potentials of charismatic politics. Liberal education in the West does not dispense with hero worship: it has transferred godlike creativity to the individual artist blessed with genius. The extolling of the artist is a cultural survival from Christianity, as words of high aesthetic value are recited and memorized with reverence by schoolchildren.

But this "religious" aspect is regarded not as indoctrination but liberal education, which opens the mind and fosters the critical faculty. If liberal critics value the artist's extraordinary creativity and imagination as evocations of the cultural ethos, quips Badiou, why should they look askance at a politically engaged artist—a political creator?

By virtue of a power to rally young students and disenfranchised workers in revolt, Mao presents the image of a popular hero, one who is out to create a new world by destroying the defunct one. If it is legitimate to valorize the artist, it is much riskier and dangerous and indeed more subversive to glorify a key agent of a political movement. This is because the political innovator seeks to change the world by rallying popular support: in Mao's case, inspiring and galvanizing young people into rebuilding society and reinventing culture. It is in fact "more meaningful," writes Badiou, "to sacralize political innovators, because political creation is rarer, more risky, and more immediately addressed to all."[54]

One reason for mass revolts was that the Chinese party-state had abandoned the revolutionary spirit and lost touch with the ordinary people. Having atrophied into a top-heavy, elitist bureaucracy, the party-state pursued policies that aggravated the divide between state and society, the elite and the grassroots, the cities and the countryside, and industry and agriculture. Although it was the vanguard of the people in the revolutionary era, the party became entrenched in the bureaucratic hierarchy and obsessed with vested power and privilege, standing aloof from the masses. There was little that could guarantee that the party represent the people or be the "source of rationality."[55]

In this vacuum of representation, there arose the need for a Rousseauian expression of the general will, for "a representation of the representation."[56] With no other institutional guarantees available, something singular and unique, something powerful and charismatic, should take the place of the routine, procedural representation. Badiou paints a scenario of religious-aesthetic representation of the popular will:

Finally, one person, a single body, comes to stand for the superior guarantee, in the classical aesthetic form of genius. It is also curious . . . to see that, trained as we are in the theory of genius in the realm of art, we should take such strong offense at it when it emerges in the order of politics. For the communist parties, between the twenties and sixties, personal genius is only the incarnation, the fixed point, of the double representative capacity of the party. It is easier to believe in the rectitude and the intellectual force of a distant and solitary man than in the truth and purity of an apparatus whose local petty chiefs are well known.[57]

Mao's hostility toward party-state bureaucracy stems from an understanding of the Paris Commune and French anarchism. Marx's *Civil War in France*, with its exultation of the people's power embodied by the Paris Commune, was one of the widely read and discussed texts in the Cultural Revolution. The Paris Commune articulated the socialist principle of mass mobilization that enables working classes to take into their own hands the direction of public affairs and their duty and rights to become the masters of their own destinies. The commune also expressed the egalitarian credo that "dictated close relations between leaders and led in accordance with the anti-hierarchical principles" of the mass line. The mass line, paradoxically, depends on "the enormous personal authority and popular prestige of Mao Zedong," whose distrust of state power goes with "a claim to the special personal relationship with the people."[58] The personality cult, in other words, functions like a religious focal image in rallying popular support in radical social movements.

Mao warned that the party-state was leading China down the road of capitalism. "Capitalism," instead of referring to private property, capital, and the free market, points specifically to the institutional atrophy and retrenchment of the postrevolutionary party-state apparatus. The charge was directed at the fact that "officials in the upper echelon of the bureaucracy, by virtue of their power and privilege in the state apparatus, were acquiring material privileges and prestige and exploiting society as a whole."[59] The party-state apparatus had a vested interest in preserving the status quo and was resistant to social change.

One appeal of the Cultural Revolution springs from Mao's attempt to go outside the party and reconnect with the people. "Mao incarnates not so much the party's representative capacity" as a personal, charismatic focus for rallying political energy from outside the party against bureaucracy within the party. Going against his own party, Mao proclaimed that it was legitimate for the revolutionary masses to rebel and to bombard the headquarters. The image of Mao, a political innovator rather than the party chief, figures prominently with a religious aura in mass movements. It is, comments Badiou, a "revenge of singularity on representation."[60]

The widespread study sessions took the form of religious hagiography, the most remarkable being Mao's *Three Constantly Read Articles* (*Lao sanpian* 老三篇). The *Lao sanpian* puts emphasis not on the leader but on everyday heroes imbued with revolutionary spirit and the self-abnegating ethos. Rather than deify the leader, Badiou elevates the people's power and gives play to the energy of the masses in political participation and social change.

In his *Théorie du sujet*, he construes Maoism as the confidence in the people's power: "la subjectivation s'ordonne au discours de la croyance pour briser l'obstacle" (subjectivity formation follows the dictates of the discourse of belief in order to smash the obstacle).[61] Invoking Mao's text "The Foolish Old Man Who Removed the Mountains," Badiou claims that confidence in the people's power is the key to galvanizing the masses as Prometheans of political participation. "The Foolish Old Man" was a speech that Mao delivered at the Seventh National Congress of the Chinese Communist Party in 1945 in Yan'an. In it, Mao recalls the Taoist fable of the indefatigable old man, who urged and led his sons in an impossible mission: digging away two mountains in front of their house. This "utopian" undertaking moved the gods, who sent down fairies from heaven to carry the mountains away. At that moment, the United Front between the Guomindang and the communists was breaking apart and the fight continued against the Japanese. Mao says, "Today, two big mountains lie like a dead weight on the Chinese people. One is imperialism, and other is feudalism. The Communist Party has long made up its mind to dig them up. We must persevere and work unceasingly, and we, too, will touch God's heart. Our God is none other than the masses of the Chinese people. If they stand up and dig together with us, why can't these two mountains be cleared away?"[62]

Rather than imposing God's top-down decrees on the people, Mao uses the fable to urge that leaders and people work together. With concerted effort, the people may match the gods and prevail over adversity. The fable offers "la conviction qu'avoir confiance en soi-même dans le mode of la scission destructrice des constraints locales généralise le processus du sujet" (the conviction that having confidence in oneself in the mode of the destructive scission of local constraints generalizes the process of the subject).[63] Instead of a paragon of virtue for mass emulation, the Foolish Old Man figures as an impetus to the masses, who are mobilized to "attaquer le reel" (attack the real). Spurred by their own power and confidence, the masses are encouraged to overcome the passive resignation to the mountainlike status quo and achieve the impossible. Linking religious dimensions to mass mobilization, Christian Sorace sees "a widening of the religious divide" between Mao and the people.[64] On the other hand, the Foolish Old Man sutures the gap between heaven and earth, the leader and the led. As Mao says, "We, too, will touch God's heart. Our God is none other than the masses of the Chinese people." Linking popular democracy to religious imagery, the fable puts the leader back among the led and renders the masses into their own leaders.

As in *On the Docks*, the working people with right ideas, political consciousness, and dynamic energy could become the master of their society and destiny. Mao's poem "Farewell to the God of Plague" illustrates the people's power in making social change. During the Great Leap Forward, a campaign was underway to wipe out the plague of schistosomiasis in Yu Jiang County, Jiangxi province. Mao wrote the poem to honor the victory of this public health campaign. Beginning with a bleak scene of desolation, the poem describes how, despite the idyllic "green mountains and emerald streams," the plague has ravaged the land and left villages inhabited by ghosts and overgrown with brambles. As peasants battle and finally prevail over the disease, the poem takes an imaginary flight toward a mythical realm, where the legendary Cowherd asks about the human conditions on Earth. Although the Cowherd and Weaving Maid are mythological figures residing in the heavens, they are from peasant stock and have humble roots. Their earthly concern is greeted with the good news of people's power over the disease:

> Borne by the breezes of spring,
> A host of soft green willow twigs dance in the air.
> In this land of ours,
> Six hundred millions are all worthy of Yao and Shun in deed and in name.
> Rain of red petals will change into waves if we so desire,
> And green mountains will turn into bridges at our command.[65]

> 春風楊柳萬千條
> 六億神州盡舜堯
> 紅雨隨心翻作浪
> 青山著意化為橋

Spring returns to the magic land of China, *shenzhou*. A handiwork not by gods but by the people, the landscape is restored to its green health and bathed in a divine aura. But the honor is due everyone involved in the health campaign: "Six hundred millions are all worthy of Yao and Shun in deed and in name." As legendary kings in Chinese antiquity, Yao and Shun are reputed for their deep commitment to the well-being of ordinary people under the mandate of tianxia. But in socialist China, ordinary working people are taking over from the ancient rulers: they are at once leaders and the led, mythical and plebeian—movers and shakers of their own destiny. Like the mythical figure of the Foolish Old Man who removed the mountains, the people are capable of transforming the sky and changing the earth:

With our silver hoes
We till the five majestic peaks that pierce the clouds;
With our arms of iron
We shape the three mighty rivers that flow across the land.[66]

天連五嶺銀鋤頭落
地動三河鐵臂搖

These lines celebrate the sovereign power of the people, who are capable of leading themselves, organizing their labor, meeting challenges, and changing the world. The poem taps into the inexhaustible reservoir of energy, intelligence, and power of the masses in shaping the future. But all these accomplishments are still graced by the aura of kingly Yao and Shun, inspired by the Foolish Old Man and Mao's charisma. These transcendent figures are the saviors of the people, leading the people in a campaign of emancipation.

Despite ruptures with its imperial past, the Chinese Revolution retained a worldview with traces of tianxia. Mao's Third Worldism articulated a new world vision and placed China as the leader of developing nations. This mix of ancient and modern sought to heal the tianxia dream broken by colonialism and imperialism. Derived from China's revolutionary experience and socialist experiment, global Maoism presented itself as a political ideology as well as a developmental strategy. In its valorization of the peasantry, mass political subjectivity, and self-reliance, Maoism made a strong appeal to Third World developing nations. The strategy of mobilizing and empowering the masses against bureaucracy and political decay inspired Badiou to shed new light on French Marxism, social movements, and the Mao cult.

The Cold War, Depoliticization, and China in the American Classroom

THE EVENTS OF SEPTEMBER 11, 2001, dealt a blow to the myth of globalization and revealed the stark relation between culture and geopolitics. Shortly afterward, a visit to the local library in a New Jersey town opened my eyes to the artifacts, weapons, and photos of war on prominent display. These relics recall the times of the world wars, military interventions, and the sacrifice of young men who grew up in the neighborhoods. If curious about China, a library patron would have no difficulty finding about thirty to forty books a few steps away. China-related books fall into two categories. One set romanticizes a long tradition of the oriental culture, and the other narrates the harrowing experiences of living in the Mao era and the Cultural Revolution. Books like *Red Azalea* by Anchee Min, *Wild Swans* by Jung Chang, *Red Flower of China* by Zhai Zhenhua, and the like belong to a familiar genre of autobiography. Under the heading of "history" at Barnes and Noble, these books tell stories of personal tragedy, tortuous bildungsroman, and purgatory experiences under the so-called totalitarian regime. The first set enshrines China in a comfort zone of oriental civilization; the second one paints a "Red China" as a menace to the free world.

An unconscious link came to the surface between weapons for national security and oriental fantasies. The memorabilia testified not only to the World Wars but also to the agenda of national security and military interventions in the Cold War. But the world in the early 1990s seemed to indulge in a celebratory mood, hailing the end of the Cold War and the end of history. The new zeitgeist declared the world flat and predicted that things would move on the level field of trade, capital flow, and consumption. The Cold War, with confrontations between the sovereign nation-states, mutually assured destruction, and ideological conflict, had somehow gone the way of the dinosaurs. The age of capitalist globalization, intoxicated with cosmopolitan sentiments and prospects, would erase national boundaries and launch individuals into a brave new world.

By conjuring up the spectra of the Cold War, the events since September 11 gave the lie to this neoliberal myth of globalization. The spectral evocations of old-fashioned geopolitics—Pearl Harbor, the world wars, the Korean War, the Vietnam War, a new wave of cold war and assertive nationalism—returned with a vengeance. It is as if the world had lived in a daydream of global connection and harmony, only to be rudely awakened to the rugged terrain of geopolitics, interstate conflict, security threat, border tightening, and national self-preservation. Beneath the euphoria of globalization, the ashes of the Cold War seemed to be smoldering all along. Does globalization signal any change in the system of nation-states? How does the end of history affect the production of subjectivity and area studies?

Globalization obscures the century-old intertwinement of capital and interstate geopolitics in the mist of cosmopolitanism. The triumph of a new-fangled cosmopolitanism goes with the waning of socialist internationalism and Third Worldism. This has led to a general trend of depoliticization that hollows out political dynamics and subjectivity by erasing memories of social movements of the global sixties. A recall of the revolutionary past will hopefully provide an alternative political language and shed critical light on Chinese studies in the American classroom.

The post–Cold War rise of transnational capitalism obscures the stark geopolitical landscape of tension and alignment between major nation-states during the Cold War, recasting the world as a cosmopolitan, free marketplace. In its unceasing expansion, global capitalism is said to be hostile to national territory and sovereignty, which resists and limits capital's horizontal "free" flow. Although the powerful nation-states were the real drivers of global capital expansion since the nineteenth century, capitalism in the late twentieth century appeared to cut loose from state control and wield a power "over a bounded and segmented social terrain."[1] For Gilles Deleuze and Félix Guattari, late capitalism in the high Cold War era already evinced a boundless appetite for world markets, labor, and resources, morphing into globalized flows and massive deterritorialization and breaking down geopolitical boundaries and state sovereignty.[2] Pitting capital's centrifugal dispersal against national sovereignty, Michael Hardt and Antonio Negri see the entire history of modernity in terms of a tension between the modern state and denationalized capital. Globalization, beginning in the Cold War's waning years, bears witness to a "one-sided movement from sovereignty's transcendent position toward capital's plane of immanence."[3]

"The plane of immanence" captures capital's inherent transnational tendency marked by a self-running, inexorable logic. Like a natural law, the logic of capital is apparently unchecked and unimpeded by the nation-state. In the Cold War era, however, capital's freewheeling profile was not so obvious. Caught in the confrontation between sovereign nation-states engaged in what Mearsheimer calls "great power politics," the nation-state played a pivotal role in powering and advancing capitalism and modernization.[4] Examining the cozy alliance between the imperialist state and market expansion, and between the military-industrial complex and culture, Virginia Carmichael designates the cultural and intellectual dimension of the Cold War as "Cultural Cold War" or the military-industrial-academic complex. Integrating technoscientific knowledge with power and capital with overseas intervention, the Cold War was also an ideological and religious war, featuring a rhetoric, a narrative, a moral drama propelled by the Manichean clash between good and evil, capitalism and communism, modernity and tradition. The intertwined operation of power and legitimacy, of colonial domination and civilizational missions, ran on a dual track: the hard-core strategies went hand in hand with ideological justification. Scholars, researchers, media, and think tanks participated in the cultural cold war to furnish myth, imaginations, and narratives as part of the military-industrial megamachine.[5] Cold War ideology reflects a "cosmopolitan" impulse to picture foreign affairs as a liberal agenda of promoting human rights and democracy for all mankind. In the era of globalization, this liberal tendency escalated into a utopian vision of market, trade, and growth as the conduit for international cooperation and global democracy, generating a cosmopolitan aura of freedom, empire, rule of law, norms, and transnationalism.

A closer look, however, reveals that the Cold War rhetoric of democracy and freedom barely veiled the stark geopolitical aggressiveness of the powerful nation-states. Consider the Cold War rationale raised by George Kennan. In a 1948 secret State Department memorandum, Kennan urged that the United States should invest in the realpolitik of military and economic domination rather than indulge in moralistic rhetoric of human rights, development, and improved living standards. Alert to the fact that the United States had 6.3 percent of the world's population but possessed 50 percent of its wealth, Kennan warned of inflammable situations of social upheavals, such as revolution or anti-hegemonic movement. "Our real task" in the coming period, wrote Kennan, "is to devise a pattern of relations which will permit us to maintain this position of disparity without positive detriment to our national security."[6] The long-term interests of the United States would be best served by policy directed toward the maintenance and concentration of wealth, capital, and resources.[7] However, human rights rhetoric has never dropped out. The strategy combining realpolitik and modernization allowed a powerful nation to emerge, which "wielded a military stick and dollar carrot to forge imperialist empire such as man has never known before."[8]

In the name of modernization and development, capitalism during the Cold War spread a myth of cosmopolitanism. What lay behind the myth was military occupation, arms race, interfering with affairs of other nations, violation of treaties, and regime change, causing constant hot wars in peripheral regions. Driven by national self-interests and neocolonialism, capitalist expansion depended heavily on the military-industrial machinery for its smooth operation at home and abroad. The state and capital worked in cahoots to manage America's world agenda. As Carmichael writes, the Cold War agenda included "the national security state, with foreign policy priority over domestic; massive military development and buildup; overt and covert non-democratic political, economic, military, and cultural intervention in and manipulation of the affairs of the other nations; and the most effective and enduring dispersal and silencing of dissent in a (legally) totally enfranchised and constitutional democracy in history."[9]

Recent talk of globalization, with its fiction of postnational, cosmopolitan world order, has thrown a veil over this realpolitik condition. The cultural and economic aspects of the Cold War came to the fore in the media and in public discourse. As culture and commodity, capital flows across a flat world of market, free trade, transnational trends, and financial investment. With the bipolar Cold War structure out of the way, the global superhighway seemed wide open for the realization of a liberal cosmopolitan order. Yet for all the euphoria, the rift has deepened between claims for democratic self-rule and military intervention.

The new cosmopolitanism arose on the heels of waning socialist internationalism and Third World movements of the global sixties. It has reshaped Chinese studies by hollowing out the political dynamics of social movements and by sweeping revolution into the dustbin. Fabio Lanza's recent book *The End of Concern* offers refreshing insights into this process. By unearthing the history of a group of Asian scholars buried under the rubble of the Cold War, Lanza invoked memories of Third World movements and China's socialist experiments. The concerned scholars broke away from orthodox Asian studies and rallied around the journal *Bulletin of Concerned Asian Scholars*. Sharing an affinity with the French Maoists such as Badiou and Jacques Rancière, the young radicals "framed themselves in opposition to the imperialist venture of Vietnam and to US policy in Asia in general."[10] They embraced revolutionary changes in China and rural reconstruction in developing Asian countries, drew lessons and critical insights from the socialist experiment, and identified with the aspiration for an alternative world. Their anti-imperial and anti-colonial stance prompted them to reflect and critique the separation of scholarship and politics in American academe. Decrying the complicity of mainstream Asian studies with the hegemonic powers, they probed into ideologies that undergirded the developmental model premised on modernization, orientalism, and neocolonialism. Although Lanza laments the retreat of the cohort's theoretic critique and the tragic fates of some scholars in the post–Cold War era, his work pulls the chestnuts from the flame, offering a critical perspective from the past to illuminate the present.

One major problem with contemporary Asian studies is the retreat of political consciousness in terms of depoliticization. To reiterate, "depoliticization" (*qu zhengzhi hua* 去政治化) describes the absence of public debate, intellectual reflection, ideological argument, and concern about public issues and global crises. In the amnesia of these big-picture issues, China's image has been neutralized into a developmental process on track with global capital. In the era when all nations seem to be jumping on the neoliberal bandwagon, the poignant irony is that China is back to square one, back to its old bourgeois beginning that Mao dubbed "old democracy." We recall that the bourgeois nation building, led by Sun Zhongshan and the Guomindang, was to make China in the image of the West. The Chinese Revolution under "New Democracy" reoriented the bourgeois national project into a socialist path, predicated on the people's democracy, mass mobilization, and social transformation. But beginning with the post–Cold War era, area studies reverted back to the shopworn modernization paradigm that cookie-cuts every nation to fit into the capitalist orbit. Chinese studies began to demonstrate how China has returned to the universal norm of West-led modernity. Scholars began to celebrate the positive role of foreign capital in breaking down the isolated and centralized system.[11]

This situation was precisely what the concerned Asian scholars critiqued and rebelled against. They looked at China as a mirror to reflect on and critique the scholarship trapped in Cold War ideology. Scholarly works on Asia "too often spring from a parochial, cultural perspective and *serve self-interest and expansion.*"[12] Mortgaged to a depoliticized, objective approach rooted in a positivistic epistemology, the modernization paradigm sees China as a local instance that is being enfolded into the international norm. China was scrambling to "become like us."

As one of the concerned Asian scholars, Paul Cohen reexamined the links between the modernization paradigm, Cold War ideology, and imperialist expansion. American historians, as part of the system in shaping the American image of modern China, in the postwar years had also "taken a leading part in the creation of conceptual paradigms for understanding it."[13] Pitting modernity against tradition, they perceived Chinese culture as being devoid of real history and dynamic change. Imperial China had been stagnant in an immutable tradition until it was jolted out of its age-old slumber by impacts from the West. Modern changes in China are to be measured by how well or miserably the country is able to make the grades in catching up with the West. With economic growth and political reform as the sole measures, the modernization paradigm writes off as tragic aberrations a whole history of revolutionary China, trashing its national liberation, decolonization, socialism, aid to the Third World, and internationalism. In short, the paradigm invalidates the experiences of the Chinese people in taking charge of their destiny and entering the world stage.

The recoil from the paradigm, however, seems to be a retreat into an ahistorical notion of China-centered history. Self-contained, aloof, and unscathed by imperialist and capitalist penetration, an "authentic" China emerges behind the bamboo curtain, enclosed in the millennia tradition and closed to the world. Despite this mystified assumption of the Other, one may give the benefit of the doubt. Cohen's inquiry into a "history inside China," whose legacy remains active in modernity, challenges the objectivity and neutrality of area studies. Pointing to an alternative worldview rooted in Chinese history and tradition, the China-centered lens reinstates ideological and intellectual debate back into Asian studies. Targeting US involvement in Vietnam and Indochina, the oil embargo of 1973, and the Iran hostage crisis of 1979–81, Cohen perceives a symbolic meaning of Vietnam as a subject of criticism, which opened up a space for soul-searching, guilt, and heightened political consciousness. The meaning of Vietnam "confronted us with the limits of our power, the very real constraints upon our capacity to bend the world to American purposes. This second meaning of Vietnam also . . . had a profound impact on American historians of China. By exposing the myth of American global supremacy—political, moral, cultural—it freed American historians, perhaps for the first time, to abandon Western norms and measures of significance and to move toward a more genuinely *other*-centered historiography, a historiography rooted in the historical experience not of the West but of China."[14] It is an irony that Cohen's critical vigilance in the Cold War seems to be swallowed up in the post–Cold War return to the modernization paradigm and neoliberal development.

Depoliticization in Asian scholarship is most evident in the methodological reduction of the sovereign people and political collectives into inert objects for "scientific" inquiry. As political, world-making subjects, a national people is the vital link between a socialist nation and Third World movements. Socialist internationalism and anti-colonialism were the ideological grounds for national-popular movements to reach out and connect with the world. But the modernization paradigm breaks the link between the people and the world. Challenging that method, the concerned Asian scholars took a new look and approached China and its influence in the Third World "as a subject of its own history and politics."[15] This affirms the revolutionary claim that the people are the motive force for world-historical change. In the spirit of Third World internationalism, the Chinese and peoples in Asia, Africa, and Latin America actively participated in the movement of decolonization and pursued socialist values and self-reliant development. As masters of their own societies, they made domestic changes in order to overcome the pitfalls of colonialism and capitalism. Revolutionary and socialist China represented a hotbed of activity and vibrant transformations. In the post–Cold War era, however, China became a mere "geopolitical location."[16] Forgotten are "Maoist economic experiments, land redistribution in liberated Vietnam, Indian peasant rebellions," among other concerns.[17]

Predicated on the mobilized Chinese people as political subjects, China's socialist experience defined its political identity as grounded in the working-class leadership and the worker-peasant alliance. The notion of the people's democracy opens the door to an internationalism based on people-to-people connections. To Lanza, this characterization is not only Chinese but also international. "It was on the basis of these categories that transnational connections, such as the relationship between the Second and Third World, the alliance of formerly colonized people—and . . . the very recognition of political subjects across the continents—was possible."[18]

Depoliticization and China's Self-Image

With the global sixties as a reference, two conflicted Chinas emerged on the world stage. One China pursued socialist and Third World internationalism; the other is now engaging "socialism with Chinese characteristics," a process that seems to abandon socialism, and is dubbed by some critics "capitalism with Chinese characteristics."[19] Before, solidarity and alliance among decolonized and independent nations defined China's world image; now, a globalism partaken by China becomes crystallized with the catchphrase "get on track with the world." Culturally, this agenda has fueled a cosmopolitanism of commodity, style, finance, and consumerism.

For many, a global China has emerged from the dark world of Mao's era. In the previously mentioned biographies loaded with harrowing narratives of repression and victimhood, Mao's China trailed miserable track records in human rights and freedom. But China is different now and is moving on a racetrack to catch up with "our" modernity. The trashing of revolutionary China continues the Cold War imaginary by positing an evil other so as to assure voters of the righteousness of liberal democracy and a "national" security in East Asia. The globalized China, on the other hand, goes with the neoliberal world picture. Both perceptions depoliticize China—by treating it as a shadowy entity whose significance is granted by external agencies and observers. China is seen either as a reluctant member of the world community or a threatening empire ready to wield its ominous power. These views ignore China as an autonomous nation-state capable of charting its own course and taking control of its future.

China's global image corresponds with its liberal self-understanding. It is a China that has finally awakened to the universal history of worldwide economic development. China moves to the world by repudiating more than a half century of revolutionary and socialist experience. Despite its preservation of the "red legacy," the official policy seems to favor further integration into the global market and unbridled economic growth. China's deepening involvement and increasing power in the global financial superstructures reflect a desire to make a clean break with the historical "aberrations" of the socialist past.

The revisionist negation of dark and tragic pasts is most evident in the narrative of trauma and memory. Numerous books have contributed to a culture industry that cashes in on the theme of trauma and victimhood, recounting harrowing experiences of individuals living under communist rule. These eyewitness and personal accounts of hunger, oppression, and repression correspond strongly to the indictment and the search-for-roots literature of the mid-1980s. The main plotlines feature tales of bildungsroman or the saga of freedom seekers in a fight against tyranny (the victims all come out scarred but unscathed). But rescues and redemption often come from the West, especially the United States. It is no accident the writers are mostly immigrants safely nestled in the United States, who look back at the other shore with fear and trembling. It is disturbing to see books of this kind arranged in libraries and touted by online retailers as the "true history" of modern China.

Easy acceptance of these narratives as historical truths puts to rest the historical and massive drive by millions of people in shaping their own destiny. Individual accounts of trauma and suffering personalize history and dissolve the persistent, unresolved problems of modern China—problems that do not end with the Cold War and integration into the global market. As Dirlik and Meisner observed, personal narratives reduce the historical understanding of complex, long-term problems embedded in Chinese history to "spatially and temporally limited tropisms" or figures.[20] Wielding an aesthetic power by couching personal experience in a melodramatic form, the trope privileges personal encounters over reflection, inquiry, and historical examination of collective problems and systemic issues. The reader is called on to like or dislike out of personal preference, not to delve into the historical context and social implications. Here we get an aesthetic that says what you see is what you get and there is nothing behind or off the screen. The personal is political or rather erases politics. The testimonies are proffered not "in explicit arguments or by systematic analyses that bring up concrete issues for discussion and debate."[21] They play on the desire for black-and-white clarity, enforcing the Cold War divide of freedom versus authoritarianism.

The individualistic account rests on the premise of history as a melodramatic, dog-eat-dog fight rather than motivated collective movements geared toward emancipation and social progress. Buttressed further by individualistic methodology and atomistic individualism, this narrative creates superficial entertainment by erasing systematic, political, and social reflection. This type of history writing has affected "Third World cinema," which is now oriented increasingly toward the cinematic staging of the spectacle of the historical past as melodramatic clashes of individual desire, ambition, and power. Merging with the aesthetic flow of capitalist culture industry, Chinese cinema is getting on the bandwagon as an instance of capital's worldwide expansion.[22] To get a sense of this trend, we may consider a Chinese film titled *Once Upon a Time in Shanghai* (*Shanghai jishi* 上海紀事, 1998).

Made in 1998 and directed by Peng Xiaolian, the film was commissioned and funded by the Shanghai municipal government to commemorate the fiftieth anniversary of the communist liberation of the city. Receiving favorable reviews and a major prize, the film was successful in rewriting Shanghai's history as a replenished icon of capitalist modernity. With its focus on Shanghai's liberation by the communists, the film may fall into the category of "red classics." Nicolai Volland cautions that the revival of the red classics or the main melody (*zhuxuanlü* 主旋律) in the 1990s could be "exploited by crass commercialism" and betrayed a vaunted "national pride" and "transnational trends."[23] *Once Upon a Time in Shanghai* is such a superficial work of the main melody. Far from affirming the history of liberation, the film replaces the genuine melody of class struggle and mass politics with the flying colors of global capitalism.

The film begins with a series of melodramatic mise-en-scènes of chaos resulting from the Guomindang leader Chiang Jieshi's ill-conceived plan to regulate the financial market. The rush on banks and stores, the street riots, the battles with the People's Liberation Army, and the crackdown on financial speculation invoke the cinematic clichés of war and the collapse of a Third World nation embroiled in turmoil. These retro-style scenes strip the volatile and potentially dynamic circumstances of political agendas. The economic and financial turmoil underscores the city's woes as a managerial and economic issue rather than a political struggle. The battles between the communists and nationalists, the day-to-day political activities of the population, the military action, the restoration of social order—all these seem to be bubbles in the film's single-minded gravitation toward the bottom line of Shanghai's financial and economic fate.

The managerial logic has its counterpart in characterization. The real hero with a mission to pull the city out of the woods is not communists, workers, soldiers, or revolutionary leadership. Instead, a Western-educated, management-savvy woman, Li Huirong, steps up as the savior and liberator. Li manages a textile factory jointly owned by her father and father-in-law, who reside in America as overseas capitalists. The overseas connection highlights her role as the harbinger of global capitalism in China. As an offspring of the national bourgeoisie with the dream of industrialization, she would have been a negative image in any work of red classics. In this film, however, she takes on an unequivocally heroic and "progressive" flare. With little support from the communists and workers, Li works single-handedly to preserve the abandoned industrial infrastructure against terrorist sabotage by retreating nationalists. It seems as though Shanghai's economic survival and revival all hang on the courage, will, and ingenuity of this capitalist daughter.

This image of progressive capitalism takes on a romantic, feminine aura, as Li is portrayed as a lovely young wife and a street-smart, sophisticated Shanghai girl. The film's romantic episodes revolve around her as the object of affection for her husband, Guo. On the eve of liberation, Guo debates with himself over taking his wife to America or joining her in rebuilding national industry—a conflict of personal desire entangled with the dilemma of shaping China's future. A freelance journalist based in America, Guo professes to take an "objective" stance toward reporting Shanghai's liberation and new order. He grounds his "objectivity" on his eyewitness accounts to tell Chinese stories to the "outside world," but the objectivity is undercut by his ideological leaning toward his wife's patriotism. The "outside world" for his reports is the United States, which is in the midst of implementing the Cold War policy against a China being lost to communism. Objectivity is meaningless and useless at that moment—except for the film's retrospective look at the dawn of Shanghai's capitalism.

Toward the end of the film, a spy attempts to sabotage the industrial infrastructure by blowing up a power plant. In safeguarding the plant, Li gets into a fight and is killed by the saboteur, who turns out to be her classmate in a business school back in America. As she lies dying in her husband's arms, the spectacular fire, explosions, and destruction on the screen seem to celebrate the tragic sacrifice of the capitalist daughter, leaving no doubt as to the seeds planted for China's future. From the scene of death and destruction, the camera cuts, magically traversing fifty years to the present, to Guo standing on the Bund of Shanghai against a dazzling array of neon-lit signs, advertisements, and a glaring silhouette of towering financial buildings—a metaphor of the phoenix rising to meet the skylines. Guo has retreated to America after his wife's death and returns half a century later in the era of globalization to Shanghai, only to find her image forever young and refreshing. Consecrated in his memory, the capitalist wife magically blends into the new financial zone of Pudong bathed in mesmerizing simulacra, complete with skyscrapers, screen towers, and myriad lights—a virtual Manhattan in the Orient.

This cinematic spectacle glosses over the rugged historical terrain by linking a personal and melodramatic scenario to capitalist modernity: the personal story sows the seeds of capital, ironically, at the dawn of Shanghai's liberation. This nostalgic evocation, as Rebecca Karl observes, makes ostensible references to its prerevolutionary past but actually empties out socialist revolution.[24] The film reflects a desire to return to a past Shanghai as the outpost of semicolonial modernity and cosmopolitanism. Foretelling its future at the moment of its liberation, this Shanghai romance creates a myth of Chinese capitalism and recasts the history of Chinese socialism as aberrant and mistaken. This back-to-the-future strategy signals contemporary China as a capitalist juggernaut, with a booming economy that renders social contradictions and conflict into a culture of management and consumerism. Holding a return ticket to the glamorous future, the film affirms the hidden teleology of China's rush to the global market. By replenishing Shanghai as the vanguard of capitalist modernity, it erases the fifty years of Chinese revolutionary history, which, ironically, is what the film commemorates.

Consuming China in the American Classroom

Not just the media treat Chinese people as capitalists and consumers. College students also approach China with a consumer gaze. This reflects the imperial attitude toward the "Chinese difference." Critics have characterized the United States not as a nation but as an empire. Although it is difficult to convince a student that he or she may be an imperial subject, much evidence from the classroom suggests what may be called imperial attitude. "Imperial" does not simply mean superior or number one; it means my culture is "all under heaven." Although Coca-Cola or Hollywood may seem to be part of world culture, they are both thoroughly American and hence national in origin, products of a particular place and time. Yet this is precisely what eludes the imperial attitude, which assumes that what originates in America is not just American but the universal norm. This mentality resembles the nonchalant, "all under heaven" mindset criticized by Liang Qichao, who associated private morality with individuals unconcerned with the national community. Is this a tianxia with American characteristics?

Liang charged that Chinese knew their families, kin, and communities— discrete units under the Mandate of Heaven—but did not know themselves as a people. Living in the long shadow of dynastic empires, they did not know who they were as a political community. For the imperial attitude, there is only genealogy, no history; there is patriarch, no political participation of citizens; there is private affair, no public good.

Many students indulge in this imperial mentality, which is utterly at odds with the image of the citizen worthy of a nation, much less of the world. This attitude affects their understanding of a foreign culture. A Chinese culture class is designed to tell stories of Chinese society and history. "Chinese culture" entails a national character with fraught relations with cosmopolitanism. Understood in the sense of a certain national origin, of public activity, a stream of political events, and a drive to forge a people's destiny, the idea of national culture is increasingly foreign to college students. Writing against the self-advertising spectacle of pan-African culture, Frantz Fanon argues that every culture is primarily national, rooted in political struggles of a people on the ground.[25] Fredric Jameson also contends that an individual's fate in a Third World culture points to a collective project.[26] But this national dimension of culture is being displaced by a denationalized, cosmopolitan flatness, and so when "Chinese" is mentioned, you may be accused of being a bloody nationalist.

The supposition "My culture is the world" links individualism to a superficial cosmopolitanism. This self-centered attitude came under fire by the concerned Asian scholars during the Cold War. Looking to revolutionary China and Third World movements for alternative global relations, Mark Seldon has critiqued "atomized individuals" bent on private interest at the expense of the public good and saw the attitude as a sign of political decay and breakdown of republicanism and civic virtue.[27] In his 1987 book *The Closing of the American Mind*, published at the moment of transition from the Cold War to globalization, Alan Bloom diagnosed the obsessive inner-directedness of American students under the rubric of "self-centeredness." Students are preoccupied with their own relationships, sexuality, and career prospects, and "the affairs of daily life rarely involve concern for a large community in such a way so as to make public and private merge in one's thought."[28] Free from the constraints of nation, religion, family, and politics—all tragic burdens of the past—students experience American culture not as "a common project but as a framework within which people are only individuals, where they are left alone."[29] Dropping all cultural belonging and communal ties, they worry about making it economically in the marketplace and about seeking personal fulfillment, success, and status. This individualistically based culture regresses to a realm where the individual resides in a naked state of nature, stripped of all national backgrounds and historical memories. With regard to other cultural traditions, the attitude leads to a bland globalism that permits anything as long as it does not infringe on the individual's rights and privacy, placing the student at an equal distance from diverse cultures. World cultures amount to little more than a playground to project personal preferences and give vent to self-expression.

This self-absorption shuts students out from geopolitical events of the day and immures them from the ongoing events that grip the attention of concerned scholars in Chinese studies. This mindset stems from a deeper moral problem that Alasdair MacIntyre has theorized as "emotivism." Cutting oneself off from culture, history, and moral evaluation, the emotivist self bears directly on self-other relations. In conceiving moral judgments as "nothing but expressions of preference, expressions of attitude or feeling," emotivism removes the question of good or bad, of truth and falsehood, from moral debate. When the individual is entitled exclusively to their opinion and feelings, moral judgments are seen as neither true nor false. Consensus "is not to be secured by any rational method, for there are none. It is to be secured, if at all, by producing certain non-rational effects on the emotions or attitudes of those who disagree with one."[30] Whoever dominates and aestheticizes a show controls perception and shapes feelings. The moral question is thus turned into a theatrical performance for the purpose of producing aesthetic effects.

In social interaction, emotivism obliterates any distinction between manipulative and nonmanipulative relations. MacIntyre reminds us that in modern moral discourse, a human relationship bereft of morality differs radically from one informed by rational communication. The former denotes a relation in which "each person treats the other primarily as a means to his or her ends"; the latter is one in which "each treats the other as an end."[31] To treat someone as an end is to treat them not as an inert object but as a sovereign subject endowed with reason and discretion. In conversation, I may offer reasons and facts to show what is good, but I should refrain from influencing another "except by reasons which that other he or she judges to be good." On the basis of Kantian universalism, this moral reason appeals to a common, shared ground, which is not dictated by you and me from a particular vantage point. Further, treating the person as the end entails mutual respect for the integrity and dignity of people who are party to a conversation: "By contrast, to treat someone else as a means is to seek to make him or her an instrument of my purposes by adducing whatever influences or considerations will in fact be effective on this or that occasions."[32] Referencing Henry James's *The Portrait of a Lady*, MacIntyre illustrates the rendering of the individual as an aesthetic object of consumption. Rich aesthetes in European villas preoccupy themselves with seeking thrills and warding off boredom. They get their daily diet of amusement by "contriving behavior in others that will be responsive to their wishes, that will feed their sated appetite."[33] Treating the other as a consumer item, the emotivist individual behaves as the consumer of persons.

The Kantian maxim "to treat someone as an end" contains a genuine cosmopolitan ethic. It could be extended to "treat a nation as an end." This means to treat each sovereign nation and its people as the master of their own destiny; to respect a nation's culture, history, and national development. The self-centered, imperial stance, however, encourages students to treat China as a means for their own private purposes. One could list five ways of approaching China. First, China is a commodity; it is a flavor of food in a multinational, multiethnic buffet and thus a source of pleasure. Second, a student may act like a connoisseur of national geographical exotica, seeking to satisfy touristic wanderlust. Third, utilitarianism motivates students to study China and its culture, prompting them to see the country in terms of market value and profit in global capital expansion. The question of China's own way of sociopolitical development or historical trajectory is irrelevant. Fourth, students view China from the capacity of a therapist, believing that as a pathological case, China is a maladjusted country that needs to receive shock therapy for it to become normal. Finally, China supplies a canvas to project the individual's ego, attitudes, feelings, and preferences.

Such self-absorption shuts students out from geopolitical events of the day and from the ongoing drama and traumas. They do not have to be concerned with the questions of what China was and is striving for. The country's unique way of sociopolitical development and history is not their concern. What this nation has been doing on its own terms, its revolutionary movements, the creativity and agency of the Chinese people, are irrelevant.

Chinese Literature and the World

Is "Chinese literature" a meaningful concept? Should it be replaced with "world literature"? There are two pitfalls in thinking about national and world literature. On the one hand, it is myopic to pin the culture down to the allegiance to the nation-state. On the other hand, a world vision is not a transcendent observation over and above the nation but an awareness of human conditions linked to a particular nation's aspirations for a common world.

In Chinese culture classes, the historical coverage of reading material plays an important role in the selection of authors and periods. How does one pick seven or eight authors for a literature course? A genuinely historical appreciation of Chinese culture and history hinges on a particular curve of historical events and a choice of authors. For example, students may not like to study old films made before the reform era of the 1980s and prefer newer films made in the twenty-first century. This presentist preference gets them excited quickly about familiar images of urban youth and juvenile delinquency, romantic relationships, consumerist lifestyle, and so on. Never mind these have become stale and uninteresting in the American media. Students readily relate to the familiar scenes and characters dressed up in Chinese trappings.

Motivated by a sense of continuous history, the older films are selected for teaching in order to showcase China's creative as well as tragic attempts to deal with problems and challenges in modern times. Without a sense of the crisis-ridden trajectory in dealing with themes of colonialism, imperialism, and upheavals, the student's perception of China would remain a series of unconnected, shallow snapshots, palatable, consumable, touristic. Worse, serving up quick snapshots caters more to a narcissist navel gazing than critical inquiry into Chinese history.

Although some students may be open minded and curious about China, this attitude can only go so far. China should be manageable and containable. Numerous threats loom large: A powerful China will inevitably disturb the power balance in East Asia and is posing a threat to US interests and security in the Asia-Pacific region. A fast-developing China will be a grave rival for oil, high tech, capital, and natural resources. A prosperous China will lead to military buildup and expansionism and the pursuit of the hegemon in Asia.[34] The sense of existential threat plays a role in shaping students' plans for China-related careers. In a recent Chinese-language class at a university in Texas, students professed that they had basically two goals in studying China. The professor, a former student of mine, said that more than half of the students were from the oil tycoon families with private jets and thought of themselves as future leaders of America. They would deal with China as diplomats, statesmen, or businessman. It is hard to underestimate the utilitarian implications of Chinese pedagogy in the geopolitical landscape: China is an object, a target, an enemy, and a rival for the United States. Chinese culture does not matter; it is a means, not an end. The point of learning the Chinese language is to facilitate intelligence gathering as a means of containing the country. With the goal of maintaining American domination in the Pacific and other regions, Chinese studies was and is the academic arm of the State Department, an enterprise of strategic importance and interstate rivalry, and academic research is no different from strategic think tanks.

Geopolitical rivalry goes with the notion of China as a cultural museum. Derived from the essentialist view of a national community, this belief goes back to cosmopolitanism and multiculturalism. As Robert Hymes puts it, the essentialist approach tends to regard diverse materials in a culture as "contained in one complete, logically compelling package or structure." A culture is typecast in "a shared and unitary system, all of its parts somehow dependent on one another or informed by a single principle of ethos, and all of its parts common property."[35]

This essentialist view resurfaces in the pervasive notion of civilizational clash. Samuel Huntington sees political and social changes in China in the post–Cold War era as a recipe for coming cultural clashes. A litany of Asian cultural patterns in opposition to universal Western values underscores the differences between Asian and American civilizations. The Confucian ethos "stressed the values of authority, hierarchy, the subordination of individual rights and interests, the importance of consensus, the avoidance of confrontation, 'saving faces,' and in general, the supremacy of the state over society and of society over the individual."[36] By contrast, Americans hold on to "beliefs of liberty, equality, democracy, and individualism." It is quintessentially American to distrust government, oppose authority, promote checks and balances, encourage competition, sanctify human rights, forget the past and ignore the future, and focus on maximizing immediate gains.[37] Thanks to these absolute, irreconcilable differences, cultural clashes are inevitable.

The world vision of cultural clash sees China as a lag in the modernization timeline. In my Chinese literature classes, works of the earlier period by Lu Xun, Shen Congwen, Ding Ling, and Eileen Chang are prominent on the reading list. In addition, more recent works from the reform era, such as *Raise the Red Lantern* by Su Tong and *To Live* by Yu Hua, help students understand China's economic reforms and cultural changes. For a time, the favorite was Dai Sijie's novel *Balzac and the Little Chinese Seamstress* and its film adaption. I would suggest that the preference for this film reflects a stance of cultural clash with Eurocentric implications.

The film *Balzac and the Little Chinese Seamstress* tells the story of two educated youth, sent down to the countryside for reeducation during the Cultural Revolution. While trapped in a mountainous village, they steal a box of books from another youth and get to read books by Balzac and other Western literary masters. An ironic jab at the reeducation campaign of Chinese youth during the Cultural Revolution, the reading experience is depicted as a religious revelation. Reading Balzac awakens the educated youth to universal values of freedom, individualism, love, and sex. Taking the text as sacred, Ma Jianling, one of the two sent-down youths, piously inscribes a whole chapter of Balzac's book on a sheepskin coat. This parchment signals the "godsend" of Western culture bequeathed to uncivilized and unenlightened Chinese youth and peasants. The Western classics change the youth's lives and, through their dissemination, the lives of the villagers, who have never seen a car or been to a modern city. The two youths develop a romantic relation with the seamstress, and under their tutelage the illiterate girl quickly becomes "enlightened" and savvy about female beauty, modern ways, and consumer fashions, including the use of bras. The seamstress's decision to leave her village signals the triumph of civilization over barbarian backwardness and benighted tradition.

Playing out on the civilizational hierarchy between a superior "us" and inferior "them," the film extends the divide to the tension between freedom and authoritarianism, modernity and tradition. The first episode pits Western civilization against a backwater of barbarism and was so compelling and irresistible as to generate glowing comments in the media. On *The Diane Rehm Show* on National Public Radio in 2003, every "China hand" pundit raved about it. The scenario begins with the urban youth's arrival in the mountain village. As peasants crowd around the young men in a dimly lit, rickety house, they spot a mysterious object: a violin. They condemn the violin as an evil bourgeois toy and hasten to burn it. The owner of the violin, Ma, protests that it is a musical instrument and wants to demonstrate by playing a Mozart sonata. With remarkable ingenuity, his friend comes up with the name for the piece: "Mozart Thinks of Chairman Mao." Having passed the ideological test, Ma begins to play the violin and the peasants immediately fall under the spell of the elegant music. With the sweet, graceful melody of Mozart's sonata flowing from the house to the crowd watching at the window, and from the crowd to the mountain ridges, the peasants seem to be undergoing an epiphany. They are discovering their "innate" human potentials for this gift of universal culture. The camera slowly backs off from the house and takes a long, panning shot over the mountain ridges and the open sky. For the first time since time immemorial, the mountain village is ringing with heavenly music and awakening to a taste of high culture from the West.

Students in my class welcome these signs of Chinese becoming enlightened about freedom, love, sex, and individualism. The irony, alas, is that Balzac is no longer a familiar name for students. We recall that Balzac was at the top of Zhou Libo's list in the world literature class in Yan'an (chapter 3). Mozart may be more familiar, but few students can name a Mozartian piece. The pundits on NPR would not fare better. How do we account for this gap between the ignorance of one's own culture, which is yet coupled with self-pride and superiority? Probably the knowledge of Balzac or Mozart does not matter so much: it is gratifying enough to see the unenlightened Chinese peasants rush to embrace our Western culture.

In this self-love, "our" Western culture is not just any particular culture; it is unconditioned by historical time and particular places; it is universal civilization, the bottom line of humanity. Culture and enlightenment here turn into a code word for superiority, progress, and advance. In the film, the religious inscribing of Balzac's words on the sheepskin overcoat is coupled with another scenario about a Chinese priest's deathbed confession. As he lies dying in the hospital, the priest has lost the memory of his mother tongue, Chinese. Yet as he struggles to utter parting words to his children, what comes out of his mouth is a stream of Latin phrases from the Latin Bible that he cherished in his early years. The students and talk show pundits take this linguistic switch for granted, as if it were the most natural things that a good Chinese can do, affirming the power of the West's civilizing mission. The message is clear: these suffering, benighted Chinese, political victims of their own country, will be able to redeem themselves, body and soul, by abandoning their own culture and prostrating before the icons of Balzac or Latin scriptures.

To see Balzac as cosmopolitan godsend is to ignore the history of Balzac's reception in China in connection with the Chinese Revolution and Chinese literature. Balzac has long been an important motif in modern Chinese criticism and literature, and generations of Chinese writers and critics studied and loved the French writer. The best-known Chinese translator of French literature, Fu Lei, translated Balzac's major novels since the 1940s. A huge body of artworks, the Balzac translations educated generations of Chinese readers, critics, and writers. In the complete oblivion of this side of Balzac, *Balzac and the Little Chinese Seamstress* becomes patently Eurocentric. This forgetfulness goes with another lack: the educated youth, while having access to the whole box of books, is indifferent to Chinese books. Books by Lu Xun and the highly regarded classics are passed over and remain unread.

The Eurocentric elevation of Balzac's fiction raises the question of world literature in the national-international nexus, harking back to Zhou Libo's lecture on world masterpieces at the Lu Xun Academy of Arts. Zhou explained

Balzac's significance not only for the novel but also for socialist realism, popular democracy, and mass movements. Balzac represents a mode of realism that discerns in naturalistic details historical and social movements. Driven by emergent people and popular nationalism, these trends run counter to the conservative elements and the power elites. Balzac's importance in Chinese literary criticism derives from the Marxist analysis of "typicality" in Balzac's fiction. In his letter to Margaret Harkness regarding her novel *City Girl*, Friedrich Engels wrote that rather than naturalist descriptions of wretched victims in *City Girl*, Balzac described the bourgeois and popular classes as an emergent historical trend and social force. Although a conservative and affiliated with the waning aristocracy, Balzac rubbed against the grain of his own politics and worldview. His novels depict the emergent characters who were representative of the lower classes and rising popular masses. A treasure trove of sociological details and motifs, Balzacian realism is nothing less than an archive of materialist history, loaded with "facts" about French society that are more insightful and objective than all Engels had learned from historians, economists, and statisticians. Balzacian realism creates an epic of historical transformation driven by "the real men of the future" as they emerge on the world arena. Engels's reading came to shape a cottage industry around Balzac, which was a forerunner of socialist realism and gestured toward the notion of world literature rooted in a national people. Just as the French Revolution attracted Liang Qichao for its creation of a republic linked to cosmopolitan aspirations, Balzac's fiction appealed to modern Chinese writers for its consciousness of historical change and realistic depictions of French society.

In the realistic and world-historical dimension, Balzac inspired Chinese critics and writers who believed literature to be a vehicle of national liberation and social emancipation. Rather than consecrated into a world republic of letters and accumulated capital and commodity, the lessons from Balzac forge the links between one nation and another and facilitate people-to-people communication. This, I think, is what Liang Qichao had in mind when he referred to the scenes of cultural exchange in the World Expo as datong in *The Future of a New China*.

A recall of the revolutionary tradition should allow students to steer clear of Eurocentrism and move to a historical understanding of modern China. A close reading of texts and a deeper awareness of the context may challenge the Cold War labels of communism, authoritarianism, and freedom. Watching the film *Yellow Earth*, for example, the students are readily drawn to the depiction of rural poverty, hopelessness, the depleted soil and nature, arranged marriage, women's suffering, and the desperate search for a new life in Yan'an. Emancipatory motifs based on an affinity with liberal ideas of freedom, individual well-being, and people's rights are recognizable and comprehensible. Why do these themes, presumably communist, make so much sense to the American students who know little about the historical backgrounds in Shaanxi province in North China? Why do they readily sympathize with the peasant girl Cui Qiao when she attempts to join the communist army and become a soldier? Why do students wish that she crosses the Yellow River to find a new home?

To close national and ideological differences, the American Revolution and Valley Forge come to mind. Surely the two revolutionary histories are far apart in space and time, but the different pursuits converge in the perception of a people trying to gain freedom and achieve independence from colonial rule. When it comes to the anti-colonial fight by soldiers led by George Washington and the Eighth Route Army's battle against Japanese aggressors, the difference between China's liberation and the American Revolution narrows and becomes unimportant. This imaginative leap narrows and transcends the East-West divide and explains China's century-long acceptance of the Western intellectual currents of cosmopolitanism, socialism, the Enlightenment, humanism, and national self-determination.

Revolution is not to create a gloomy future drenched in war, slogans, or blood: it is to change the status quo in pursuit of well-being, livelihood, and political freedom. A revolutionary narrative makes sense to an audience born and bred on the liberal-democratic tradition, precisely because it is an endeavor of seeking freedom and justice. By placing a revolution in its historical context and by discerning sharable aspirations, one may discover a method of teaching China called "historicization." Historicization is politicization: it blends sociopolitical history with a history of ideas and sensibility, and illuminates the way Chinese experiences become aligned with worldwide movements beyond national and cultural boundaries.

In the new round of cold war geopolitical conflict, what fatally obstructs mutual understanding, sympathy, and communication stems from the myth of the absolute difference and cultural clash. This myth divides and places America and China in different universes, maintaining that two countries have entirely different cultures and systems, that the difference is so huge that the two powers cannot coexist under one heaven and on planet Earth. The history of US-China cultural and intellectual exchange has constantly given the lie to the myth. People of both countries have always been able to understand and sympathize with each other and share certain values—

as human beings and even in their distinct identity as Chinese and Americans. The Chinese revolutionaries admired George Washington and Martin Luther King Jr.; Chinese citizens applauded and supported America's civil rights movement and anti-racialist movement. With sharable values and sympathy and in constant communication and mutual leaning, Chinese and American cultures, in Levenson's words, can be "nationalist and internationalist at the same time."[38]

Using the Past   Eight
to Understand the Present

INSPIRED BY LEVENSON'S MOTTO of going "against the world to join it" and Wang Hui's thesis of "modernity against modernity," this book reconsiders how the ideas of tianxia took on new forms and reverberated in different eras since the beginning of the twentieth century.[1] Chinese thinkers and writers carried over inherited outlooks as they positioned China in the world. Beginning with Kang Youwei's datong and Liang Qichao's cosmopolitan nation, articulations of worldviews went through controversy, renovation, and transformation. Based on national independence and appropriations from the West, a Chinese world vision emerged in the prospect of a cosmopolitan state, metamorphosed into socialist internationalism, and surged in Third World movements in the Cold War era, giving way to a new cosmopolitanism in the age of globalization.

Rethinking the enduring questions and unfulfilled aspirations, this book purports to provide insights into how China has moved from empire to modern nation and to ascertain how the old worldviews inform new outlooks. Rather than asserting a Chinese particularism or exceptionalism, the analysis seeks to understand how Chinese thinkers depart from empire and engage nation-state discourse yet strive to combine and go beyond both. In this concluding chapter, I offer further reflection on philosophical premises that undergird the historical accounts of events, figures, and intellectual trends in the chapters.

Empire and Nation-State

The shift from empire to nation-state informs Qing China's transformation to the modern world. The perception of empire as an oversize nation-state is limited and problematic. It fuels fears of China as a new hegemon. Indebted to orientalism, the fear is mortgaged to a long-entrenched image of oriental empire whereby China is classed with Mogul India or Persia. Centralized, despotic, and closed, the oriental empire has lurked in the Western imagination for centuries and has been looming large in recent decades. The militant empire in the garb of a modern nation also informed Sinology and spawned media spectacles, images, and foreign policy.

Is China in the past three hundred years to be understood as an empire or a nation-state? The image of oriental empire presupposes a "prehistorical" community that was reluctantly forced into a world history spearheaded by leading Western nation-states. In this light, historians have seen a nation-state in the making under Western influence since the late Qing era. Jolted out of lethargy and stagnation by the West, China broke away from its dynastic tradition and embarked on the fast track of modernization, industrialization, and nation building. This approach claims many luminous observers, including Karl Marx, Joseph Levenson, and John Fairbank, as well as Chinese modernizers and revolutionaries. The nation-state perspective also helps Asian scholars distance from Western-led modernity and move to "discover history in China."[2] The Japanese historians of the Kyoto School, for instance, viewed Song dynasty China as the dawn of East Asia's homegrown modernity, discerning early signs of a national economy, trade, and urbanization in an embryonic, premodern nation-state. The nation-state lens permits a perception of an imperial China charting its own course into modernity well into the late nineteenth century, when Qing China began to pursue modernity in earnest by virtue of industrialization, modernization, and political institution.

Premised on a rigid dichotomy of nation-state and empire, this perception has been belied by the fact that the modern Chinese nation-state has been built as much on the legacy of the Qing and millennial Chinese civilization as borrowing from the West. As the Qing dynasty was swept into the system of nation-states, Kang Youwei, in the spirit of New Text Confucianism, proposed strategies for thinking about world governance along with nation building.[3] Kang's Confucian universalism, as Wang Hui writes, mobilizes the ancient legacy as a source of political culture with the potential to critique the nation-state. As the country embarked on the trajectory of self-transformation, Chinese writers tapped into the Confucian resources while engaging in national projects. They realized that the tianxia legacy enabled the ethnic Manchus to shore up their legitimacy as a "Chinese" dynasty by incorporating diverse ethnic communities, populations, localities, and religions "into a flexible and pluralistic political structure."[4] Although nation building was imperative for China to survive in the world of national competition, Chinese thinkers aspired to a different kind of world order.

Kang Youwei reclaimed a traditional universalism to meet the challenges of the modern world. Treating Confucianism as flexible and adaptive, Kang envisaged a reformist agenda that drove renewal and innovation. Over the centuries, a critical form of Confucianism has engaged in reflection, self-critique, and institutional reforms in meeting challenges and responding to contingencies. As the late Sinologist Kung-chuan Hsiao noted, the Confucian tradition is at once moral, intellectual, and practical: it was "not as a complex of doctrines held by any Confucian sect or individual Confucian thinker, but [as] a broad stream of thought that had been running its course ever since its inception in the sixth century before Christ."[5] This critical, pragmatic strategy presents the image of empire and its intellectual heritage as a dynamic process fraught with inner contradictions and untapped possibilities. Institutionally, the empire appears to be an unstable, evolving system of centralized prefecture and local feudalism as well as tributary networks spanning adjacent areas. Modern China was built as much on the resources of empire as by borrowing from and adapting to the modern world.

Modern political concepts, by presuming a nation-state's clean break with the past, cut China loose from its moorings in millennial tradition. Unhappy with the nation versus empire dichotomy, historians in recent decades have reconsidered the continuous role of China's imperial legacy and contemporary implications. Scholars like David Kang, Yuri Pines, Brantly Womack, Wang Gungwu, James Hsiung, and many others have elaborated on modern China's enduring ties to its imperial legacy, tracing the persistent strains of thought and practice to the Qing dynasty and earlier.[6] As Philip Kuhn notes, "Although China's revolution wrought many changes, its constitutional agenda reflected some basic concerns of the late imperial and Republican states."[7] Chinese nation builders "took certain contents and characteristics of a syncretic universal imperial system and brought them into the inner structure of the nation-state."[8]

In this light, modern China appears to be a process of political and cultural innovation from the combined resources of tradition and modernity, empire and nation. In chapter 1, I discuss how Kang Youwei responded to the collapse of the tianxia order under the assault of the international system. In the manner of Kantian cosmopolitanism, Kang resorted to universal reason and intersubjective, cross-cultural humanism by way of aesthetic experience, revising a moral language of empathy and benevolence for the conflicted world. Liang Qichao called for a public ethos requisite of a national citizenry while updating tianxia into the idea of public morality. Initially linked to private morality of family and kinship ties, tianxia was seen as moral deficiencies of particularism and parochialism, making Chinese unfit for a national community. But a moral reform would enable individuals to build up the scope of attachment and obligation from family through community to nation. The citizens would be able to push private sympathies outward in a widening gyre, extending the horizon to civic virtue and to the public ethos for the common good. This trajectory underpins Liang's concept of the cosmopolitan state through a rite of moral passage. Embarking on an ascending curve of cultivation, the individual would build up character, learn to harmonize with the family, and live up to the duty of a national community, culminating in the harmony of all under heaven.

Ethnic Diversity and Transethnic Unity

The issue of ethnicity is integral to the empire-nation nexus and concerns the geography and belonging of ethnic minorities in China. The nation-state lens sees the empire as a nation-state writ large, teetering on the verge of ethnic separation and regional conflict. In the spirit of "multiculturalism" and regionalism, scholars attend to the interaction of different ethnic people, flows of cultural goods and ethnic traditions in terms of "hybridity," without giving much thought to the modern agenda of enfolding diverse cultures and ethnicities into a unity. Favoring ethnic differences as potentially centrifugal and separatist forces breaking the empire apart, historians take aim at the empire as a colonizing "nation-state," "Qing imperialism," or Sinocentric colonialism.

The ethnonational lens defines the empire as a nation-state with imperialist agendas to colonize and dominate diverse ethnicities, races, and regions. A distinction, however, needs to be made between empire and imperialism. Imperialism is a modern world system driven by powerful nation-states in the service of capitalist expansion and colonial domination. Empire, on the other hand, denotes a premodern, noncapitalist system that includes multiethnic groups, traditions, and cultures in a shared network of norms, values, and beliefs. The Chinese empire has accumulated a welter of ethnic minorities and regions into a sociopolitical order. The oft-quoted "Han" as the equivalent of "Chinese" is a distortion: it drastically reduces the empire's ethnic complexity and multiplicity. Instead of an ethnic category, "Han" in connection with "Chinese" reveals a fluid process of political legitimation and cultural unity. The Manchus, for example, were a large ethnic group from North China that came to settle in "China" and carried on the Mandate of Heaven, self-styling their identity as "Chinese." As the founders of Qing China, the Manchus were not accepted as legitimate rulers of Chinese until they assimilated themselves into the empire they had conquered. When the dust settled, the Manchus became Chinese. Ethnic groups adjacent to the Qing's porous frontiers were not sovereign nationalities. They were areas within the empire's prefectural structure and loosely connected tributary networks. Flows of goods and people, as well as the grafting of different cultures, had been going on between the center and peripheries across porous borders.

Time and again, "outside" minorities settled on the central territories (*ruzhu zhongyuan* 入主中原), founded a dynasty, and ruled the areas inhabited by Chinese, becoming themselves Chinese. In modern times, *Zhonghua* 中華 developed into an umbrella term that includes heterogeneous ethnicities and cultural identities but also enfolds them into a shared political identification with a modern republic. A placeholder with varying ties to diverse ethnic groups over time, the term *Chinese* serves as a palimpsest open to rewriting by variable ethnic, cultural, and political regimes throughout history. Designations like "Chinese colonialism" or Qing imperialism are problematic because they rest on the assumption that China's ethnic identity remained homogeneous and frozen throughout the centuries; and that the Qing empire, like a nation, is defined by a clear-cut ethnicity, ruled by a central sovereignty, and bounded by a territory. But the so-called Han Chinese has always been a myth and misnomer. The unbroken Han identity becomes irrelevant when one looks at the recurrent pattern by which wave after wave of "minorities"—Mongols, Jurchens, Xianbei, Chuoba, Muslims, and Jews—migrated to the "central kingdom" and blended into a larger community while retaining their distinct ways of life and ethnic features.[9]

My analysis of ethnic minority in *Five Golden Flowers* in chapter 5 draws on the imperial residues with respect to ethnic composition. Although China's nation building dismantled the ancient empire and the Chinese revolutionaries built a socialist nation-state, the PRC carried over certain imperial legacies in multiethnic populations, regional diversity, and territories. As Wang Hui notes, socialist China presents a three-pronged synthesis of "imperial legacy, the nation-state, and socialist values."[10] The structure of centralized administration and ruling authority remained, taking over territories, landmass, populations, transethnic linkages, and cross-cultural networks. The socialist minority agendas appreciate cultural differences among minorities but recognize their equality, rights, and autonomy in relation to other groups. Designed to bring diverse ethnic groups into common prosperity, socialist modernization placed national unity at the center of the complex ethnic landscape to avoid the tendencies of nationalist separatism. While ethnic tensions have always existed and divided the majority from minorities, the challenge was not to rule over minorities but to combat Han chauvinism. The mainstay of socialist minority policy consisted in the arrangement of an administrative system of autonomous regions to facilitate social progress and economic development: "The goal of regional ethnic autonomy was to allow different ethnicities to progress together, not to isolate them from one another; expanding the autonomous regions and encouraging interethnic cooperation became the means by which different ethnicities could share the fruits of progress."[11]

Universalism and Cosmopolitanism

Rooted in ancient cosmology, tianxia has a lineage in *tianli* 天理 (Principle of Heaven). Dong Zhongshu of the Han dynasty elevated this universal moral authority to a natural order where humans live in tune with heavenly designs. Song neo-Confucianists conceived the Principle of Heaven as inner-directed reflection but also deployed it to critique the corrupt political system. In Zhu Xi, the Principle of Heaven comes to light through an arduous practice of self-cultivation, reflection, and learning. This moral activity is both personal and political, both moral and institutional: it expands from the inner mind outward and becomes embodied in the fabric of community and affairs of governance. Deemed immanent within rituals of everyday experience, the Principle of Heaven takes on flesh and blood by being enacted in the daily conduct of serving families and fulfilling mutual obligation toward fellow humans. Participation in a dense welter of everyday moral duty and deed not only generates spiritual meaning but also promotes institutional reform.

For Kang Youwei and Liang Qichao, the Principle of Heaven mutated to the universal principle (gongli) and humanist principle (*rendao* 人道). The

League of Nations' peace initiatives reminded Liang of these ancient heritages. Provoked by the French philosopher Émile Boutroux's complaint of China's reluctance to share its culture, Liang recalled ancient humanist universals such as "all men are brothers," economic equality, and universal love advocated by philosopher Mozi. Acutely aware of social ills on his European trips, Liang realized that China had something to offer to the world. Addressing "Chinese Responsibility to World Civilization" in his *Travel Impressions of Europe*, Liang suggests that the datong ideal calls on Chinese intellectuals to absorb Western civilization to expand Chinese civilization—in such a way to contribute our share to aid the West. Such convergence will make it possible to create a new world community.

The ancient principles also provided a lens for Liang to understand the struggle for national independence. In a translation of the Japanese novel *Chance Encounters with Beautiful Women* (*Jiaren qiyu ji* 佳人奇遇記), Liang invoked gongli to explain the uprising of black slaves in the Haitian Revolution (1791–1804). Under the banner of human liberty and rights, black slaves summoned the universal principle in their fight against colonial oppression.[12] A half-million slaves in the French colony of Saint-Domingue, an island in the Caribbean, "took the struggle for liberty into their own hands" and forced France to acknowledge the abolition of slavery and built an independent nation. In Susan Buck-Morss's account, these "black Jacobins" surpassed the metropolis in realizing the Enlightenment goal of human liberty. The European humanists mouthed such slogans as "Man is born free" and "All men are created equal" while turning a blind eye to slavery. Although the French anthem "La Marseillaise" denounced "l'esclavage antique," it is the black slaves who struggled to attain freedom and dignity with their own hands and sacrifices.[13] Amid battles, French soldiers heard the tunes of what they thought was a tribal chant, which turned out to be "La Marseillaise." They were confused about whom they were fighting.[14] The black slaves took the principles of liberty, equality, and fraternity far more seriously than the French themselves, and their self-emancipation reasserted the universal ideals.

The Haitian Revolution marked the birth of the worldwide movement to break colonial shackles, anticipating bandung and Third World movements.[15] Paradoxical to some but in tune with the internationalist ear, "La Marseillaise" sung by black slaves signals not an act of yielding to colonialism but an assertion of universalism and humanism. In the revolutionary era, Chinese singers of the French anthem were not Francophiles or enamored of cosmopolitan culture but fighters for socialist internationalism. Although France was one of the imperialist powers out to colonize China, Chinese revolutionaries—many of them to become the party leaders—studied social-ism and cosmopolitanism in Paris. James Bertram, a British journalist who traveled widely in China and interviewed Mao in Yan'an, witnessed the Red Army soldiers singing foreign songs in battlefields and marches. "It was a curious experience," Bertram wrote, "to hear those mountain gores ringing with the 'Internationale,' or 'La Marseillaise,' or a theme-song from a Russian film—all rendered, with a difference, in throaty Chinese dialect."[16] In the War of Resistance against Japanese Aggression, "La Marseillaise" inspired the mu-sician Nie Er to compose the Chinese anthem.

To Marx, the French Revolution not only was about national liberation but also inspired a new universalism. Writing in 1850 in the wake of the First Opium War about Britain's territorial claims on China, Marx discerned so-cialist implications in the Taiping rebellion's denouncement of gaps between rich and poor and the demand for the "redistribution of property." "The oldest and the most shattered empire on this earth has been pushed," wrote Marx, "by the cotton ball of the British bourgeoisie toward the brink of social upheaval that must have most profound consequences for civilization."[17] The European reactionaries, when reaching the Great Wall on their next flight through Asia, were shocked to see the following inscription on the Wall:

République Chinoise
Liberté, Equalité, Fraternité.[18]

This gesture—of stoking flame of universalism from the far-flung ashes—became a pattern of socialist internationalism. For Chinese "Marseillaise" singers, France or even "Europe," as Lin Chun notes, "signals the struggle for freedom, equality, and fraternity."[19] For Mao Zedong, the universalism of the Western Enlightenment came as a source of inspiration for Chinese social-ists. In a speech at the founding of the PRC in 1949, Mao stated that Chinese nation builders since Kang Youwei and Liang Qichao had been eager to ac-quire "the new learning" from Western "teachers." But the chairman won-dered aloud, "Why were the teachers always committing aggression against their pupils?"[20] Yet with little regret, Mao noted how progressive and socialist ideas indeed came to China under the West's rod. The chairman urged revolu-tionaries to absorb not only socialism but also the "progressive culture of the age of Enlightenment"—with the caveat of exercising the critical faculty and using the foreign to benefit China.[21] Levenson remarked on this universalism by stating that revolutionary cosmopolitans go "against the world to join it."[22]

Critics of postcolonialism may find the embrace of Western universalism disturbing. Protective of the integrity and difference of marginalized groups, discourses of postcolonialism valorize particular identities against all forms of Western universalism. But flaunting cultural difference as an end in itself risks dropping the universal as the foundation of a common world. The claims of cultural or ethnic difference, as Pheng Cheah has argued, "do not seek to retrieve a lost authentic tradition oppressed by universalism. In rejecting the false universalism of cosmopolitan culture," these discourses "already desire access to a true universal."[23]

> The argument for the autonomy of the local presupposes the universal value of autonomy and proposes to apply it to every group or collective unit. This desire for a polymorphous universal capable of respecting the particularities of its constituent units sublates the opposition between the universal and the particular, modernity and tradition. Consequently, political claims for cultural specificity posit the autonomy of cultural identity . . . as an ideal-normative goal: all cultural groups should have equal excess to the social, economic and political forces that constitute the world system and the freedom to direct these forces to their own interests.[24]

Cheah's insight resembles Kang Youwei's notion of universal access to datong. Kung-chuan Hsiao identified three ways for Chinese thinkers to approach the West. The first is the outright dismissal of "learning from the barbarians" by insisting that China, boasting five thousand years of civilization, already has the best. The second view bemoans that China is ill-equipped for modernity, and a partial or total embrace of Western civilization is the way to move forward. But Kang followed a more synthetic and universal path. Upholding the tianxia principle that conceives human knowledge to be common property for all, Kang assumed that "differences between East and West were more nominal than basic."[25] To transform "China's outmoded political, economic, and educational systems was not Westernization but in reality universalization—bringing Chinese culture up to that stage of civilization to which all mankind should do well to attain." This universalism dates back at least to Song dynasty Confucianism, with its motto that "The truth permeates all under Heaven" and that the same principle holds good for all.[26]

Today, rising nationalist sentiments are fueling chauvinist pride and stoking tensions between China and the West. This situation makes intercultural learning extremely urgent and significant. A genuine universalism needs to separate the imperialist agenda from what has become the common property of a global society. Rather than a structure of domination by the elites and culture industry, Western culture has been a source for Chinese writers to draw on in the endeavor to envisage a cosmopolitan world.

Tianxia embodies a moral authority and a tradition of critical evaluation, political reform, and social critique. This critical gesture recalls Levenson's distinction of value and history. While the Principle of Heaven guided ritual, music, and classics, historical reality always falls short of ideals and aspiration. Frequent contradictions and gaps flare up and destroy the temporary equilibrium, severing ideals from reality. But the tradition of Confucian commentary wades into the rift and thrives on the gap between value and history, engaging the tension as a discursive battleground for polemics and renovation.

The Confucian tradition sees the rift as a divorce between name and substance and the estrangement of ritual and music from the warped institutions (禮樂與制度的分化). *The Spring and Autumn Annals*, a rectification of the travesties and collapse of ritual and music (禮崩樂壞), seeks to reinstate the ethico-political order modeled on the Golden Age of the Three Dynasties. Over the centuries, scholar-officials continued to exercise this discursive capability to repair ruptures and fix corruption. The rift between morality and politics, ritual and institution became a self-conscious and well-practiced critical strategy. Wang Hui writes,

> As the Song Neo-Confucianists posited a principle above ritual to redefine its practice, they believed that the established ritual and institutions have lost their intrinsic value and degenerated into empty forms or functioned in promo forma fashion. In response, they sought to reconstruct the intrinsic relation between principle and ritual and restore ritualistic practice to its proper value and sacredness. Their affirmation of everyday life amounts to an endorsement of ritual's holiness. For this reason, Confucianism refuses to regard everyday life as a random, whimsical process but a pattern steeped in principles and ritual, corresponding intimately with the Principle of Heaven. Thus, tianli, rather than a secular development, was a renewed attempt to internalize and give fresh aura to ritual. As ritual practice fell into disarray, Neo-Confucianism strove, through the subject's sincerity and respect, to endow the ritual with substantive content.[27]

In Confucian thought, culture is interchangeable with morality. The moral norm is the heart that animates the body politic and transmits vital ethical meanings through daily ritual and cultivation. The moral-political linkages "maintain political order by resorting to morality," granting the centrality of moral virtue and compassion to tianxia politics.[28] Kang Youwei and Liang Qichao contrasted the public sphere of modern politics with the private loyalty of imperial autocrats. The public dimension is fundamentally cultural and moral. As Charlotte Furth suggests, the concept of gong (public, commonality, public authority) derives from the Confucian assumption that "correct political action must be based upon commonly recognized principles." Instead of an institutional mechanism for mediating pluralistic interests, as in Western public assemblies or parliaments, the political realm manifests itself as the "spirit of public morality" and functions as "educative and expressive instruments for achieving a common consensus" and "a community of understanding and purpose."[29] This accounts for the proposal of political and social reform by means of voluntary societies of study and enlightenment advocated by Tan Sitong, Kang Youwei, Liang Qichao, and others. The study society presents a platform for the common pursuit of enlightenment, moral improvement, and sympathy among social members, serving to form a unity of value by linking thought with action and conduct. This ethico-political turn is evident in Liang, who placed top priority on morality and proposed to renovate Chinese moral character and educate them as modern citizens.

Revolutionary thinkers shifted the moral emphasis to the relations of culture and politics, theory and practice, spirit and machine. In global Maoism and Third World movements, the exhortation "politics in command" was in fact culture in command—a reign of virtue and spirit. Cultural politics lies at the heart of attempts to empower a collective and forge political subjects by means of shared visions, consciousness, solidarity, and ethos. Rejecting the vulgar Marxist claim that the advanced relations of production—the ethico-political realm—would automatically move in sync with a higher mode of economic production, Maoism gravitates overwhelmingly to culture, which bears "the burden for the transformation to socialism," wrote Dirlik. Cultural transformation must play a key role and take on an independent life vis-à-vis economic production.[30] From the Great Leap Forward to the Cultural Revolution, the gap between socialist ethos and bureaucratic, technocratic tendencies grew wider. Wave after wave of cultural campaigns intervened and seized upon consciousness and morality as the decisive battlefield for shaping new personalities and sociopolitical change. The autonomy of culture vis-à-vis economy and technology resonated with the sociocultural transformations underway in the Third World and the First World.

Cultural politics places value above history, culture above politics, and spirit over machine, stamping myriad episodes and events with symbolic aura and significance under the aegis of "cultural revolution." It may not be an exaggeration to claim that the impulse for cultural change has been regarded as a crucial driving force for modern China's social and economic development. Mao's belief in the power of mass political subjectivity put the legendary mountain-removing Yugong (Foolish Old Man) on the pedestal. The primacy of public spirit lay behind Liang Qichao's proposal of moral reform and creation of civic ethos. Zhou Libo's humanist education in Yan'an aimed to raise political consciousness in the manner of Gramsci's humanist culture, marking an extended moral education toward the self-understanding of human worth and equality. The Lu Xun Academy of Arts was designed to educate minds, cultivate sentiments, teach arts and literature, and forge the peasants into political subjects. The concept of "class nation" is not only a socioeconomic category for stratification and classification. Rather, "class" denotes class consciousness, structures of feeling, solidarity, and common purposes. The voluntary soldiers in the Korean War embodied internationalist spirit as part of a proletarian class. They fought and made sacrifices because they acquired a world-class consciousness about the shared history of colonialism and foreign invasion, and because they were empathetic to the pain and suffering of Korean people. Their spirit was amplified into a weapon more powerful than the atomic bomb, unleashing vast amounts of energy—a spiritual bomb prevailing over advanced weaponry.

Globalization and Depoliticization

Since the late 1970s, the world witnessed the waning of socialist internationalism and Third World movements. The post–Cold War era saw the rise of a new empire, which peaked from the 1990s to the first decade of the new millennium. Maintaining the mirage of a flat world of neoliberal networks of trade and capital, the empire presided over the world to keep it safe for transnational corporations and the affluent lifestyle of Western metropolises. Dubbed "American tianxia" by Salvatore Babones, the empire is said to govern the world via soft power—through consent and inculcation of universal values of trade, growth, technology, and consumerism.[31]

China observers are now familiar with the country's spectacles of wealth and prosperity. But just beneath the fanfare and sheen lurks the widening gulf between rich and poor, between urban prosperity and rural impoverishment, between elites and working people. Dispossessed peasants riot in the streets against the plundering of land. Rural migrants build the gleaming high-rises yet can barely scrape out a subhuman existence. Rural kids quit school and toil as underage laborers to feed themselves. Glaring inequality and degraded human life raise the pressing questions of social justice, class inequality, and class polarization, conjuring up the harsh conditions of primitive accumulation and exploitation in the colonial years.

There is no denying that old problems of capitalist modernity are haunting today's China. As a campaign to overcome the traps of the capitalist world system, the Chinese Revolution got off the ground to combat the economic meltdown, class divides, and social disintegration. It was both a national resistance to colonialism and a social movement to lift the population out of poverty, oppression, and inequality. Socialist China pursued a self-reliant agenda and sought independence from the dictates of global capital and superpower hegemony. Committed to a fair redistribution of goods and income, socialism strove to narrow the gap between town and countryside, mental and manual labor, industry and agriculture, striking out an alternative development path.

The rise of neoliberal globalization, however, hollows out the memories of revolution, socialist experiments, anti-colonial mass movements, and Third World movements. The concept of depoliticization has proved fruitful in understanding contemporary China's place in the world. The term describes the disappearance of a forum of public deliberation and conversation on values and policy in the party-state and in society at large. Absent such a forum, political institutions shrivel into an arena of power rivalry, faction fight, and coercive policing. A series of development since the 1970s reveals the collapse of collective politics across East and West. Jumping on the bandwagon of economic globalization, historians and critics turn away from the significant debate about China's future. In the total negation of the revolutionary past, the unresolved questions and issues are dismissed. The legitimate revolutionary changes are interpreted as signs of the inner party power struggle, violence, and repression. The blind rejection of the socialist development swept into the dustbin China's pursuit of alternative modernity for more than half a century.

In the age of globalization, China has shifted from a leader of the anti-hegemonic Third World to a "strategic partner" or a competitor in capitalist globalization.[32] Getting on track with capitalism, the CCP seems to be abandoning its legacy of ideological debate, grassroots organization, and mass mobilization. Although the Cultural Revolution has been deemed a calamity, the mass activities signaled the last gasp of political energy and radicalism: it challenged the atrophied, depoliticized party-state. In a brief spasm of remobilization of political life and debate, factories across China were reorganized along the lines of the Paris Commune, and "schools and work units engaged in discussion, polemics, and social experimentation."[33] Challenged by pressure from below, the party-state recognized the crisis and sought to "carry out a self-renewal." The momentum unfolded in the "currents that hoped to smash the absolute authority of the party and the state, in order to further the goal of progress toward genuine popular democracy."[34] But these short-lived activities of political revitalization were quickly crushed.

The symptoms of depoliticization are apparent when the party-state has ceased to be a platform of ideological debate and becomes a state apparatus ruled by partisan and vested interests. No longer an organization serving the public good, it decays into a mechanism of power. Its role to ensure the smooth functioning of the market recalls Lenin's well-known definition of the bourgeois state: a committee for managing the common affairs of the bourgeoisie at the expense of working people. Bureaucratic red tape, rigid hierarchy, and factionalism erode the vibrant sphere of discussion and evaluation.

Embedded in the tradition of rectification of rifts between culture and politics, critiques of depoliticization are associated with two meanings of "hegemony." The first meaning is imperialist in the sense of wielding domination through coercion. The second meaning is the idea of cultural leadership conceived by Gramsci. Thus, in upholding socialist internationalism and supporting the Third World, China was regarded, writes Wang Hui, as "hegemonic" in the sense of demonstrating "the ruling group's strategic ability of proposing solutions to common problems," while "allocating exceptional powers to itself."[35] Mao's Third World theory applied the first sense of hegemony as domination to two superpowers and appealed to the second sense of moral leadership whose function was to rally independence-seeking people to break the hegemons' sway. The two meanings of hegemony could be traced further back to *The Spring and Autumn Annals* and the *Zuo Commentary*. The two classics "use the concept of ducal authority (control by force) and hegemonic authority (domination through rites and rituals) to differentiate two types of power" as the ancient kingdoms of Qi, Jin, Chu, and Qin alternately clashed and aligned with each other.[36]

Depoliticization zeros in on a form of politics devoid of moral and cultural dimensions. This insight sheds light on the episodes from the global sixties to the era of globalization. Global Maoism came on the scene as a counter-discourse to seal ruptures of culture and politics. Reasserting the faith in the peasantry as a source of revolutionary virtue and political energy, mass-line mobilization fostered and created robust political subjects and devoted workers. The mass line relied on the subjective factor, consciousness, and drive of a dedicated people, not on technocratic elites and administrative cadres. Energized grassroots momentum challenged the malaises of modernity marked by urbanization, industrialization, institutional corruption, and the distance between state and society. Mao's utopianism also inspired the French Maoist Alain Badiou. Engaging the politics of mobilizing workers and peasants and following the credo of "Going to the people," Badiou worked closely with workers and peasants with the goal of raising their consciousness and unleashing radical energy. His criticism of Althusser's theory of state targeted the hollowing out of politics as manifest in the claim of "history without a subject," which deprives social change of popular agency and political subjectivity. The Cultural Revolution and May 1968 student rebellion in France signaled the power of a new wave of resurgent political subjectivity against the party-state establishment. In Chinese cultural studies, China is increasingly depoliticized into a sideshow of capitalist market development. Instead of socialist internationalism and mass politics, studies of Chinese culture and literature gravitated toward how China has returned to the universal norm of West-led modernity.[37]

I hope this book offers some clues to the puzzle: Is China an empire or a nation-state? Does the country aspire to a genuine cosmopolitanism or does it pursue an aggressive nationalism? I am convinced that a deep-seated desire for a cosmopolitan world prevails over assertions of nationalism. Indebted to the legacy of tianxia and empire, Chinese thinkers and writers have demonstrated an unceasing aspiration for universal recognition and norms. Unfolding in writing, literature, and image, this world vision reasserted itself in discourses of Confucian universalism, cosmopolitanism, humanism, socialist internationalism, Third World agendas, and globalization. This quest is as pertinent in the present as in the past. Neoliberalism claims to be the standard bearer of universalism, and the recent rise of nationalism and tribalism is turning the world into a new cold war of arms race, nationalist fervor, and geopolitical conflict. Will China join the old game of interstate rivalry and conflict? Or will China play a responsible cosmopolitan role? Is China wielding its new power and influence in the name of national self-interest? Could the country keep its tianxia vision alive and contribute to the world community and peace? There can be no clear and unequivocal answers.

This book attempts to offer some answers to how Chinese tradition informs its present and future. The imperial legacy persists in the making of modern China, providing insights and perspectives on contemporary issues. Confucianism has been enacted to diagnose and critique corrosive consequences of capitalist modernity. The classical nexus of culture and politics, of morality and institution, continues to shed light on political decay and breakdowns of intersubjectivity and the fabric of the world community. Socialist internationalism offers justification for self-determination of the wretched of the earth, decolonization, and anti-hegemonic movements.

Even in its apparent repudiation of the socialist legacy, China cannot throw the baby out with the bathwater. It must keep alive certain memories of revolutionary spirit and socialist values, if only to legitimate the ruling body in the eyes of Chinese society. As Wang Hui notes, socialist value works as an "internal restraint" on state reforms and market agenda, and the Chinese leadership has to conduct a dialogue with this tradition.[38] The party-state has to harmonize policy orientation with the proclaimed goal of serving the general population and offering legitimate channels to discuss and address issues of inequality, corruption, and environmental crises.

On the international scene, China seems to be on track as well as on a collision course with global capitalism. Will China be a source of order or disorder, a threat or contributor to the stability and harmony in the world? In combatting hegemony in Third World alliances, Mao repeatedly said China has no ambition to become a hegemonic power (*bu chengba* 不称霸). Being poor and developing, China was in no position to be a chauvinist nation. But what would become of China in the future? In November 1975, invoking Mao's disclaim of hegemony to Japanese diplomats, Deng Xiaoping explained: "Frankly, a poor and backward country such as ours has no qualification and right to be a hegemonic power. But the question is that in thirty or fifty years, when we become a developed country, shall we claim to be a hegemonic power? Mao's call is 'Never become a hegemon' [*yongyuan bu chengba* 永遠不称霸]. This strategy speaks not only to the present, but also to the future."[39]

Deng's future of a developed China is now. With Mao's disclaimer, with the revolutionary tradition of supporting poor countries, and with the legacy of tianxia and socialist internationalism, will China rule the world or bring harmony to it?

Notes

Series Editor's Foreword

1 Ricci, *True Meaning of the Lord under Heaven*, 31–32. The full opening line is "平治庸理, 惟竟於一," which Ricci's English translators render as "All doctrines about making the whole world peaceful and governing correctly are focused on the principle of uniqueness."
2 Lewi and Hseih, "*Tianxia* and the Invention of Empire in East Asia."
3 Schuessler, ABC *Etymological Dictionary of Old Chinese*, 495; Purchas, *Purchas His Pilgrimage*, cited in the *Oxford English Dictionary* entry for "tian."

Introduction

1 Pye, *The Spirit of Chinese Politics*, 235.
2 Fairbank, *The Chinese World Order*, 5.
3 Jacques, *When China Rules the World*, 201.
4 Larson, *Zhang Yimou*, 333–45.
5 Liang, *Liang Qichao quanji*, 3031–32.
6 Liang, *Liang Qichao quanji*, 2978.
7 Liang, *Liang Qichao quanji*, 2986. All translations are mine unless otherwise indicated.

8 Christopher Coker conceives civilization in terms of culture history and inherited values, antithetical to cosmopolitanism. Coker, *The Rise of the Civilizational State*.

9 Zhao, *Tianxia tixi*.

10 Pines, *The Everlasting Empire*, 2–11.

11 Luo Mengce, *Zhongguo lun*, 11–12.

12 Schwartz, "Themes in Intellectual History," 100.

13 Schwartz, "Themes in Intellectual History," 104.

14 Schwartz, "Themes in Intellectual History," 104.

15 Huters, *Bringing the World Home*.

16 Liu, *Translingual Practice*; Liu, *The Clash of Empires*.

17 Karl, *Staging the World*, 16.

18 K. Qian, *Imperial-Time-Order*; Volland, *Socialist Cosmopolitanism*.

19 Hsiung, *China into its Second Rise*, xviii–xix, 245.

20 Sun, *Sun Zhongshan quanji*, 9:226.

21 Quoted in Schram, *Mao Tse-tung*, 201.

22 Wang Gungwu, *Renewal*, 1.

23 Wang Hui, *Xiandai Zhongguo*.

24 Wallerstein, *Geopolitics and Geoculture*, 217.

25 Rowe, *China's Last Empire*, 284.

26 Wang Gungwu, *Renewal*, ix, x.

27 Wang Hui, *China from Empire to Nation-State*, 33.

28 Wang Hui, "From Empire to State," 49.

29 Wang Hui, *Xiandai Zhongguo*, 21.

30 Wang Hui, *Xiandai Zhongguo*, 21.

31 Wang Hui, *The Politics of Imagining Asia*, 32.

32 Wang Hui, *The Politics of Imagining Asia*, 32.

33 Wang Hui, *The Politics of Imagining Asia*, 86.

34 See chapter 1 for Kang's Confucian universalism.

35 Liang, *Liang Qichao quanji*, 661.

36 Liang, *Liang Qichao quanji*, 5610.

37 Smith, *An Inquiry*, 2:141. Kant, *Critique of the Power of Judgment*, 301.

38 Levenson, *Revolution and Cosmopolitanism*, 19.

39 Daruvala, *Zhou Zuoren*, 40–46.

40 Zhou Zuoren, "Humane Literature," 154.

41 Zhou Zuoren, "Humane Literature," 161.

42 Shih, *Lure of the Modern*, 153.

43 Qian Suoqiao, *Liberal Cosmopolitanism*, 6.

44 Qian Suoqiao, *Liberal Cosmopolitanism*, 60.

45 Qian Suoqiao, *Liberal Cosmopolitanism*, 61.

46 Shen, *Cosmopolitan Publics*, 42.

47 Shen, *Cosmopolitan Publics*, 4.

48 Marx and Engels, *The Marx-Engels Reader*, 338–39.

49 Levenson, *Revolution and Cosmopolitanism*, xx.

50 Casanova, *The World Republic of Letters*, 12.

51 Cheah, "What Is a World?," 33.
52 Schwarzmantel, "Nationalism and Socialist Internationalism," 637.
53 Li Dazhao, *Li Dazhao quanji*, 259.
54 Marx, "Draft of an Article," 280.
55 Fitzgerald, *Awakening China*, 31.
56 Wang Hui, *The Politics of Imagining Asia*, 35.
57 Mao Zedong, *Selected Works*, 2:343.
58 Mao Zedong, *Selected Works*, 2:342.
59 Mao Zedong, *Selected Works*, 2:344.
60 Snow, *Red Star over China*, 406–7.
61 Snow, *Red Star over China*, 406.
62 Levenson, *Revolution and Cosmopolitanism*, 28, 30.
63 Schwartz, *China and Other Matters*, 169.
64 Anderson, "Internationalism," 6.

Chapter One. Morality and Global Vision in Kang Youwei's World Community

Portions of chapter 1 were published in *Chinese Vision of World Order*, ed. Ban Wang (Durham, NC: Duke University Press, 2017), 87–105.

1 Linklater, *Men and Citizens*, 4.
2 Quoted in Linklater, *Men and Citizens*, 4.
3 Mearsheimer, *The Tragedy of Great Power Politics*, 2.
4 Huntington, *The Clash of Civilizations*, 21.
5 Linklater, *Men and Citizens*, 26.
6 Levenson, *Revolution and Cosmopolitanism*, 24.
7 De Bary and Bloom, *Sources of Chinese Tradition*, 343, translation modified.
8 Kang Youwei, *Kang Youwei jingdian wenchun*, 10.
9 Kang Youwei, *Datong shu*, 69; Kang Youwei, *Ta T'ung Shu*, 80. I modified the English translation by Laurence Thompson. Further references to Kang's book appear parenthetically in the text with two sets of page numbers, for the original and its translation by Thompson.
10 Schwartz, *The World of Thought in Ancient China*, 260–61.
11 De Bary and Bloom, *Sources of Chinese Tradition*, 343, translation modified.
12 Kant, *Political Writings*, 44.
13 Kant, *Political Writings*, 44.
14 Kant, *Critique of the Power of Judgment*, 301.
15 Kant, *Critique of the Power of Judgment*, 73–75.
16 Cheah, *Inhuman Conditions*, 96.
17 Eagleton, *The Ideology of the Aesthetic*, 96.
18 Quoted in Muthu, *Enlightenment against Empire*, 148.
19 Muthu, *Enlightenment against Empire*, 144.
20 Levenson, *Revolution and Cosmopolitanism*, 20.
21 Kang Youwei, *Datong shu*, 5. I use Jonathan Spence's translation of this passage. See Spence, *The Gate of Heavenly Peace*, 66.

22 Mencius, *The Works of Mencius*, book 1, chapter 1, part 7. I use James Legge's translation.

23 Eagleton, *The Ideology of the Aesthetic*, 13.

24 Mencius, *The Works of Mencius*, book 1, part 2.

25 Mencius, *The Works of Mencius*, book 1, part 2, chapter 1.

26 Kant, *Political Writings*, 100.

27 Eagleton, *The Ideology of the Aesthetic*, 24.

28 Eagleton, *The Ideology of the Aesthetic*, 24.

29 Eagleton, *The Ideology of the Aesthetic*, 24.

30 Kang Youwei, *Kang Youwei quanji*, 145–59.

31 Fung, *A Short History of Chinese Philosophy*, 202.

32 Tang Zhijun, *Kang Youwei zhuan*, 75.

33 Furth, "Intellectual Change," 20.

34 Furth, "Intellectual Change," 20.

35 Tang Zhijun, *Kang Youwei zhuan*, 24.

36 Schwartz, *The World of Thought*, 386–87.

37 Schwartz, *The World of Thought*, 387.

38 Gan, *Jiangcuo jiucuo*, 259.

39 Liang Qichao, *Liang Qichao quanji*, 72.

Chapter Two. Nationalism, Moral Reform, and *Tianxia* in Liang Qichao

Parts of chapter 2 appeared in "Morality, Aesthetics, and World Literature in Liang Qichao," *Chinese Literature Today* 5, no. 1 (2015): 93–101.

1 Liang, *Liang Qichao quanji*, 5610. Further references appear parenthetically in the text.

2 Calhoun, *Nationalism*, 92.

3 See Luo Zhitian, "Lixiang yu xianshi."

4 Gu Yanwu distinguished the collapse of a dynastic state from the demise of tianxia. The state dies when a new state replaces it and changes its title. Tianxia, a civilization based on moral principles of ritual, sociality, and reciprocity, is imperiled when the state elites brutalize people and plunge society into chaos and mutual butchering. See Gu, *Rizhilu*, 590.

5 Wang Hui, *Xiandai Zhongguo*, 821–29.

6 Liang, *Liang Qichao quanji*, 170.

7 Fukuyama, *Political Order*, 16.

8 Sun, *Sun Zhongshan quanji*, 9:226.

9 Sun, *Sun Zhongshan quanji*, 9:253.

10 Liang, *Liang Qichao quanji*, 5615.

11 Levenson, *Revolution and Cosmopolitanism*, 7–8.

12 Liang, *Liang Qichao quanji*, 5611.

13 Zhao, "Cong shijie wenti kaishi de tianxia zhengzhi," 69.

14 Fukuyama, *Political Order*, 86. Fukuyama regards China of Qin and Han dynasties as the first modern state with an impersonal bureaucracy and meritocracy. But the patrimonial pull of private and kinship ties eroded the

"public" administrative system, which was in fact the tianxia order. Liang was deploring the similar patrimonial relationship.

15 Liang, *Liang Qichao quanji*, 661.
16 Liang, *Liang Qichao quanji*, 413–14.
17 Zhao, "Cong shijie wenti kaishi de tianxia zhengzhi," 50; 56.
18 Wakeman, *History and Will*, 30, 100.
19 This well-quoted passage is reproduced in the section "The Public Principle, Selfishness, and Equality" in chapter 1. See also de Bary and Bloom, *Sources of Chinese Tradition*, 343.
20 Eagleton, *The Ideology of the Aesthetic*, 24.
21 Sun, *Sun Zhongshan quanji*, 9:327.
22 Liang, *Liang Qichao quanji*, 3605.
23 Hsia, *C. T. Hsia on Chinese Literature*, 223–46.
24 Hsia, *C. T. Hsia on Chinese Literature*, 237.
25 X. Tang, *Global Space*, 137.
26 Liang, *Liang Qichao quanji*, 5629–30.
27 Liang, *Liang Qichao quanji*, 5630.
28 Liang, *Liang Qichao quanji*, 5631.
29 Gu's distinction between demise of tianxia and loss of a country is exemplified in a public-minded warrior. Scholar and lexicographer Liu Jiexiu found that Liang turned Gu's discourse into an eight-character stock phrase. See Liu Jiexiu, "Who coined *tianxia xingwang* phrase?," http://zhidao.baidu.com/question/98878177.html, accessed October 27, 2016.
30 Liang, *Liang Qichao quanji*, 5634.
31 Lu, *Lu Xun quanji*, 1:79. The English translation is based on Jon Kowallis's excellent translation. See Kowallis, *Warriors of the Spirit*.
32 Lu, *Lu Xun quanji*, 1:79.
33 Lu, *Lu Xun quanji*, 1:80.
34 Lu, *Lu Xun quanji*, 2:78.
35 Lu, *Lu Xun quanji*, 1:81.
36 Lu, *Lu Xun quanji*, 1:82.
37 Quoted in Brady, *Making the Foreign Serve China*, 36.
38 Liang, *Liang Qichao quanji*, 3043.
39 Liang, *Liang Qichao quanji*, 3044.
40 Liang, *Liang Qichao quanji*, 3044–45.
41 Liang, *Liang Qichao quanji*, 3048.
42 Liang, *Liang Qichao quanji*, 3144.
43 Liang, *Liang Qichao quanji*, 3688.

Chapter Three. World Literature in the Mountains

A portion of chapter 3 appeared in "The People in the Modern Chinese Novel," *Novel* 47, no. 1 (2014): 43–56.

1 He et al., *Luyi shihua*, 104.
2 He et al., *Luyi shihua*, 104–6.

3 Volland, *Socialist Cosmopolitanism*, 39–61.

4 Li Zehou, *Zhongguo xiandai sixiang shi lun*, 7–49.

5 Said, *Humanism and Democratic Criticism*, 11.

6 Said, *Humanism and Democratic Criticism*, 11–12.

7 United Nations, *The Universal Declaration*, 1.

8 Marshall Berman viewed socialism as inheriting and fulfilling the emancipatory promises of bourgeois humanism: "Marx's vision of modern *subjectivity* is his central theme." He shares Georg Wilhelm Friedrich Hegel's idea that the "principle of the modern world is freedom of subjectivity." Freedom of subjectivity is the vital center of Marx's critique of modern capitalism. In "Private Property and Communism," Marx conceives the historical subject as "the rich human being": "established society produces man in the entire richness of his being, produces the rich man profoundly endowed with all the senses, as its enduring reality." This "being in need of a totality of human life-activities" is bound to feel alienated and crushed by capitalism. In *The Communist Manifesto*, Marx defines communist society as one where "the free development of each is the basis for the free development of all." See Berman, "Themes for China," 433–35.

9 Quoted in Althusser, *For Marx*, 224.

10 Althusser, *For Marx*, 226.

11 Roche, "Marx and Humanism," 336.

12 Dirlik, "The Predicament of Marxist Revolutionary Consciousness."

13 Gramsci, *The Antonio Gramsci Reader*, 56.

14 Gramsci, *The Antonio Gramsci Reader*, 57.

15 Gramsci, *The Antonio Gramsci Reader*, 58.

16 He et al., *Luyi shihua*, 3.

17 Mao Zedong, *Selected Works*, 3:369.

18 See Holm, *Art and Ideology in Revolutionary China*; Huang, *Yan'an wenxue yanjiu*; Melvin and Cai, *Rhapsody in Red*.

19 Mao Zedong, *Selected Works*, 3:82.

20 Quoted in He et al., *Luyi shihua*, 3.

21 Mao Zedong, *Selected Works*, 2:369.

22 Lu, *Lu Xun quanji*, 1:56. I use Jon Kowallis's unpublished translation of Lu's text.

23 Lu, *Lu Xun quanji*, 1:56.

24 Quoted in Huang, *Yan'an wenxue yanjiu*, 30–31.

25 Snow, *Red Star over China*, 407–8.

26 Apter and Saich, *Revolutionary Discourse*, 224.

27 For a comprehensive examination of "brainwashing," see Gao, *How the Red Sun Rose*.

28 Quoted in Apter and Saich, *Revolutionary Discourse*, 238.

29 Calhoun, "Imagining Solidarity," 148; Arendt, *Between Past and Future*, 221.

30 Gao, *How the Red Sun Rose*, 369.

31 Zhou Libo, *Zhou Libo luyi jianggao*, 6. Further references appear parenthetically in the text.

32 Goldman and Lee, *An Intellectual History of Modern China*, 184.

33 See Muthu, *Enlightenment against Empire*, chapter 6.

34 Lukács, *The Historical Novel*, 25.
35 Lukács, *The Historical Novel*, 28.
36 Mao Zedong, *Mao Tse-tung on Literature and Art*, 31–32.
37 Zhou Libo, *Zhou Libo luyi jianggao*, 94.
38 Zhou Libo, *Sanxiang ju bian*, 109.
39 Marx and Engels, *The Communist Manifesto*, 84.
40 Marx famously wrote: "The nationality of the worker is neither French, nor English, nor German, it is labor, free slavery, self-huckstering. His government is neither French, nor English, nor German, it is capital." Marx, "Draft of an Article," 280.
41 Mao, *Selected Works*, 2:196.
42 Mao, *Selected Works*, 3:67.
43 Zhou Libo, *Sanshi niandai wenxue pinglun ji*, 92–120.
44 Zhou Libo, *Zhou Libo wenji*, 5:86.
45 Zhou Yang, *Zhou Yang wenji*, 1:173.
46 See Shu, *Buglers on the Home Front*, 38.
47 Quoted in Wang Hui, *The Politics of Imaging Asia*, 101.
48 Levenson, *Revolution and Cosmopolitanism*, 7.
49 Levenson, *Revolution and Cosmopolitanism*, 7.
50 Casanova, *The World Republic of Letters*, 74–76.
51 Levenson, *Revolution and Cosmopolitanism*, 7.
52 Mao, *Selected Works*, 3:84.
53 Mao, *Selected Works*, 3:81.
54 Zhou Yang, *Zhou Yang wenji*, 1:298.
55 Zhou Yang, *Zhou Yang wenji*, 1:298–300.
56 Calhoun, "Imagining Solidarity," 162–64.
57 Levenson, *Revolution and Cosmopolitanism*, 6.
58 Levenson, *Revolution and Cosmopolitanism*, 8.
59 Levenson, *Revolution and Cosmopolitanism*, 8.
60 Schram, *Mao Tse-tung*, 201.
61 Sun, *Sun Zhongshan quanji*, 9:226.
62 Mao Zedong, *Selected Works of Mao Tse-tung*, 4:414.

Chapter Four. Art, Politics, and Internationalism in Korean War Films

A different version of chapter 4 was published as "Art, Politics, and Internationalism: Korean War Films in Chinese Cinema," in *The Oxford Handbook of Chinese Cinema*, ed. Carlos Rojas and Eileen Chow (New York: Oxford University Press, 2013), 251–66.
1 Quoted in Schram, *Mao Tse-tung*, 201.
2 Saunders, *The Cultural Cold War*.
3 X. Wang, *Modernity with a Cold War Face*.
4 Chen Jian, *Mao's China and the Cold War*, 87.
5 Cummings, *North Korea*, 5–6; Cummings, *Korea's Place in the Sun*, 193–94.
6 Wang Hui, *China's Twentieth Century*, 143.

7 Mao Zedong, *Selected Works*, 2:512. Charles Tilly has argued that European state building was driven by the need of the monarchs to wage war. See Fukuyama, *The Origins of Political Order*, 110.

8 Mao Zedong, *Quotations*, 99.

9 Meng, "Xin xieshi yu yingxiong shishi," 52.

10 Meng, "Xin xieshi yu yingxiong shishi," 52.

11 Etherton, "Reading against the Gun," 109.

12 Schram, "Mao Tse-tung's Thought," 309.

13 S. Zhang, *Mao's Military Romanticism*, 1–11.

14 Wang Zhi, "*Yingxiong ernü* beihou de gushi," 18.

15 Wu Rongbin and Wen Shijiang, "Cong 1978 nian qianhou," 121.

16 Mao Zedong, *Selected Works*, 3:70.

17 Mao Zedong, *Selected Works*, 2:143–44.

18 Larson, *From Ah Q to Lei Feng*, 91.

19 Cook, *Mao's Little Red Book*, 9–11.

20 Schwartz, *China and Other Matters*, 169.

21 Schumann, *Ideology and Organization*, 521.

22 Schumann, *Ideology and Organization*, 521.

23 Schumann, *Ideology and Organization*, 526–27.

24 Lin, *Renmin zhanzheng shengli wansui*, 3.

25 Schwartz, *China and Other Matters*, 174.

26 Lin, *Remin zhangzheng shengli wansui*, 24–26.

27 Levenson, *Revolution and Cosmopolitanism*, 25.

28 Mao Zedong, *Selected Works*, 2:196.

29 Mao Zedong, *Selected Works*, 4:97–102.

30 Yang, "A Chinese Variation."

31 Cummings, *Korea's Place in the Sun*, 241.

32 Zhu, "Nationalism and Chinese Foreign Policy."

33 Levenson, *Revolution and Cosmopolitanism*, 7–8.

34 Gramsci, *The Antonio Gramsci Reader*, 363.

35 Levenson, *Revolution and Cosmopolitanism*, 10.

36 Levenson, *Revolution and Cosmopolitanism*, 10.

Chapter Five. National Unity, Ethnicity, and Socialist Utopia in *Five Golden Flowers*

Parts of chapter 5 were published in "Laughter, Ethnicity, and Socialist Utopia: *Five Golden Flowers*," in *Maoist Laughter*, ed. Ping Zhu, Zhuoyi Wang, and Jason McGrath (Hong Kong: Hong Kong University Press, 2019), 19–36.

1 Lin, "China's Lost World of Internationalism," 183–84.

2 Jie Chen, "Nation, Ethnicity, and Cultural Strategies," 35–36.

3 Wang Hui, *The Politics of Imagining Asia*, 177.

4 Gladney, *Muslim Chinese*; Harrell, "Civilizing Projects and the Reaction to Them," 3–36; Mullaney, *Coming to Terms with the Nation*.

5 Harrell, "Civilizing Projects," 10.

6 Harrell, "Civilizing Projects," 14.
7 McCarthy, *Communist Multiculturalism*, 3.
8 McCarthy, *Communist Multiculturalism*, 9.
9 Liang, *Liang Qichao quanji*, 3344.
10 Wang Hui, *The Politics of Imagining Asia*, 160.
11 Wang Hui, *The Politics of Imagining Asia*, 186.
12 Quoted in Wang Hui, *The Politics of Imaging Asia*, 187. See also Fei, "Zhonghua minzu," 1.
13 Committee on Ethnicity Policy, *Minzu zhengce wenxuan*, 108.
14 Jie Chen, "Nation, Ethnicity, and Cultural Strategies," 44.
15 Yingjin Zhang, *Screening China*, 165. See also Bao Ying, "In Search of Laughter," 100; Jie Chen, "Nation, Ethnicity, and Cultural Strategies," 63.
16 Bao, "In Search of Laughter in Maoist China," 35–36.
17 Jie Chen, "Nation, Ethnicity, and Cultural Strategies," 26.
18 Jie Chen, "Nation, Ethnicity, and Cultural Strategies," 14.
19 Lü, "Xin Zhongguo shaoshu minzu yingxiang shuxie," 23.
20 L. Zhang, "Navigating Ethnicity, Gender, and Space," 154.
21 Zhang Zhaofu and Yan, *Wuduo Jinhua*, 8.
22 Bao, "In Search of Laughter in Maoist China," 95.
23 L. Zhang, "Navigating Ethnicity, Gender, and Space," 156.
24 L. Zhang, ""Navigating Ethnicity, Gender, and Space," 155, 157, 168.
25 See Zhou Yang, *Zhou Yang wenji*, 3:2.
26 Zhuoyi Wang, *Revolutionary Cycles in Chinese Cinema*, 136–38.
27 Barton, "The Philosophy of Humor."
28 Rea, *The Age of Irreverence*, ix–x.
29 Bao, "The Problematics of Comedy," 186.
30 Bao, "In Search of Laughter in Maoist China," 35–36.
31 Bao, "In Search of Laughter in Maoist China," 81.
32 Barton, "The Philosophy of Humor."
33 Mao Zedong, *Mao Tse-tung on Literature and Art*, 33–34.
34 Mao Zedong, *Mao Tse-tung on Literature and Art*, 34.
35 Snow, *Red Star over China*, 109. Further references appear parenthetically in the text.
36 Schiller, *Essays*, 179–201.
37 Cai Chusheng et al., "*Jintian wo xiuxi* zuotan hui," 34–46.
38 Li Zehou, *Meixue lunji*, 225.
39 Meisner, *Mao's China and After*, 179–80.

Chapter Six. The Third World, Alternative Development,
and Global Maoism

Portions of chapter 6 were published in "Third World Internationalism: Films and Operas in the Chinese Cultural Revolution," in *Listening to China's Cultural Revolution*, ed. Paul Clark et al. (New York: Palgrave Macmillan, 2015), 85–106.

1 Monson, *Africa's Freedom Railway*, 3, 6.

2 Quoted in Monson, *Africa's Freedom Railway*, 6.
3 Monson, *Africa's Freedom Railway*, 2.
4 Kissinger, *On China*.
5 D. Kang, *East Asia before the West*.
6 Levenson, *Revolution and Cosmopolitanism*, 26.
7 Wakeman, "Foreword," xvi.
8 Levenson, *Revolution and Cosmopolitanism*, 28.
9 Mao Zedong, *Selected Works*, 4:97–101.
10 Yang, "A Chinese Variation."
11 Wang Hui, "Depoliticized Politics," 29.
12 Monson, *Africa's Freedom Railway*, 3; Mao quoted in Schram, *Mao Tse-tung*, 201.
13 X. Chen, *Acting the Right Part*, 148–50.
14 X. Chen, *Acting the Right Part*, 151.
15 Meisner, *Marxism, Maoism, and Utopianism*, 65.
16 Luxemburg, *The Accumulation of Capital*, 432.
17 Lin, "China's Lost World of Internationalism," 180–81.
18 Dirlik, "Globalization and National Development."
19 Maxwell, *China's Road to Development*, 8.
20 Yu Zhang, *Going to the Countryside*, 3–4.
21 Yu Zhang, *Going to the Countryside*, 4.
22 Meisner, *Marxism, Maoism, and Utopianism*, 60.
23 Meisner, *Marxism, Maoism, and Utopianism*, 60.
24 Schmalzer, *Red Revolution, Green Revolution*, 3.
25 Schmalzer, *Red Revolution, Green Revolution*, 3.
26 Meisner, *Mao's China and After*, 114, 119.
27 Selden, *The Yenan Way*, 210.
28 Schmalzer, *Red Revolution, Green Revolution*, 4.
29 Riskin, *China's Political Economy*, 184.
30 Riskin, *China's Political Economy*, 184.
31 Sidel, "The Barefoot Doctors," 1294.
32 Victor Li, "Politics and Health Care in China," 827.
33 Fang, *Barefoot Doctors and Western Medicine*, 2.
34 Gorz, *Écology et politique*, 192, 232.
35 Illich, *Medical Nemesis*, 68–69.
36 Illich, *Medical Nemesis*, 59.
37 Hou, *Building for Oil*, 6–8.
38 Mao Huahe, *The Ebb and Flow of Chinese Petroleum*, 12–13.
39 Hou, *Building for Oil*, 6.
40 Foster-Carter, "North Korea."
41 Dirlik, "Globalization and National Development," 248.
42 Dirlik, "Globalization and National Development," 248.
43 Murphey, *The Fading of the Maoist Vision*, 41–42.
44 Cook, *Mao's Little Red Book*, 96.
45 Wolin, *The Wind from the East*, 11.

46 Wolin, *The Wind from the East*, 11.
47 Cai Xiang, a leading Chinese literary critic, has quoted Badiou frequently in *Revolution and Its Narratives*.
48 Wolin, *The Wind from the East*, 159.
49 Wang Hui, "Depoliticized Politics."
50 Apter and Saich, *Revolutionary Discourse in Mao's Republic*, 3.
51 Kalyvas, *Democracy and the Politics of the Extraordinary*, 47.
52 Kalyvas, *Democracy and the Politics of the Extraordinary*, 52, 57.
53 Badiou, "The Cultural Revolution," 504.
54 Badiou, "The Cultural Revolution," 505.
55 Badiou, "The Cultural Revolution," 505.
56 Badiou, "The Cultural Revolution," 505.
57 Badiou, "The Cultural Revolution," 505.
58 Meisner, *Mao's China and After*, 248.
59 Meisner, *Mao's China and After*, 370.
60 Badiou, "The Cultural Revolution," 506.
61 Badiou, *Théorie du sujet*, 340–41.
62 Mao, *Selected Works*, 3:321–22.
63 Badiou, *Théorie du sujet*, 341.
64 Sorace, "Saint Mao," 176.
65 Translation by Ma, *Snow Glistens on the Great Wall*, 110–11.
66 Ma, *Snow Glistens on the Great Wall*, 111.

Chapter Seven. The Cold War, Depoliticization, and China in the American Classroom

1 Hardt and Negri, *Empire*, 326.
2 Deleuze and Guattari, *Anti-Oedipus*, 224.
3 Hardt and Negri, *Empire*, 327.
4 Mearsheimer, *The Tragedy of Great Power Politics*, 2. Mearsheimer argues the realistic theme that power conflict and war will remain the basic condition for the twenty-first century.
5 Carmichael, *Framing History*, 120.
6 Quoted in Carmichael, *Framing History*, 36–37.
7 Carmichael, *Framing History*, 37.
8 Lens, *The Forging of the American Empire*, 2.
9 Carmichael, *Framing History*, 36.
10 Lanza, *The End of Concern*, 177.
11 Lanza, *The End of Concern*, 180.
12 Lanza, *The End of Concern*, 33.
13 Cohen, *Discovering History in China*, 150.
14 Cohen, *Discovering History in China*, 7.
15 Lanza, *The End of Concern*, 180.
16 Lanza, *The End of Concern*, 183.

17 Lanza, *The End of Concern*, 35.
18 Lanza, *The End of Concern*, 183.
19 Lin, "China's Lost World of Internationalism," 197.
20 Dirlik and Meisner, *Marxism and the Chinese Experience*, 5.
21 Dirlik and Meisner, *Marxism and the Chinese Experience*, 7.
22 For a discussion of cinema as the image of capital, see Beller, "Capital/Cinema."
23 Volland, *Socialist Cosmopolitanism*, 7.
24 Karl, *The Magic of Concepts*, 156–58.
25 Fanon, *The Wretched of the Earth*, 216.
26 Jameson, "Whether World Literature Has a Foreign Policy?"
27 Lanza, *The End of Concern*, 36.
28 Bloom, *The Closing of the American Mind*, 84.
29 Bloom, *The Closing of the American Mind*, 85.
30 MacIntyre, *After Virtue*, 12.
31 MacIntyre, *After Virtue*, 22.
32 MacIntyre, *After Virtue*, 24.
33 MacIntyre, *After Virtue*, 24.
34 Bernstein and Munro, *The Coming Conflict with America*.
35 Hymes, *Way and Byway*, 6.
36 Huntington, *The Clash of Civilizations*, 225.
37 Huntington, *The Clash of Civilizations*, 225.
38 Levenson, *Revolution and Cosmopolitanism*, 7.

Chapter Eight. Using the Past to Understand the Present

1 Wang Hui, "Contemporary Chinese Thought," 14; Levenson, *Revolution and Cosmopolitanism*, 1.
2 Cohen, *Discovering History in China*.
3 New Text Confucianism refers to the study of the classical Confucian texts recovered after the Qin emperor's burning of the classics. The New Text scholars defend the authenticity of Confucian doctrines in the new as opposed to the old texts. The themes relevant to Kang Youwei are the image of Confucius as a reformer, the valorization of *The Spring and Autumn Annals* over the *Zuo Commentary*, and transhistorical and normative principles over realpolitik. See Hsiao, *A Modern China and a New World*, 66–67.
4 Wang Hui, *The Politics of Imagining Asia*, 90.
5 Hsiao, *A Modern China and a New World*, 43.
6 D. Kang, *East Asia before the West*; Womack, *China among Unequals*.
7 Kuhn, *Origins of the Modern Chinese State*, 92.
8 Wang Hui, *Xiandai Zhongguo*, 21.
9 Wang Hui, *Xiandai Zhongguo*, 82. Further references appear parenthetically in the text.
10 Wang Hui, *The Politics of Imagining Asia*, 160.
11 Wang Hui, *The Politics of Imagining Asia*, 186.

12 Liang, *Liang Qichao quanji*, 5531.
13 Buck-Morss, *Hegel, Haiti, and Universal History*, 35–39.
14 Žižek, *First as Tragedy, Then as Farce*, 112.
15 Prashad, "Dream History of the Global South," 43.
16 Quoted in Howard, "Music for a National Defense," 3.
17 Avineri, *Karl Marx on Colonialism and Modernization*, 44–45.
18 Avineri, *Karl Marx on Colonialism and Modernization*, 45.
19 Lin, *China and Global Capitalism*, 189.
20 Mao, *Selected Works*, 4:413.
21 Mao, *Selected Works*, 2:380.
22 Levenson, *Revolution and Cosmopolitanism*, 1.
23 Cheah, *Inhuman Conditions*, 101.
24 Cheah, *Inhuman Conditions*, 101.
25 Hsiao, *A Modern China and a New World*, 413.
26 Hsiao, *A Modern China and a New World*, 413.
27 Wang Hui, *Xiandai Zhongguo*, 113.
28 Zhao, "Cong shijie wenti kaishi de tianxia zhengzhi," 69.
29 Furth, "Intellectual Change," 35.
30 Dirlik, "Globalization and National Development," 245.
31 Babones, *American Tianxia*.
32 Wang Hui, *The End of the Revolution*, 5.
33 Wang Hui, *The End of the Revolution*, 9.
34 Wang Hui, *The End of the Revolution*, 9.
35 Wang Hui, *The End of the Revolution*, 15.
36 Wang Hui, *The End of the Revolution*, 15.
37 Lanza, *The End of Concern*, 180.
38 Wang Hui, *The End of the Revolution*, 18.
39 Research Bureau for Documents of the CCP, *Chronicles of Deng Xiaoping's Thoughts*, 3–4.

Bibliography

Althusser, Louis. *For Marx.* New York: Penguin, 1969.

Anderson, Perry. "Internationalism: A Breviary." *New Left Review,* no. 14 (March 2002): 5–25.

Apter, David, and Tony Saich. *Revolutionary Discourse in Mao's Republic.* Cambridge, MA: Harvard University Press, 1994.

Arendt, Hannah. *Between Past and Future.* New York: Viking Press, 1961.

Avineri, Shlomo, ed. *Karl Marx on Colonialism and Modernization.* New York: Doubleday, 1968.

Babones, Salvatore. *American Tianxia: Chinese Money, American Power, and the End of History.* Bristol: Policy Press, 2017.

Badiou, Alain. "The Cultural Revolution: The Last Revolution?" *positions: east asia cultures critique* 13, no. 3 (Winter 2005): 481–514.

Badiou, Alain. *Théorie du sujet.* Paris: Éditions du seul, 1982.

Bao Ying. "In Search of Laughter in Maoist China: 1949–1966." PhD diss., Ohio State University, 2008.

Bao Ying. "The Problematics of Comedy: New China Cinema and the Case of Lü Ban." *Modern Chinese Literature and Culture* 20, no. 2 (Fall 2008): 185–228.

Barton, Adrian. "The Philosophy of Humor." In *Comedy: A Geographic and Historical Guide,* vol. 2, edited by Maurice Charney, 462–76. Westport, CT: Greenwood, 2005.

Beller, Jonathan. "Capital/Cinema." In *Deleuze and Guattari*, edited by Eleanor Kaufman and Kevin Heller, 77–95. Minneapolis: University of Minnesota Press, 1998.

Berman, Marshall. "Themes for China: Modern Arts, Modern Conflict." In *Culture and Social Transformations in Reform Era China*, edited by Cao Tian Yu, Zhong Xueping, and Liao Kebin, 433–35. Leiden: Brill, 2010.

Bernstein, Richard, and Ross H. Munro. *The Coming Conflict with America*. New York: Vintage, 1998.

Bloom, Allan. *The Closing of the American Mind: How Higher Education Has Failed Democracy and Impoverished the Souls of Today's Students*. New York: Simon and Schuster, 1987.

Brady, Anne-Marie. *Making the Foreign Serve China: Managing Foreigners in the People's Republic*. Lanham, MD: Rowman and Littlefield, 2008.

Buck-Morss, Susan. *Hegel, Haiti, and Universal History*. Pittsburgh: University of Pittsburgh Press, 2009.

Cai Chusheng 蔡楚生 et al. "*Jintian wo xiuxi* zuotanhui" 今天我休息"座談會 [Forum on *Jintian wo xiuxi*]. *Dianying yishu* [Film art], no. 6 (1960): 34–46.

Cai Xiang. *Revolution and Its Narratives*. Durham, NC: Duke University Press, 2016.

Calhoun, Craig. "Imagining Solidarity: Cosmopolitanism, Constitutional Patriotism, and the Public Sphere." *Public Culture* 14, no. 1 (Winter 2002): 147–71.

Calhoun, Craig. *Nationalism*. Minneapolis: University of Minnesota Press, 1997.

Carmichael, Virginia. *Framing History: The Rosenberg Story and the Cold War*. Minneapolis: University of Minnesota Press, 1993.

Casanova, Pascale. *The World Republic of Letters*. Cambridge, MA: Harvard University Press, 2004.

Cheah, Pheng. *Inhuman Conditions*. Cambridge, MA: Harvard University Press, 2006.

Cheah, Pheng. "What Is a World? On World Literature as World-Making Activity." *Daedalus* 137, no. 3 (Summer 2008): 26–38.

Chen Jian. *Mao's China and the Cold War*. Chapel Hill: University of North Carolina Press, 2001.

Chen, Jie. "Nation, Ethnicity, and Cultural Strategies: Three Waves of Ethnic Representation in Post-1949 China." PhD diss., Rutgers University, 2008.

Chen, Xiaomei. *Acting the Right Part: Political Theater and Popular Drama in Contemporary China*. Honolulu: University of Hawai'i Press, 2002.

Cohen, Paul. *Discovering History in China: American Historical Writing of the Recent Past*. New York: Columbia University Press, 1984.

Coker, Christopher. *The Rise of the Civilizational State*. Cambridge: Polity, 2019.

Committee on Ethnicity Policy, ed. *Minzu zhengce wenxuan* 民族政策文選 [Selected works on policy toward ethnic minorities]. Urumchi: Xinjiang renmin, 1985.

Cook, Alexander, ed. *Mao's Little Red Book: A Global History*. New York: Cambridge University Press, 2014.

Cummings, Bruce. *Korea's Place in the Sun: A Modern History*. New York: Norton, 1997.

Cummings, Bruce. *North Korea: Another Country*. New York: New Press, 2004.

Daruvala, Susan. *Zhou Zuoren and an Alternative Response to Modernity*. Cambridge, MA: Harvard University Press, 2000.

de Bary, Theodore, and Irene Bloom, eds. *Sources of Chinese Tradition*. 2nd ed. New York: Columbia University Press, 1999.

de Tocqueville, Alexis. *Democracy in America*. New York: Bantam, 2000.

Deleuze, Gilles, and Félix Guattari. *Anti-Oedipus: Capitalism and Schizophrenia*. Minneapolis: University of Minnesota Press, 1983.

Dirlik, Arif. "Globalization and National Development: The Perspective of the Chinese Revolution." *New Centennial Review* 3, no. 2 (Summer 2003): 241–70.

Dirlik, Arif. "The Predicament of Marxist Revolutionary Consciousness: Mao Zedong, Antonio Gramsci, and the Reformulation of Marxist Revolutionary Theory." *Modern China* 9, no. 2 (April 1983): 182–211.

Dirlik, Arif, and Maurice Meisner, eds. *Marxism and the Chinese Experience*. New York: M. E. Sharpe, 1989.

Eagleton, Terry. *The Ideology of the Aesthetic*. Oxford: Blackwell, 1990.

Etherton, Ross. "Reading against the Gun: The Machine Gun and *Sturm*." *Telos*, no. 190 (Spring 2020): 93–115.

Fairbank, John, ed. *The Chinese World Order: Traditional China's Foreign Relation*. Cambridge, MA: Harvard University Press, 1968.

Fang, Xiaoping. *Barefoot Doctors and Western Medicine in China*. Rochester, NY: University of Rochester Press, 2012.

Fanon, Frantz. *The Wretched of the Earth*. New York: Grove Press, 1963.

Fei Xiaotong 費孝通. "Zhonghua minzu de duoyuan yiti geju" 中華民族的多元一體格局 [Unity in diversity of the Chinese nation]. In *Zhonghua minzu de duoyuan yiti geju*, edited by Fei Xiaotong et al., 1–36. Beijing: Zhongyang minzu xueyuan, 1989.

Fitzgerald, John. *Awakening China: Politics, Culture, and Class in the Nationalist Revolution*. Stanford, CA: Stanford University Press, 1996.

Foster-Carter, Aidan. "North Korea: Development and Self-Reliance: A Critical Appraisal." In *Korea, North and South: The Deepening Crisis*, edited by Gavan McCormack and Mark Selden, 115–49. New York: Monthly Review Press, 1978.

Fukuyama, Francis. *The Origins of Political Order*. New York: Farrar, Straus and Giroux, 2011.

Fukuyama, Francis. *Political Order and Political Decay*. New York: Farrar, Straus and Giroux, 2014.

Fung Yu-lan. *A Short History of Chinese Philosophy*. New York: Free Press, 1948.

Furth, Charlotte. "Intellectual Change." In *An Intellectual History of Modern China*, edited by Merle Goldman and Leo Ou-fan Lee, 13–96. New York: Cambridge University Press, 2002.

Gan Yang 甘揚. *Jiangcuo jiucuo* 將錯就錯 [Live with mistakes]. Beijing: Sanlian, 2002.

Gao Hua. *How the Red Sun Rose: The Origins and Development of the Yan'an Rectification Movement, 1930–1945*. Hong Kong: Chinese University Press, 2018.

Gladney, Dru. *Muslim Chinese: Ethnic Nationalism in the People's Republic*. Cambridge, MA: Harvard University Press, 1991.

Goldman, Merle, and Leo Ou-fan Lee, eds. *An Intellectual History of Modern China.* New York: Cambridge University Press, 2002.

Gorz, André. *Écology et politique.* Paris: Galilée, 1975.

Gramsci, Antonio. *The Antonio Gramsci Reader: Selected Writings, 1916–1935.* New York: New York University Press, 2000.

Gu Yanwu 顧炎武. *Rizhilu* 日知錄 [Collected annotations of *Daily Reflections*]. Shanghai: Shanghai guji, 2013.

Hardt, Michael, and Antonio Negri. *Empire.* Cambridge, MA: Harvard University Press, 2000.

Harrell, Stevan, "Introduction: Civilizing Projects and the Reaction to Them." In *Cultural Encounters on China's Ethnic Frontiers,* edited by Stevan Harrell, 3–36. Seattle: University of Washington Press, 1995.

He Zhiqiang 賀志強 et al., eds. *Luyi shihua* 魯藝史話 [History of Lu Xun Academy of Arts]. Xian: Shaanxi renmin, 1991.

Holm, David. *Art and Ideology in Revolutionary China.* New York: Oxford University Press, 1991.

Hou, Li. *Building for Oil: Daqing and the Formation of the Chinese Socialist State.* Cambridge, MA: Harvard University Press, 2018.

Howard, Joshua. "Music for a National Defense: Making Martial Music during the Anti-Japanese War." *CrossCurrents: East Asian History and Culture Review* 13 (December 2014): 1–50. http://cross-currents.berkeley.edu/e-journal /issue-13.

Hsia, Chih-tsing. *C. T. Hsia on Chinese Literature.* New York: Columbia University Press, 2004.

Hsiao, Kung-chuan. *A Modern China and a New World: Kang Yu-Wei, Reformer and Utopian, 1858–1927.* Seattle: University of Washington Press, 1975.

Hsiung, James C. *China into its Second Rise: Myths, Puzzles, Paradoxes, and Challenge to Theory.* Hackensack, NJ: World Scientific, 2012.

Huang Ke'an 黃科安. *Yan'an wenxue yanjiu* 延安文學研究 [Study of Yan'an literature]. Beijing: Wenhua yishu, 2009.

Huntington, Samuel. *The Clash of Civilizations and the Remaking of World Order.* New York: Touchstone, 1996.

Huters, Theodor. *Bringing the World Home: Appropriating the West in Late Qing and Early Republican China.* Honolulu: University of Hawai'i Press, 2005.

Hymes, Robert. *Way and Byway: Taoism, Local Religion, and Models of Divinity in Sung and Modern China.* Berkeley: University of California Press, 2002.

Illich, Ivan. *Medical Nemesis: The Expropriation of Health.* London: Calder and Boyars, 1975.

Jacques, Martin. *When China Rules the World: The Rise of the Middle Kingdom and the End of the Western World.* New York: Penguin, 2009.

Jameson, Fredric. "Whether World Literature Has a Foreign Policy?" Speech at the reception of the Holberg International Memorial Prize, Franklin Humanities Institute, Duke University, November 10, 2008.

Kalyvas, Andreas. *Democracy and the Politics of the Extraordinary: Max Weber, Carl Schmitt, and Hannah Arendt.* New York: Cambridge University Press, 2008.

Kang, David. *East Asia before the West: Five Centuries of Trade and Tribute*. New York: Columbia University Press, 2010.

Kang Youwei. *Datong shu* 大同書 [Book of great community]. Shenyang: Liaoning renmin, 1994.

Kang Youwei. *Kang Youwei jingdian wenchun* 康有为经典文存 [Selected classics by Kang Youwei]. Shanghai: Shanghai University Press, 2003.

Kang Youwei. *Kang Youwei quanji* 康有為全集 [Complete works of Kang Youwei]. Vol. 1. Edited by Jiang Yihua and Zhang Ronghua. Beijing: Renmin University Press, 2007.

Kang Youwei. *Kongzi gaizhi kao* 孔子改制考 [Confucius as reformer]. Vol. 3, *Kang Youwei quanji* 康有為全集 [Complete works of Kang Youwei], edited by Jiang Yihua and Zhang Ronghua. Beijing: Renmin University Press, 2007.

Kang Youwei. *Ta T'ung Shu: The One-World Philosophy of K'ang Yu-wei*. Translated by Laurence Thompson. London: Routledge, 2011.

Kant, Immanuel. *Critique of the Power of Judgment*. Translated by Paul Guyer and Eric Mathews. New York: Cambridge University Press, 2000.

Kant, Immanuel. *Political Writings*. Edited by H. S. Reiss. Translated by H. B. Nisbet. New York: Cambridge University Press, 1991.

Karl, Rebecca. *The Magic of Concepts: History and the Economic in Twentieth-Century China*. Durham, NC: Duke University Press, 2017.

Karl, Rebecca. *Staging the World: Chinese Nationalism at the Turn of the Twentieth Century*. Durham, NC: Duke University Press, 2002.

Kissinger, Henry. *On China*. New York: Penguin, 2011.

Kowallis, Jon Eugene von. *Warriors of the Spirit: The Early Wenyan Essays of Lu Xun*. Berkeley: University of California, Institute of East Asian Studies Monographs, forthcoming.

Kuhn, Philip. *Origins of the Modern Chinese State*. Stanford, CA: Stanford University Press, 2002.

Lanza, Fabio. *The End of Concern: Maoist China, Activism, and Asian Studies*. Durham, NC: Duke University Press, 2017.

Larson, Wendy. *From Ah Q to Lei Feng: Freud and Revolutionary Spirit in 20th Century China*. Stanford, CA: Stanford University Press, 2009.

Larson, Wendy. *Zhang Yimou: Globalization and the Subject of Culture*. Amherst, NY: Cambria, 2017.

Lens, Sidney. *The Forging of the American Empire*. New York: Thomas Y. Crowell, 1971.

Levenson, Joseph R. *Revolution and Cosmopolitanism*. Berkeley: University of California Press, 1971.

Lewis, Mark Edward, and Mei-yu Hseih. "*Tianxia* and the Invention of Empire in East Asia." In *Chinese Visions of World Order: Tianxia, Culture, and World Politics*, edited by Ban Wang, 34–68. Durham, NC: Duke University Press, 2017.

Li Dazhao 李大釗. *Li Dazhao quanji* 李大釗全集 [Complete works of Li Dazhao]. Vol. 2. Beijing: Renmin chubanshe, 2006.

Li, Victor H. "Politics and Health Care in China: The Barefoot Doctors." *Stanford Law Review* 27, no. 3 (February 1975): 827–40.

Li Zehou 李澤厚. *Meixue lunji* 美學論集 [Essays on aesthetics]. Shanghai: Shanghai wenyi, 1980.

Li Zehou 李澤厚. *Zhongguo xiandai sixiang shi lun* 中國現代思想史論 [On the history of modern Chinese thought]. Beijing: Dongfang, 1987.

Liang Qichao 梁啟超. *Liang Qichao quanji* 梁啟超全集 [Complete works of Liang Qichao]. Beijing: Beijing chubanshe, 1999.

Lin Biao 林彪. *Renmin zhanzheng shengli wansui* 人民戰爭勝利萬歲 [Long live the people's war]. Beijing: Renmin chubanshe, 1965.

Lin, Chun. *China and Global Capitalism*. New York: Palgrave, 2013.

Lin, Chun. "China's Lost World of Internationalism." In *Chinese Visions of World Order: Tianxia, Culture, and World Politics*, edited by Ban Wang, 177–211. Durham, NC: Duke University Press, 2017.

Linklater, Andrew. *Men and Citizens in the Theory of International Relations*. 2nd ed. London: Macmillan, 1990.

Liu, Lydia. *The Clash of Empires: The Invention of China in Modern World Making*. Cambridge, MA: Harvard University Press, 2004.

Liu, Lydia. *Translingual Practice: Literature, National Culture, and Translated Modernity*. Stanford, CA: Stanford University Press, 1995.

Lü Xinyu 呂新雨. "Xin Zhongguo shaoshu minzu yingxiang shuxie" 新中國少數民族影像書寫 [Writing minority film images in new China]. *Shanghai daxu xuebo* 32, no. 5 (2015): 13–51.

Lu Xun 魯迅. *Lu Xun quanji* 魯迅全集 [Complete works of Lu Xun]. Vol. 1. Beijing: Renmin wenxue, 2005.

Lukács, György. *The Historical Novel*. Lincoln: University of Nebraska Press, 1983.

Luo Mengce 羅夢冊. *Zhongguo lun* 中國論 [On China]. Shanghai: Shangwu yinshuguan, 1944.

Luo Zhitian 羅誌田. "Lixiang yu xianshi: Qingji minchu shijie zhuyi yu minzu zhuyi de guanlian yu hudong" 理想與現實：清季民初世界主義與民族主義的關聯與互動 [Ideal and reality: Relations and interactions between nationalism and cosmopolitanism during the Qing and early Republican eras]. In *Xiandai Zhongguo sixiang de hexin guannian* 現代中國思想的核心觀念 [Key concepts in modern Chinese thought], edited by Xu Jilin and Song Hong, 335–50. Shanghai: Shanghai renmin, 2011.

Luxemburg, Rosa. *The Accumulation of Capital*. New York: Routledge, 2003.

Ma Wen-yee. *Snow Glistens on the Great Wall: A New Translation of the Complete Collection of Mao Tse-tung's Poetry*. Santa Barbara, CA: Santa Barbara Press, 1986.

MacIntyre, Alasdair. *After Virtue*. 2nd ed. Notre Dame, IN: University of Notre Dame Press, 1984.

Mao Huahe. *The Ebb and Flow of Chinese Petroleum: A Story Told by a Witness*. Translated by Mao Yiran and Thomas Seay. Leiden: Brill, 2019.

Mao Zedong. *Mao Tse-tung on Literature and Art*. Peking: Foreign Languages Press, 1967.

Mao Zedong. *Quotations from Chairman Mao Tse-tung*. Beijing: Foreign Languages Press, 1972.

Mao Zedong. *Selected Works of Mao Tse-tung.* 4 vols. Peking: Foreign Languages Press, 1961.

Marx, Karl. "Draft of an Article on Friedrich List's Book *Das nationale System der politischen Ōkonomie.*" In *Collected Works,* vol. 4, edited by Karl Marx and Friedrich Engels, 265–93. New York: International Publishers, 1975.

Marx, Karl, and Friedrich Engels. *The Communist Manifesto.* New York: Penguin, 1985.

Marx, Karl, and Friedrich Engels. *The Marx-Engels Reader.* Edited by Robert C. Tucker. New York: Norton, 1972.

Maxwell, Neville, ed. *China's Road to Development.* 2nd enlarged ed. Oxford: Pergamon Press, 1979.

McCarthy, Susan K. *Communist Multiculturalism: Ethnic Revival in Southwest China.* Seattle: University of Washington Press, 2009.

Mearsheimer, John. *The Tragedy of Great Power Politics.* New York: Norton, 2001.

Meisner, Maurice. *Mao's China and After.* 3rd ed. New York: Free Press, 1999.

Meisner, Maurice. *Marxism, Maoism, and Utopianism.* Madison: University of Wisconsin Press, 1982.

Melvin, Sheila, and Jindong Cai. *Rhapsody in Red.* New York: Algora, 2000.

Mencius. *The Works of Mencius.* Translated by James Legge. New York: Dover, 1970.

Meng Liye 孟犁野. "Xin xieshi yu yingxiong shishi" 新寫實與英雄史詩 [New realism and epic of heroism]. *Dangdai dianying* 5 (2002): 52–57.

Monson, Jamie. *Africa's Freedom Railway: How a Chinese Development Project Changed Lives and Livelihood in Tanzania.* Bloomington: Indiana University Press, 2009.

Mullaney, Thomas. *Coming to Terms with the Nation: Ethnic Classification in Modern China.* Berkeley: University of California Press, 2011.

Murphey, Rhoads. *The Fading of the Maoist Vision: City and Country in China's Development.* New York: Methuen, 1980.

Muthu, Sankar. *Enlightenment against Empire.* Princeton, NJ: Princeton University Press, 2003.

Pines, Yuri. *The Everlasting Empire: The Political Culture of Ancient China and Its Imperial Legacy.* Honolulu: University of Hawai'i Press, 2009.

Prashad, Vijay. "Dream History of the Global South." *Interface* 4 (May 2012): 43–53.

Purchas, Samuel. *Purchas His Pilgrimage; or, Relations of the World and the Religions Obserued in All Ages and Places Discouered.* London, 1613.

Pye, Lucian. *The Spirit of Chinese Politics.* Cambridge, MA: Harvard University Press, 1992.

Qian, Kun. *Imperial-Time-Order: Literature, Intellectual History, and China's Road to Empire.* Leiden: Brill, 2016.

Qian Suoqiao. *Liberal Cosmopolitanism: Lin Yutang and Middling Chinese Modernity.* Leiden: Brill, 2011.

Rea, Christopher. *The Age of Irreverence.* Oakland: University of California Press, 2015.

Research Bureau for Documents of the CCP, ed. *Chronicles of Deng Xiaoping's Thoughts.* Beijing: Press of Research Bureau of Documents of the CCP, 2011.

Ricci, Matteo. *The True Meaning of the Lord under Heaven*. Edited by Thierry Meynard. Translated by Douglas Lancashire and Peter Hu Kuo-chen. Boston: Institute of Jesuit Sources, Boston College, 2016.

Riskin, Carl. *China's Political Economy: The Quest for Development since 1949*. New York: Oxford University Press, 1988.

Roche, John. "Marx and Humanism." *Rethinking Marxism* 17, no. 3 (July 2005): 335–48.

Rowe, William T. *China's Last Empire: The Great Qing*. Cambridge, MA: Harvard University Press, 2012.

Said, Edward. *Humanism and Democratic Criticism*. New York: Columbia University Press, 2004.

Saunders, Frances S. *The Cultural Cold War: The CIA and the World of Arts and Letters*. New York: New Press, 1999.

Schiller, Friedrich. *Essays*. Edited by Walter Hinderer and Daniel Dahlstrom. New York: Continuum, 1993.

Schmalzer, Sigrid. *Red Revolution, Green Revolution: Scientific Farming in Socialist China*. Chicago: University of Chicago Press.

Schram, Stuart. *Mao Tse-tung*. Harmondsworth, UK: Penguin, 1966.

Schram, Stuart. "Mao Tse-tung's Thought to 1949." In *An Intellectual History of Modern China*, edited by Merle Goldman and Leo Ou-Fan Lee, 267–348. New York: Cambridge University Press, 2002.

Schuessler, Axel. *ABC Etymological Dictionary of Old Chinese*. Honolulu: University of Hawai'i Press, 2007.

Schumann, Franz. *Ideology and Organization in Communist China*. Berkeley: University of California Press, 1971.

Schwartz, Benjamin. *China and Other Matters*. Cambridge, MA: Harvard University Press, 1996.

Schwartz, Benjamin. "Themes in Intellectual History: May Fourth and After." In *An Intellectual History of Modern China*, edited by Merle Goldman and Leo Ou-fan Lee, 97–141. New York: Cambridge University Press, 2002.

Schwartz, Benjamin. *The World of Thought in Ancient China*. Cambridge, MA: Harvard University Press, 1985.

Schwarzmantel, John. "Nationalism and Socialist Internationalism." In *The Oxford Handbook of the History of Nationalism*, edited by John Breuilly, 635–54. New York: Oxford University Press, 2013.

Selden, Mark. *The Yenan Way in Revolutionary China*. Cambridge, MA: Harvard University Press, 1974.

Shen, Shuang. *Cosmopolitan Publics: Anglophone Print Culture in Semi-Colonial Shanghai*. New Brunswick, NJ: Rutgers University Press, 2009.

Shih, Shumei. *The Lure of the Modern*. Berkeley: University of California Press, 2001.

Shu, Yunzhong. *Buglers on the Home Front: Wartime Practice of the Qiyue School*. Albany: State University of New York Press, 2000.

Sidel, Victor W. "The Barefoot Doctors of the People's Republic of China." *New England Journal of Medicine* 286, no. 24 (June 1972): 1292–1300.

Smith, Adam. *An Inquiry into the Nature and Causes of the Wealth of Nations*. London: Methuen, 1961.

Snow, Edgar. *Red Star over China*. New York: Random House, 1944.

Sorace, Christian. "Saint Mao." *Telos*, no. 151 (Summer 2010): 173–91.

Spence, Jonathan. *The Gate of Heavenly Peace*. New York: Penguin, 1981.

Sun Zhongshan 孫中山. *Sun Zhongshan quanji* 孫中山全集 [Complete works of Sun Zhongshan]. 11 vols. Beijing: Zhonghua shuju, 1986.

Tang, Xiaobing. *Global Space and the Nationalist Discourse of Modernity: The Historical Thinking of Liang Qichao*. Stanford: Stanford University Press, 1996.

Tang Zhijun 湯志鈞. *Kang Youwei zhuan* 康有為傳 [Biography of Kang Youwei]. Taipei: Taiwan Shangwu, 1997.

United Nations. *Universal Declaration of Human Rights, 1948*. n.p.: United Nations, 2015.

Volland, Nicolai. *Socialist Cosmopolitanism*. New York: Columbia University Press, 2017.

Wakeman, Frederic, Jr. "Foreword." In Levenson, *Revolution and Cosmopolitanism*, ix–xxix. Berkeley: University of California Press, 1971.

Wakeman, Frederic, Jr. *History and Will: Philosophical Perspectives of Mao Tse-tung's Thought*. Berkeley: University of California Press, 1973.

Wallerstein, Immanuel. *Geopolitics and Geoculture*. New York: Cambridge University Press, 1991.

Wang, Ban, ed. *Chinese Visions of World Order: Tianxia, Culture, and World Politics*. Durham, NC: Duke University Press, 2017.

Wang Gungwu. *Renewal: The Chinese State and New Global History*. Hong Kong: Chinese University Press, 2013.

Wang Hui. *China from Empire to Nation-State*. Translated by Michael Gibbs Hill. Cambridge, MA: Harvard University Press, 2014.

Wang Hui. *China's Twentieth Century*. New York: Verso, 2016.

Wang Hui. "Contemporary Chinese Thought and the Questions of Modernity." *Social Text 55*, no. 2 (Summer 1998): 9–44.

Wang Hui. "Depoliticized Politics, from East to West." *New Left Review 41* (September–October 2006): 29–45.

Wang Hui. *The End of the Revolution and Limits of Modernity*. London: Verso, 2009.

Wang Hui. "From Empire to State: Kang Youwei, Confucian Universalism, and Unity." In *Chinese Visions of World Order: Tianxia, Culture, and World Politics*, edited by Ban Wang, 49–64. Durham, NC: Duke University Press, 2017.

Wang Hui. *The Politics of Imagining Asia*. Translated and edited by Theodor Huters. Cambridge, MA: Harvard University Press, 2011.

Wang Hui 汪晖. *Xiandai Zhongguo sixiang de xingqi* 現代中國思想的興起 [Rise of modern Chinese thought]. Beijing: Sanlian, 2004.

Wang, Xiaojue. *Modernity with a Cold War Face*. Cambridge, MA: Harvard University Press, 2013.

Wang Zhi 王直. "*Yingxiong ernü* beihou de gushi" 英雄兒女背後的故事 [The story behind *Heroic Sons and Daughters*]. *Fujian dangshi yuekan* 15 (2011): 13–19.

Wang, Zhuoyi. *Revolutionary Cycles in Chinese Cinema, 1951–1979*. New York: Palgrave Macmillan, 2014.

Wolin, Richard. *The Wind from the East: French Intellectuals, the Cultural Revolution, and the Legacy of the 1960s*. Princeton, NJ: Princeton University Press, 2010.

Womack, Brantley. *China among Unequals: Asymmetrical Foreign Relations in Asia*. Hackensack, NJ: World Scientific, 2010.

Wu Rongbin 吳榮彬 and Wen Shijiang 文仕江. "Cong qi ba nian qianhou zhanzheng pian kan dianying shengyin chuangzuo chayi" 從七八年前後戰爭片看電影聲音創作差異 [Considering differences in the creation of filmic sound in war films before and after 1978]. *Dianying wenxue* 6 (2011): 120–21.

Yang, Kuisong. "A Chinese Variation during Sino-American Reconciliation: An Analysis of Mao Zedong's Three Worlds Theory." In *Frail Alliance: Cold War and Sino-Soviet Relations*, edited by Shen Zhihua and Douglas Stiffler, 457–81. Beijing: Social Science Academic Press, 2010.

Zhang, Ling. "Navigating Gender, Ethnicity, and Space: *Five Golden Flowers* as a Socialist Road Movie." In *The Global Road Movie: Alternative Journeys*, edited by Timothy Corrigan and José Duarte, 150–71. Chicago: Intellect, 2018.

Zhang, Shuguang. *Mao's Military Romanticism: China and the Korean War, 1950–1953*. Lawrence: University Press of Kansas, 1995.

Zhang, Yingjin. *Screening China*. Ann Arbor: University of Michigan Press, 2002.

Zhang, Yu. *Going to the Countryside: The Rural in the Modern Chinese Cultural Imagination, 1915–1965*. Ann Arbor: University of Michigan Press, 2020.

Zhang Zhaofu 張照富 and Yan Kai 嚴鍇, eds. *Wuduo Jinhua* 五朵金花 [Five golden flowers]. Changchun: Jinlin chuban jituan, 2012.

Zhao Tingyang 赵汀阳. "Cong shijie wenti kaishi de tianxia zhengzhi" 從世界問題開始的天下政治 [Tianxia politics derived from the world question]. In *Dongya zhixu: Guannian, zhidu, yu zhanlue* 東亞秩序：觀念、制度與戰略 [East Asian order: Ideas, institution, and strategy], edited by Zhou Fangyin 周方銀 and Gao Chen 高程, 44–84. Beijing: Shehui kexue wenxian, 2012.

Zhao Tingyang 赵汀阳. *Tianxia tixi* 天下體系 [Tianxia system]. Nanjing: Jiangsu jiaoyu chubanshe, 2005.

Zhou Libo 周立波. *Sanshi niandai wenxue pinglun ji* 三十年代文學評論集 [Collection of literary reviews in the 1930s]. Shanghai: Shanghai wenyi chubanshe, 1984.

Zhou Libo 周立波. *Shanxiang ju bian* 山鄉巨變 [Great changes in a mountain village]. Changsha: Hunan renmin, 1983.

Zhou Libo 周立波. *Zhou Libo luyi jianggao* 周立波魯藝講稿 [Zhou Libo's lecture notes in the Lu Xun Academy]. Shanghai: Shanghai wenyi, 1984.

Zhou Libo 周立波. *Zhou Libo wenji* 周立波文集 [Collected works]. 5 vols. Shanghai: Shanghai wenyi, 1985.

Zhou Yang 周扬. *Zhou Yang wenji* 周楊文集 [Selected works of Zhou Yang]. 3 vols. Beijing: Renmin chubanshe, 1984.

Zhou Zuoren. "Humane Literature." In *Modern Chinese Literary Thought*, edited by Kirk Denton, 151–61. Stanford, CA: Stanford University Press, 1996.

Zhu, Tianbiao. "Nationalism and Chinese Foreign Policy." *China Review* 1, no. 1 (Fall 2007): 1–27.

Žižek, Slavoj. *First as Tragedy, Then as Farce*. New York: Verso, 2009.

Index